Gender and the
Archaeology of Death

GENDER AND ARCHAEOLOGY SERIES

Series Editor
Sarah Milledge Nelson
University of Denver

This series focuses on ways to understand gender in the past through archaeology. This is a topic poised for significant advances in both method and theory, which in turn can improve all archaeology. The possibilities of new methodological rigor as well as new insights into past cultures are what make gendered archaeology a vigorous and thriving subfield.

The series welcomes single authored books on themes in this topical area, particularly ones with a comparative focus. Edited collections with a strong theoretical or methodological orientation will also be considered. Audiences are practicing archaeologists and advanced students in this field.

BOOKS IN THE SERIES

Volume 1, *In Pursuit of Gender: Worldwide Archaeological Approaches,*
    Sarah Milledge Nelson and Myriam Rosen-Ayalon, Editors
Volume 2, *Gender and the Archaeology of Death,* Bettina Arnold and Nancy
    L. Wicker, Editors

Submission Guidelines

Prospective authors of single or co-authored books and editors of anthologies should submit a letter of introduction, the manuscript or a four to ten page proposal, a book outline, and a curriculum vitae. Please send your book/manuscript proposal packet to:

Gender in Archaeology Series
AltaMira Press
1630 North Main Street #367
Walnut Creek, CA 94596
(925) 938-7243
www.altamirapress.com

Gender and the Archaeology of Death

BETTINA ARNOLD
and
NANCY L. WICKER

ALTAMIRA
PRESS

A Division of
ROWMAN & LITTLEFIELD PUBLISHERS, INC.
Lanham • Boulder • New York • Toronto • Plymouth, UK

ALTAMIRA PRESS
A division of Rowman & Littlefield Publishers, Inc.
4501 Forbes Boulevard, Suite 200
Lanham, MD 20706

Estover Road
Plymouth PL6 7PY
United Kingdon

British Library Cataloguing in Publication Information Available

Library of Congress Cataloging-in-Publication Data

Gender and the archaeology of death / edited by Bettina Arnold and Nancy L. Wicker.
    p.   cm.—(Gender and archaeology series ; v. 2)
    Includes bibliographical references and index.
    ISBN 0-7591-0136-1 (cloth : alk. paper)—ISBN 0-7591-0137-X (pbk. : alk. paper)
    1. Social archaeology. 2. Sex role—History. 3. Funeral rites and ceremonies—History. 4. Death—Social aspects—History. 5. Human remains (Archaeology)
6. Excavations (Archaeology) 7. Ethnoarchaeology. 8. Feminist archaeology.
9. Women, Prehistoric. I. Arnold, Bettina. II. Wicker, Nancy L. III. Series.
CC72.4 .G44 2001
304.6′4—dc21   2001018225

Printed in the United States of America

Contents

Weapons, Women, Warriors

Introduction

Bettina Arnold and Nancy L. Wicker

Gender has been late in making an appearance as a subject of systematic study in the discipline of archaeology. Historically, there are a number of reasons for this institutional neglect. (For a discussion of the historical context of this area of archaeological research, see Claassen 1992; Gilchrist 1991; Nelson 1997; Whitehouse 1998; Wright 1996; Wylie 1991a, 1991b, 1992, among others.) One of these is undoubtedly the androcentric nature of the discipline, historically primarily focused on, and practiced by, men. Another is the widespread assumption that patriarchal systems like those that dominate the world today have always existed and are a reflection of biological imperatives as much as a product of cultural influences (Hager 1997, among others). This has resulted in the naturalization of the male-centered reconstruction of the past that has dominated the discipline since its inception as a profession in the nineteenth century.

The history of the archaeology of gender has been extensively documented in the last two decades (see Bacus et al. 1993, Nelson 1997, among others), and based on the avalanche of publications related to this topic since 1990 (recent examples include Rautman 2000 and Sweely 1999), it is safe to say that the archaeology of gender has at last come into its own. Unfortunately, this emerging awareness of the importance of gender as a component of archaeological interpretation has so far tended to ghettoize its practitioners, a trend to which this volume regrettably contributes by singling out gender as a "special" area of inquiry. It is still possible to justify this disciplinary specialization on the grounds that we are a long way from redressing the more than two centuries of androcentric bias in the reconstruction of the past. Researchers interested in encouraging the investigation of gender configurations in archaeologically documented cultures still benefit from explicitly defined studies like the ones in this and similar volumes. However, while the centrality of gender configurations to all cultures, past and present, has proven too important to be ignored in archaeological interpretation, this does not mean that adequate methodological approaches have been developed to cope with that recognition of centrality. The ultimate goal should be to make gender an integral part of all archaeological research, from research design conception to publication of results; perhaps within the next decade that goal will be achieved.

A perusal of the existing literature on the archaeology of gender reveals two thought-provoking trends: first, the most effective applications of gender theory to archaeological interpretation are those that make use of archaeological evidence in conjunction with written records, and second, there has so far been a notable absence, at least in the American archaeological literature, of volumes (or even articles in edited volumes) dedicated to applications of gender theory to mortuary analysis. There are a few exceptions, but these are rare enough to make the point even more forcibly: a recent edited volume by Rautman (2000, chapters 3–7), Cohen and Bennett (1993), McCafferty and McCafferty (1994), and Wilson (1997).

The first of these phenomena is not perhaps surprising, since gender falls within the realm of cognitive archaeology (Renfrew and Bahn 1996, 207–10), and the identification and interpretation of gender configurations in the archaeological record are undoubtedly significantly richer in texture if supported by written sources. The implications for the engendering of societies without written sources, particularly pre–state-level societies, could be interpreted as a problem, but as several of the chapters in this volume show, the outlook for an engendered mortuary archaeology of preliterate societies is far from hopeless.

The second phenomenon also requires an explanation, particularly in view of the fact that burials constitute a category of evidence that could be expected to yield an especially close and nuanced association with gender. In fact, in the European literature such studies have been conducted with considerable success (recent examples include Anderson and Boyle [1996]; Hayden [1998]; Jensen and Nielsen [1997]; Kästner [1997]; Leighton [1998]; Lillie [1997]; Lucy [1997]; Strömberg [1993]; and Wicker [1998]).

Over the last decade, a rather counterproductive form of labor specialization seems to have developed with respect to the interpretation of gender in archaeological mortuary contexts: the American contribution has thus far tended to focus on theoretical exegesis, whereas the European publications have been more concerned with applying these theoretical approaches to specific archaeological mortuary contexts. This is not a recent phenomenon. An edited volume published in 1987 included three articles on gender in mortuary analysis that were based on a Norwegian workshop held in 1979 (Bertelsen, Lillehammer, and Naess 1987), five years before Conkey and Spector (1984) published their pioneering article in *Advances in Archaeological Method and Theory*, vol. 7.

To some extent the ambivalent attitude of American archaeologists toward developing a gendered archaeology of death and burial must be seen in the larger context of the effects of NAGPRA (the Native American Graves Protection and Repatriation Act, passed by the U.S. Congress in 1990), in which human remains have become so politically charged that avoidance of association with the subject has become almost instinctive (for two opposing perspectives, see Meighan 1994 and Zimmerman 1994). The effect of this gap in the American literature has been to isolate those archaeologists who are attempting to work on engendering mortuary analysis, for example, in historical archaeology or on the basis of already published material. A decade's worth of opportunities for cross-cultural collaboration and comparison between Old and New World archaeologists with respect to mortuary ritual and gender has been lost as a result. Nor is this an issue of significance only to archaeologists working in the Americas or in Europe; archaeologists in the Near East, east and southwest Asia, and Africa (see Kent 1997) are also in the market for theoretical and methodological approaches to the engendering of archaeological mortuary analysis.

Why is the absence of good working models for the engendering of mortuary data such a problem? Obviously, the more aspects of past cultures archaeologists have access to, the better. Ideally, we would all like to study only literate cultures whose behavior has conveniently been preserved in situ under anaerobic conditions. In real life, however, there are often significant lacunae in the archaeological record, and not all sources of data provide us with the same kinds of information. Settlement data are extremely useful in allowing archaeologists to peer into the cooking pots and poke about in the middens of past cultures; as a source of information about everyday life, settlement data cannot be bettered. Such data leave much to be desired, however, when it comes to getting a sense of the inner life of a society, the life of ideology and self-representation, including the representation of gender in all its forms—not simply gendered human life, but the gendered universe. It is in this realm, referred to variously as cognitive or symbolic archaeology, that burial data provide one of the most useful windows into the way past societies gendered their world.

There is clearly a need for a collection of papers that specifically focuses on gender in the context of mortuary ritual, and ideally the distribution of such a publication should be trans-Atlantic. It seemed particularly important to the editors that this volume focus as much as possible on methodology, rather than simply "talking about" engendering the mortuary record, which was also the main theme of the Fifth Gender and Archaeology Conference in 1998. One of the more frustrating aspects of teaching courses that either focus on engendered approaches to archaeology or deal with mortuary analysis is the dearth of exemplary applications for students looking for approaches to engendering mortuary studies within their own research areas. It is hoped that this book will serve as a useful source of applications for established as well as beginning researchers in search of detailed case studies featuring gendered approaches to mortuary analysis.

ORGANIZATION OF THE VOLUME

This book is based on a selection of papers from the Fifth Gender and Archaeology Conference, organized by the editors at the University of Wisconsin, Milwaukee, in October 1998. The chapters by Hamlin and Scott, who were not able to attend the conference, extend the geographic and temporal range of the volume. The papers from the conference were too numerous to publish in a single volume; moreover, while papers dealing variously with gender in the context of settlement data, representational media, and other forms of archaeological data generally were represented by no more than five or six papers per category, there was an especially large and interesting group of papers dealing with mortuary analysis. In part, this was because the editors who set up the conference work in Europe, and as has already been mentioned, European archaeologists have, to date, been more active in developing concrete approaches to engendering archaeological mortuary analysis. It seemed logical therefore to divide the conference papers into two volumes: one, a more conventional conference proceedings (Wicker and Arnold 1999) presenting a selection of the best papers that did not deal with mortuary analysis, and the second, this volume, dedicated to a specific methodological approach to engendering archaeological interpretation.

This book then attempts to do several things: (1) meet the evident need for a compilation of methodological approaches to the archaeology of gender in mortuary contexts from a cross-cultural perspective, (2) create a venue in which Americanist and Old World approaches to mortuary analysis can be directly compared to one another in a way that the editors hope will foster continuing cross-fertilization, (3) provide a forum in which the similarities and differences of engendered mortuary analysis in societies at very different levels of sociopolitical complexity can be more clearly defined.

The range of topics included in the volume is broad in geographic as well as temporal terms in order to demonstrate the applicability of a gendered approach to mortuary ritual in extremely varied contexts. The case studies are more or less evenly divided between the Old and New Worlds, allowing the reader to compare the different approaches to gender and mortuary analysis within these different analytical traditions. North American case studies include Inuit burials in Alaska (Crass), warfare in the northern Plains (Hollimon), U.S. eastern Woodland grave good assemblages (Doucette), early Archaic (Hamlin) and Oneota mortuary ritual in midcontinental North America (O'Gorman). Old World case studies range from Bronze Age Germany (Weglian), Viking Scandinavia (Gräslund, Stalsberg), and Neolithic China (Jiao) to an investigation of infanticide from a cross-cultural perspective (Scott). Some of the chapters present specific case studies based on one or a select group of sites, while others discuss particular issues in engendering mortuary analysis. State-level societies as well as simple foraging societies are represented; in some cases written sources, either ethnographic or self-representational, are available in the analysis; in other cases, the archaeological evidence is the only source of information.

The chapters in this volume represent a number of different but interrelated issues in the engendered analysis of mortuary ritual, as seen from various scalar perspectives. Deciding on a single organizing principle proved difficult, mainly because the theme of the volume was already so specific that the only way to construct a book around it seemed to be to provide variety in the form of contrasting examples. Nevertheless, for the sake of creating a framework for the reader, it was decided to organize the papers according to four categories that the editors felt were especially important and recurrent. Each of these became a section heading: Gender Ideology and Mortuary Analysis; Gender and Power; Gender Roles and the Ambiguity of Signification; and Weapons, Women, Warriors. Each of these categories can be further broken down into a number of important issues or methodological problems that are discussed in the next section.

APPROACHES TO ENGENDERING MORTUARY ANALYSIS

All of the papers in this volume demonstrate another truism in archaeology: you find what you look for (or, in the case of gender structures, you don't find what you don't look for). Now that archaeologists are actively looking for evidence of gender configurations, including "anomalies" of various kinds that challenge normative (and often ethnocentric) gender dichotomies, in mortuary contexts, such evidence appears to be ubiquitous, or nearly so. Several of the case studies deal specifically with issues related to gender ideology, simultaneously one of the most challenging and rewarding areas of engendered archaeological research.

Person/Non-Person

Scott's contribution is perhaps the most wide-ranging, geographically and temporally. She presents a cross-cultural analysis of infanticide, addressing the issue of the selective, gendered culling of certain individuals at the level of the population. Her case studies are drawn from contexts as diverse as Paleolithic Europe, Bronze Age Yugoslavia, Roman Israel, Phoenician Carthage, and Moche Peru. In her exploration of the archaeological narrative she calls "the killing of the female," she also addresses notions of what it means to be fully human in preindustrial and prehistoric cultures, and how this set of values intersects with variable responses to practices like infanticide. This is a topic of considerable interest in other subfields of anthropology, as demonstrated by Sarah Blaffer Hrdy (1999) in a volume dedicated to exploring the biological roots of maternal (and parental) behavior. The section on infanticide as seen from the perspective of physical anthropology is one of the most extensive in the book. Archaeology has much to contribute to this particular topic, and Scott's chapter (as well as a recent British Archaeological Reports volume on the same topic [Scott 1999]) suggests some ways in which that contribution might be made. The relative value assigned to gender and its cultural expression necessarily enters into Scott's discussion as well, particularly with respect to the concept of "expendability": when is a human being not a person? How do definitions of personhood intersect with gender ideology? With age? With other social categories? These are important questions, and Scott suggests some ways in which an engendered approach to the interpretation of mortuary ritual might be able to provide answers.

Jiao's paper on the mortuary ritual of Neolithic China deals with some of the same issues as Scott's study, particularly with respect to the issue of "personhood," and what it means to be "human"—both concepts that are extremely contextually mutable. He discusses the phenomenon of multiple burials, where it is possible that only one of the individuals in the grave is actually a "person" (in the sense of fully human), whereas any additional human remains may represent another category of grave good, comparable to any of the other categories of nonhuman material culture found in the burial. Multiple burials are a virtually cross-cultural phenomenon for societies that have reached a level of complexity that involves some form of social differentiation, but to date there has been no attempt to analyze it systematically from an archaeological perspective. This is particularly unfortunate because of the obvious potential of this category of burial to inform our understanding of the evolution of gender difference and its institutionalization in past societies.

The relatively new but potentially powerful tool of genetic analysis of ancient DNA (for a recent summary see Schurr 2000) may provide us with an additional approach to this problem. Jiao's presentation of the nature of multiple burials in Neolithic China suggests that a direct comparison of the individuals in such contexts could provide us with significant insights into gender relations during this critical period. There is as yet so little published in English on Neolithic China, let alone on the cultural construction of gender as reflected in burial ritual (but see Chang 1986, Nelson 1991) that this chapter has a significant contribution to make. Jiao's discussion underscores the tremendous potential of the archaeological record of this part of the world to contribute to our understanding of various social configurations, including gender.

Sex/Gender Disjunction

Weglian and Hollimon similarly deal with gender ideology, but in more specific cultural contexts: Bronze Age Germany and the northern Plains Indian cultures of North America. Although their analyses vary significantly in some ways (Weglian discusses a single cemetery, while Hollimon presents an osteological analysis informed by ethnographic and textual data), both chapters raise the issue of sex/gender disjunction in the mortuary context. Rautman refers to this phenomenon as "gender ambiguity," and argues that "it is more productive to consider sexual/gender categories as gradational and, in some cases, context-dependent" (2000, 3).

In her study of osteological trauma in female burials from the northern Plains, Hollimon argues that the tendency of archaeologists to create exclusionary categories is a pervasive problem. The exceptions to the "expected" patterns are often more interesting than the rule, and can be more illuminating as well. Her discussion of the potential of osteological evidence, particularly traumatic injuries, as a window on gender configurations raises an important point: additional forensic studies should be carried out to allow archaeologists to distinguish between defensive and offensive injuries as well as angle and type of trauma as a way of refining this approach. Evidence of traumatic injury alone cannot provide an adequate basis for identifying the presence of individuals who engaged in offensive as well as defensive violent interaction with others. Leg wounds or other injuries endured by women while fighting on horseback against people on foot would seem, for example, to provide better evidence of "women warriors" than some other types of injury. Patterns of trauma from the various parts of the world in which women warriors are either documented in the historical sources or suspected in the archaeological record (Plains Indian groups [Hollimon 1999; Hollimon and Owsley 1994] and Scythian/Sarmatian groups [Davis-Kimball 1997a and 1997b] are just two examples), and could perhaps be systematically compared to identify forensic commonalities.

Weglian's study highlights another problem in the interpretation of sex/gender disjunction in the mortuary context: how does one deal with burials in large or small cemetery populations that fall outside the "normative" gender pattern? This is a phenomenon that is fairly common (therefore presumably not as anomalous as it is often presented) in prehistoric European burial contexts (Arnold 1991, 1996, 2001). It is in the context of mortuary ritual, where the physical remains of the individual are associated with the material culture of gender symbolism, that the complex interplay between sex and gender is especially clearly signified (Arnold 2001). The extent to which sex/gender disjunction is present in the archaeological record, often without being recognized, or without being acknowledged, is demonstrated by the temporal and geographic range of the three case studies that explore this phenomenon in this volume.

Gender Fluidity

Weglian's paper overlaps to some extent Crass's investigations of mortuary ritual in the Arctic, where grave goods are ambiguous markers of gender, and the correlation between biological sex and culturally constructed gender that dominates Western discourse breaks down in a rich interweaving of identities that conflates past and present, male and female. Crass's paper is a cautionary tale of sorts, reminding us that the extent to which gender is represented in the material culture of burial may vary considerably from one culture to another, and that an engendered analysis of mortuary ritual may be especially problematic in contexts in which grave goods are regularly disturbed, replaced, or otherwise manipulated after deposition. Ethnographic evidence for the concept of reincarnation, irrespective of the biological sex of the child, clearly has ramifications for the utility of material culture as a gender marker in mortuary ritual. Costume, for example, which would be the best indicator of gender in Inuit cultures, is generally not preserved. Two of the papers (Crass, Hamlin) deal with unusual preservation conditions. Wood and other materials in the Arctic are in such short supply that cairns are often opened and objects removed or replaced by those in need (Crass), while the anaerobic conditions of water-logged sites represent a unique environment for the preservation of organic material impossible to duplicate in ordinary circumstances (Hamlin). Both case studies are useful object lessons for those of us dealing with more "typical" archaeological contexts—we must be careful to judge only on the basis of recoverable data, and not on the apparent absence of gender markers in areas that might include organic materials.

Interestingly enough, given their very different environmental contexts, Hamlin's case study of the early Archaic Windover site in Florida parallels Crass's in some important ways, particularly with respect to the problem of cultures that do not choose to represent gender roles in the realm of burial (or may not organize their societies according to a rigid sexual division of labor).

Like Crass (but without the help of the extensive ethnographic sources available in Crass's study), she is able to present a discussion of gender ideology as well as gender role, an important distinction (Spector and Whelan 1991). Even if the jobs men and women do are not used to differentiate them from one another, some other variable (in the case of the Windover site, the material the tools are made of) may have served such a purpose in a symbolic rather than functional sense. If the universe, and all the natural materials in it, are gendered, human labor may not need to be. That does not mean that in such societies women and men were necessarily considered identical in all respects except in the realm of reproduction. Windover represents a virtually unique, but also very valuable, archaeological example of the potential as well as the limitations of engendering the analysis of archaeological remains. In this instance, the difficulty is not an incomplete picture of the society due to preservation conditions, but rather the absence of a corresponding set of settlement data that restricts the kinds of conclusions that can be drawn about this fabulously preserved early Archaic site. Nevertheless, Hamlin has succeeded, through the application of an extremely careful and clearly articulated analysis of the material, in presenting us with a window into the complex gender ideology of this society.

Material Culture Mutability and Gender

Doucette's paper addresses a related and similarly complex issue: the multivocality of material culture function and form associations in different burial contexts. In Doucette's case study from the eastern Woodlands, the item in question is the atlatl, which seems to have been modified/disassembled for burial and was occasionally included as a grave good in women's burials. Does an atlatl minus its shaft when found in a woman's grave have the same meaning as the identical item when found in a man's burial? Spear points are occasionally found in women's burials in Iron Age Europe and later, but wear patterns in some cases suggest that they were used as weaving battens rather than weapons (Fisher n.d.), neatly illustrating the problem of the transformative power of context. The multivocality of objects in burial contexts has long been recognized (Pader 1982). Just as death is a transformative process for the deceased, the life history of an item of material culture can be transformed in the course of the mortuary ritual. Since material culture tends to be the way archaeologists "map" gender in mortuary contexts, this is clearly a major concern. If we are to move beyond simply acknowledging that burials are not a direct reflection of daily life (which by now has taken on the quality of a truism), archaeologists will have to find a way to deal with this problem. An atlatl may have had precisely the same meaning in eastern Woodland men's and women's burials, or it might have had quite a different significance in the one context versus the other. It is this paradox that Doucette illustrates in her case study.

Supporting Sources: Settlement Data and Texts

On occasion, settlement and burial data can be brought to bear together in the reconstruction of gender configurations in the archaeological past. O'Gorman shows us how this can be done in a case study that represents the best of all possible worlds from the point of view of the archaeologist: the Oneota longhouses of the Tremaine site in Wisconsin. Unfortunately, this is not typically the kind of data set most archaeologists face—burial in the domestic context with patterned spatial associations supporting the observed gender differences in both categories of evidence. Most societies seem to choose a limited number of modalities through which to express gender differences, and often this takes the form of an either/or proposition (gender is reflected either in the mortuary or the settlement context, but not in both). In other instances, archaeologists have access to only one category of evidence, either because of the conditions of discovery and recovery (as at Windover), or because of contemporary political constraints, such as those imposed by NAGPRA. O'Gorman's case study presents an enviably well-documented archaeological context elegantly analyzed; she demonstrates how tremendously nuanced a gendered analysis can be if the source material is especially good.

The best-case scenario for the interpretation of gender configurations in mortuary contexts occurs when written material as well as archaeological records are available. Crass's chapter makes it clear how problematic the interpretation of Arctic gender configurations would be without ethnographic evidence. Scott's cross-cultural study of infanticide also relies heavily on written sources. Both of the Scandinavian papers (Stalsberg, Gräslund) make use of mutually supportive textual and material culture sources to inform their discussion of gender in two different early medieval contexts.

Gräslund uses the supporting evidence of rune stone inscriptions from circa A.D. 1000 to construct a picture of high-status women in Scandinavia around this time. Stalsberg's discussion crosscuts issues of ethnic identity for Viking women in the Rus', raising another issue of importance: to what extent were women more likely than men to be buried outside their natal communities, especially if they were members of the elite? Political alliances in cultures like those of Viking Scandinavia often involved the exchange of women, and when gender, status, and ethnicity intersect, as they do in these case studies, the engendering of the mortuary record becomes even more complex.

The Intersection of Gender and Status

Sweely's (1999) edited volume *Manifesting Power* focuses on another important theme that is addressed by several chapters in this book: the extent to which certain patterns related to gender are restricted to particular social groups, especially on the basis of status. Elites, whatever their gender, are generally more visible in the archaeological record than other social groups because they control the material manifestations of power in life as well as in death. Jiao, Gräslund, Scott, and Stalsberg all deal with this phenomenon in various ways. The main pitfall to avoid here is making generalizations about gender configurations in the society as a whole on the basis of patterns observed in the mortuary ritual of elites. For example, there is good ethnographic evidence to suggest that the presence of high-status women in positions of political as well as social power within a society need not necessarily say anything about the relative status of women in relation to men in that society (Arnold 1996, 161).

An additional problem is how to identify women with actual, rather than secondhand, or reflected, power. This parallels the problem of the identification of women warriors, as described by Hollimon: traumatic injuries tend to look superficially very much the same whether suffered by a woman warrior fighting in the front lines or by a wife and mother defending her home and family, and elite women who are buried with large quantities of high quality grave goods may have acquired the right to such a burial either as appendages of high-status males, or in their own right. The difficulty lies in devising strategies for distinguishing between these patterns, and that requires a solid grasp of ethnographic analogy as well as a sufficient sample size for comparison. Various analytical techniques may be applied; the approaches presented in this volume are only a beginning.

CONCLUSION

Each of the chapters in this book contributes to the as-yet relatively undeveloped area of engendered archaeological mortuary analysis. Some are more methodologically oriented, others combine theoretical and methodological approaches to their reconstructions of past gender configurations. While one of the main messages of the chapters is clearly a call for caution in the relatively uncritical ways archaeologists tend to assign gender on the basis of grave good assemblages, at the same time, several profitable approaches are presented that suggest the endeavor is not hopeless. The more historically oriented and text-aided approaches complement the analyses that rely primarily or entirely on the archaeological record in combination with ethnographic analogy; each has its own contribution to make to the theme of the volume. Presenting case studies from both Old and New World contexts should go some way toward bridging the divide between scholars in these two areas. By providing a methodological and bibliographic resource spanning recent literature in a broad range of geographic contexts, this volume links the American and European archaeological traditions in gender studies. We hope that the door will stay open now that the conferences in this series have begun to extend their invitations to scholars overseas, and that communication will become more frequent and productive as a result of publications such as this one.

ACKNOWLEDGMENTS

The editors would like to thank the various departments and organizations at the University of Wisconsin, Milwaukee (UWM), and Minnesota State University, Mankato, that made the conference that gave rise to this volume possible in the first place: the UWM Letters and Science Dean's Office, the UWM Department of Anthropology, the UWM Anthropology Student Union, and the Minnesota State University, Mankato, Department of Art. The many UWM students who volunteered their services throughout the conference are due special thanks—we couldn't have done it without their help. We also would like to thank the contributors to this volume for putting up with constant requests for changes, new drafts, and for additional information; we hope that the wait will have been worth it. Thanks also to Eleanor Scott and Christine Hamlin, who were not able to attend the 1998 conference, but very kindly agreed to contribute to the book after the fact. Finally, the editors thank their spouses for emotional and technical support throughout the editorial process; their patience and encouragement have made this part of the journey possible.

REFERENCES

Anderson, Sue, and Katherine Boyle, eds. 1996. *Ritual treatment of human and animal remains.* Proceedings of the first meeting of the Osteological Research Group, 1994. Oxford, U.K.: Oxbow Books.

Arnold, Bettina. 1991. The deposed princess of Vix: The need for an engendered European prehistory. In *The archaeology of gender: Proceedings of the twenty-second annual Chacmool conference of the Archaeological Association of the University of Cal-*

gary. Edited by Dale Walde and Noreen Willows, pp. 366–74. Calgary: University of Calgary.

——. 1996. Honorary males or women of substance? Gender, status, and power in Iron Age Europe. *Journal of European Archaeology* 3 (2):153–68.

——. 2001. "Sein und Werden": Gender as process in mortuary ritual. In *In pursuit of gender*. Edited by Sarah M. Nelson. Walnut Creek, Calif.: AltaMira.

Bacus, Elisabeth A., Alex W. Barker, Jeffrey D. Bonevich, Sandra L. Dunavan, J. Benjamin Fitzhugh, Debra L. Gold, Nurit S. Goldman-Finn, William Griffin, and Karen M. Mudar, eds. 1993. *A gendered past: A critical bibliography of gender in archaeology*. Ann Arbor: University of Michigan Museum of Anthropology.

Bertelsen, Reidar, Arnvid Lillehammer, and Jenny-Rita Naess, eds. 1987. *Were they all men? An examination of sex roles in prehistoric society*. Stavanger, Norway: Arkeologisk Museum.

Chang, Kwang-Chih. 1986. *The archaeology of ancient China*. New Haven, Conn.: Yale University Press.

Claassen, Cheryl. 1992. Questioning gender: An introduction. In *Exploring gender through archaeology*. Edited by Cheryl Claassen, pp. 1–10. Madison, Wis.: Prehistory Press.

Cohen, Mark N., and Sharon Bennett. 1993. Skeletal evidence for sex roles and gender hierarchies in prehistory. In *Sex and gender hierarchies*. Edited by Barbara D. Miller, pp. 273–96. Cambridge, U.K.: Cambridge University Press.

Conkey, Margaret W., and Janet Spector. 1984. Archaeology and the study of gender. *Advances in Archaeological Method and Theory* 7:1–38.

Davis-Kimball, Jeannine. 1997a. Warrior women of the Eurasian Steppes. *Archaeology* 50 (1): 44–48 (January/February 1997).

——. 1997b. Sauro-Sarmatian nomadic women: New gender identities. *Journal of Indo-European Studies* 25 (3–4): 327–43.

Fisher, Genevieve. n.d. Battle-stirrers or peace-weavers? Militaristic imagery in the construction of early Anglo-Saxon female identity. Paper presented at the sixty-third annual meeting of the Society for American Archaeology, Seattle, March 25–29, 1998.

Gilchrist, Roberta. 1991. Women's archaeology? Political feminism, gender theory, and historical revision. *Antiquity* 65:495–501.

Hager, Lori, ed. 1997. *Women in human evolution*. London: Routledge.

Hayden, Chris. 1998. Public and domestic: The social background. In *Gender and Italian archaeology: Challenging the stereotypes*. Edited by Ruth D. Whitehouse, pp. 127–42. Vol. 7 of *Accordia Specialist Studies on Italy*. London: University College London.

Hollimon, Sandra E. 1999. Sex, health, and gender roles among the Arikara of the northern Plains. In *Reading the body: Representations and remains in the archaeological record*. Edited by Alison Rautman, pp. 25–37. Philadelphia: University of Pennsylvania Press.

Hollimon, Sandra E., and Douglas W. Owsley. 1994. Osteology of the Fay Tolton site: Implications for warfare during the initial middle Missouri variant. In *Skeletal biology in the Great Plains: Migration, warfare, health, and subsistence*. Edited by Douglas W. Owsley and Richard L. Jantz, pp. 345–53. Washington, D.C.: Smithsonian Institution Press.

Hrdy, Sarah Blaffer. 1999. *Mother nature: A history of mothers, infants, and natural selection*. New York: Pantheon.

Jensen, Claus K., and Karen Hoilund Nielsen, eds. 1997. *Burial and society: The chronological and social analysis of archaeological burial data*. Aarhus, Denmark: Aarhus University Press.

Kästner, Sibylle. 1997. Rund ums Geschlecht. Ein Überblick zu feministischen Geschlechtertheorien und deren Anwendung auf die archäologische Forschung. In *Vom Knochenmann zur Menschenfrau: Feministische Theorie und Archäologische Praxis*. Edited by Sigrun M. Karlisch, Sibylle Kästner, and Eva-Marie Märtens, pp. 13–35. Münster, Germany: Agenda Verlag.

Kent, Susan, ed. 1997. *Gender in African archaeology*. Walnut Creek, Calif.: AltaMira Press.

Leighton, Robert. 1998. Reflections on San Teodoro 1–7 and recent sex changes in the Upper Paleolithic. In *Gender and Italian archaeology: Challenging the stereotypes*. Edited by Ruth D. Whitehouse, pp. 45–56. Vol. 7 of *Accordia Specialist Studies on Italy*. London: University College London.

Lillie, Malcolm C. 1997. Women and children in prehistory: Resource sharing and social stratification at the Mesolithic–Neolithic transition in Ukraine. In *Invisible people and processes: Writing gender and childhood into European archaeology*. Edited by Jenny Moore and Eleanor Scott, pp. 213–28. London: Leicester University Press.

Lucy, Susan J. 1997. Housewives, warriors, slaves? Sex and gender in Anglo-Saxon burials. In *Invisible people and processes: Writing gender and childhood into European archaeology*. Edited by Jenny Moore and Eleanor Scott, pp. 150–68. London: Leicester University Press.

McCafferty, Sharisse, and Geoffrey McCafferty. 1994. Engendering Tomb 7 at Monte Albán. *Current Anthropology* 35 (2): 143–66.

Meighan, Clement. 1994. Burying American archaeology. *Archaeology* 47 (6):64–68 (November/December 1994).

Nelson, Sarah M. 1991. The "Goddess Temple" and the status of women at Niuheliang, China. In *The archaeology of gender: Proceedings of the twenty-second annual Chacmool conference*. Edited by Dale Walde and Noreen D. Willows. Calgary: University of Calgary.

———. 1997. Introduction. In *Gender in archaeology: Analyzing power and prestige*. Pp. 13–30. Walnut Creek, Calif.: AltaMira Press.

Pader, Ellen-Jane. 1982. *Symbolism, social relations, and the interpretation of mortuary remains*. British Archaeological Reports International Series 130. Oxford, U.K.: Archaeopress.

Rautman, Alison, ed. 2000. *Reading the body: Representations and remains in the archaeological record*. Philadelphia: University of Pennsylvania Press.

Renfrew, Colin, and Paul Bahn. 1996. *Archaeology*. London: Thames and Hudson.

Schurr, Theodore G. 2000. Mitochondrial DNA and the peopling of the New World. *American Scientist* 88 (3):246–53 (May–June).

Scott, Eleanor. 1999. *The archaeology of infancy and infant death*. British Archaeological Reports International Series 819. Oxford, U.K.: Archaeopress.

Spector, Janet, and Mary K. Whelan. 1991. Incorporating gender into archaeology courses. In *Gender and anthropology: Critical reviews for research and teaching*. Edited by Sandra Morgen, pp. 65–94. Washington, D.C.: American Anthropological Association.

Strömberg, Agneta. 1993. *Male or female? A methodological study of grave gifts as sex-indicators in Iron Age burials from Athens.* Jonsered, Sweden: Paul Aströms Förlag.

Sweely, Tracy L., ed. 1999. *Manifesting power: Gender and the interpretation of power in archaeology.* London: Routledge.

Whitehouse, Ruth, ed. 1998. Introduction. In *Gender and Italian archaeology: Challenging the stereotypes.* Pp. 1–8. Vol. 7 of *Accordia Specialist Studies on Italy.* London: University College London.

Wicker, Nancy L. 1998. Selective female infanticide as partial explanation for the dearth of women in Viking Age Scandinavia. In *Violence and society in the early medieval west.* Edited by Guy Halsall, pp. 205–21. Woodbridge, U.K.: Boydell Press.

Wicker, Nancy L., and Bettina Arnold, eds. 1999. *From the ground up: Beyond gender theory in archaeology. Proceedings of the fifth gender and archaeology conference.* British Archaeological Reports International Series 812. Oxford, U.K.: Archaeopress.

Wilson, Diane. 1997. Gender, diet, health, and status in the Mississippian Powers Phase Turner Cemetery population. In *Women in prehistory.* Edited by Rosemary Joyce and Cheryl Claassen, pp. 119–35. Philadelphia: University of Pennsylvania Press.

Wright, Rita. 1996. Introduction: Gendered ways of knowing in archaeology. In *Gender and archaeology.* Edited by Rita Wright, pp. 1–22. Philadelphia: University of Pennsylvania Press.

Wylie, Alison. 1991a. Gender theory and the archaeological record: Why is there no archaeology of gender? In *Engendering archaeology: Women and prehistory.* Edited by Joan M. Gero and Margaret W. Conkey, pp. 31–54. Oxford, U.K.: Basil Blackwell.

———. 1991b. Feminist critiques and archaeological challenges. In *The archaeology of gender: Proceedings of the twenty-second annual Chacmool conference.* Edited by Dale Walde and Noreen Willows, pp. 17–23. Calgary: University of Calgary.

———. 1992. The interplay of evidential constraints and political interests. *American Antiquity* 57:15–35.

Zimmerman, Larry. 1994. Sharing control of the past. *Archaeology* 47 (6):64–68 (November/December 1994).

Gender Ideology and Mortuary Analysis

1

Killing the Female? Archaeological Narratives of Infanticide

Eleanor Scott

There is a rather large body of opinion, pervasive in archaeological and historical literature, that infanticide is basically the story of the killing of the female. This is a mighty assumption; the cultural, ontological implications for women and women's history are enormous. Is there really an inexorable historical thread linking women, giving them all a common status as unwanted, disposable, and killed? It occurs to me that it is extraordinary that such a discourse has remained largely uninvestigated and indeed unquestioned for so long.

This chapter argues that it is probably a fallacy on a number of counts that infanticide is basically about disposal of unwanted females. While accepting that infanticide was widespread in the past, I argue that not only did the causes, effects, and meanings of infanticide vary from society to society, and indeed within societies, but that infant boys as well as infant girls were killed. I also explore the notion that these infants were not "unwanted," and that the problems of killing of neonates were cushioned by the construction and maintenance—through mortuary practices, for example—of a number of beliefs and rituals, such as believing that the infant could be reborn at a later date or by denying the human-ness of the newborn infant. Such beliefs may account for the virtually complete absence of neonate and infant burials from formal cemeteries in Europe from the Neolithic onward. This belief in the ontological difference of the neonate appears to have been so ingrained that even in Christian contexts neonatal burials are set apart from the rest of the community of the dead.

I raised these issues concerning infanticide in a recent publication (Scott 1999), but only briefly; and now, with hindsight, I realize that they warrant detailed and explicit analysis. Belief in widespread female infanticide as part of the human past is deeply rooted in archaeological and anthropological discourse. It pervades the secondary sources in particular and has been used to explain processes as diverse as Paleolithic population control and the demographics of Roman mortuary contexts. For example, Frere, in his seminal work *Britannia* on Roman Britain, makes the assertion that the ninety-seven infant skeletons discovered at Hambleden Roman villa were not only victims of infanticide but were the unwanted female offspring of a slave-run establishment (Frere 1978, 303–4), despite there being no evidence for this at all. Indeed, the area is very likely to have been the settlement's separate infant cemetery, interestingly in an area of agricultural processing, and the numbers of infants buried are entirely consistent with the natural infant mortality rates to be expected in such a preindustrial, rural community (Scott 1999, 110–15).

Female infanticide first entered the interpretative literature in the nineteenth century as part of the thought processes of cultural anthropologists seeking evolutionary theories of cultural development. Female infanticide was postulated as a key component in the evolution of lineage and marriage systems by McLennan ([1865] 1970), for example, who believed patriliny to have developed via polyandry from matriliny, which in turn had emerged from pristine promiscuity via female infanticide and exogamy (Cheater 1989, 19). Theories such as these were informed by ethnographic observations of hunter-gatherer societies in the latter half of the nineteenth century that were factored into evolutionary theories of human culture. So, for example, the accounts of early explorers and early ethnographers who came into contact with the Inuit were seized upon. The unequal sex ratio in some Inuit groups at the turn of the century suggested to observers and commentators that the number of dependent young were limited through female infanticide (e.g., Bates 1996, 113, citing Freeman 1971 on the Netsilik Inuit). The Netsilik remained very much in the anthropological eye during the early part of the twentieth century, and are in fact the only society for which there is any real qualitative data about the existence of the practice of female infanticide (Rasmussen 1931; Reynolds and Tanner 1983, 50). That the Old World theory was (and still is) informed by nineteenth-century observations of the New World is also apparent in the case of Australian Aborigines. The Australian Aborigines have a record of widespread infanticide and have apparently articulated reasons for their practices: "Me bin keepem one boy and one girl. No good keepem mob, him too much wantem tuckout" (Willshire 1895, quoted in Reynolds and Tanner 1983, 49). The Australian Aborigines killed both boys and girls, in order to preserve the mobility of the mother. The Yanomamo Indians of South America also practiced infanticide of both male and female babies, usually in circumstances where the mother already had an existing infant; however, the impression of observers and missionaries was that females were less desirable than males because of the way that adult females were denigrated within the family and the community, and that more female babies were killed than males (50–51).

It is also pertinent to note that the idea that female infanticide was normal practice in the past is heavily dependent upon one particular historical context—the ancient history of Greek and Roman texts—and has been lazily extrapolated to the rest of the classical past. In a number of these texts, the female infant is apparently devalued to the extent of being expendable. These texts, which survive from the classical Mediterranean civilizations, have had an almost overbearing influence, especially one frequently quoted Roman-Egyptian papyrus letter in which a husband tells his pregnant wife: "If the child is a boy, let it live; if a girl, expose it" (Shelton 1988). But to argue from this historically specific evidence to a notion of a global female infanticide in the human past is a major and risky leap in the dark. And, of course, the social and demographic implications of believing in widespread preferential female infanticide are enormous, but yet—strangely—unexamined. And just what social and economic systems cause the female infant to be so devalued in the first place, where this does occur? Or, is the presumption of female infanticide actually a modern construct that has been projected onto the past?

It has therefore become necessary to question whether female infanticide was/is a cultural universal and, further, to examine the assumption that such practices existed because female infants were less valued than males. This chapter examines these beliefs against archaeological evidence and presents some alternative interpretations, and to this extent, it is a combination of critique and historical revision. There is no room for complacency in either accepting the existence of widespread female infanticide in the past, or, concomitantly, in thinking that we understand the meanings of such postulated processes.

KILLING THE FEMALE

There are certainly a number of well-known contexts in which preferential female infanticide has very likely been practiced or is currently observed. One thinks of those cultures mentioned above, such as the Inuit, and, in addition, there is Viking society, as well as modern India and China.

The best review of the evidence for female infanticide in Iron Age and medieval Scandinavia is the one by Wicker (1998). In this important review of the mortuary evidence, situated within but not subjectively informed by the historical framework, Wicker argues that the interpretation of the known scattered archaeological traces of infants who were not buried with an adult-type burial rite is problematical, but when viewed in tandem with the dearth of adult women in cemetery remains and in literature could be suggestive of female infanticide. However, she is also careful to point out that "Even if we can demonstrate that infanticide was practiced, we have only indirect grounds for discussing the existence of preferential female infanticide" (Wicker 1998, 216). As she observes, we know much less about women (and children) of the Viking period than about men because they were not similarly commemorated in life or in death in the histories and sagas available to us or in the known burial remains (206).

Female infanticide in India exists. It has a long history and continues today. The complexity of its meanings, however, as well as its causes and effects, should not be underestimated. Harris provides an engaging and provocative discussion of female infanticide in India as part of his overall treatise that "the procreative imperative" is something of a myth.

> Northern India was [a] region where people systematically killed unwanted infants, especially females. Early nineteenth-century censuses indicated that boys outnumbered girls four to one among certain castes in Gujarat; and three to one in the northern provinces. British administrators were astounded by recurrent reports of castes and villages that prevented even one female baby from surviving past infancy. (Harris 1989, 213)

Harris looks into the historical, cultural causes and meanings of female infanticide in India, and observes that in nineteenth-century India, for example, the most lopsided ratios of young males to young females occurred among the Rajputs and other high-ranking military and land-owning castes. This might appear surprising on the surface, because the Rajputs had the resources to raise large numbers of children, both boys and girls. British officials of the time reported that among the Rajput elite, the rajahs of Mynpoorie, every female infant was killed. At the root of this practice, Harris believes, is a struggle on the part of elite men to keep their lands and other forms of wealth from being divided up between too many heirs. "It was not reproductive success that governed their behavior, but a refusal to give up the luxurious style of life to which they had grown accustomed." The Rajputs went one step further. Rather than responding to the burden of supplying dowries for their daughters, they eliminated the need to pay any dowry by eliminating their female infants (226–27). Such behaviors tend to become reinforcing, as the drive for fewer daughters in itself leads to a conceptual devaluation of the female.

China too is a well-known crucible of female infanticide. The first European explorers to reach China were shocked at the obvious prevalence of infanticide (Harris 1989, 212). For example, when census figures became available in the nineteenth century, it appeared that boys outnumbered girls four to one in the province of Fukien, where rates of direct and indirect infanticide could range from 10 percent to 80 percent of female births. Fukien, however, was something of a special case, because it was a rural area of great poverty where the inhabitants did not own the land and, traditionally, parents would not raise more than two daughters (213).

The Communist Chinese state recognized that a prime instrument of revolutionary change must be laws determining land tenure, marriage, and the family. The Chinese Marriage Law of 1950 outlawed the prevailing "feudal" marriage system, including bigamy, concubinage, child betrothal, and infanticide. The rights of women and the importance of the family were stressed as part of the new social order, and population statistics indicate that female infanticide declined quite notably. In 1980, when the Marriage Law was updated, many of the old clauses were dropped because there was simply no longer a need for them; however, it was still felt necessary to outlaw infanticide explicitly because of another piece of radical legislation. In 1979, Han families were limited to one child apiece, and this policy notably caused an upsurge in female infanticide (Cheater 1989, 234–35). But why? Exactly why should the parents of these infants choose to kill the females and not the males? The key is to look very closely, not just at traditions of land tenure and marriage, but also at the ownership of wealth and its transmission across generations. A Chinese couple do not collect a pension upon retirement; they are supported by any male children they might have and by those sons' wives. If they were not to raise a son, they would have no old-age provision. If they raised a daughter, the fruits of her labors would be absorbed by the family into which she marries. Thus, female infants are not "unwanted" per se; rather, the parents make a basically economic decision that is reinforced by all their neighbors making the same decision.

All the societies discussed in the above section present very distinct social circumstances. There is no a priori reason for female infanticide; rather the female infants are devalued as a result of particular prevailing social situations or ideologies. Thus, in modern China, there is pressure for the one permitted child to be male owing to patterns of inheritance and intergenerational movement of money; in India, the dowry system puts pressure on poorer families to produce more boys than girls. Harris's argument concerning female infanticide in Rajput India is compelling and important, for it raises the possibility that female infanticide is often elite female infanticide and has to do with movement of wealth. It has more in common with the elite male infanticide of the ancient Phoenicians and Greeks and the accumulation and movement of wealth within lineages within specific cultures than it has with any fantasy of the casual disposal of large masses of unvalued girls.

KILLING THE MALE

A glance at the Bible reveals the extent to which male infanticide was either practiced or at least passed as an idea into folk memory: the drowning of the infant boys of the Hebrews by Pharaoh in the hunt for Moses (Exod. 1:22); the smiting of Egypt's firstborn at the time of the original Passover (Exod. 13:29); and the "Massacre of the Innocents" by Herod (Matt. 3:16). These are not isolated examples. The Nayars of southern India are reported at one time to have sacrificed their firstborn sons to the goddess of smallpox (Sherring 1872, 81; Reynolds and Tanner 1983, 54).

There is also evidence from the classical Mediterranean of elite male infanticide. The example of the Phoenicians is discussed below. The other well-documented example comes from ancient Greece, where we must contextualize infanticide through reference to this society's particular construction of the family, inheritance, and political structure known as *demokratia*. The Athenians did not actually have a word for "family," but spoke of the *oikos*, a household unit comprising all the inhabitants, including slaves, as well as the buildings and land belonging to it. Preserving the *oikos*, and the number of *oikoi*, was a preoccupation of the *demokratia*. Landed property was the basis of an Athenian's social status and political influence, and land could only be possessed by a legitimate Athenian male citizen. Thus, although the acknowledged purpose of Athenian marriage was the procreation of legitimate children, contradictory pressures operated on parents. There was a real risk of producing too many children; the property would be fragmented among the male heirs or depleted by dowries. In response to these pressures, the Athenians practiced infanticide, exposing newborn infants to die, a fate that befell male as well as female infants. In this sense, the primary object of Athenian infanticide was the same as the object of reproduction: to secure the continuity of the *oikos* with all its social, religious, political, and military implications (Jones 1984, 157–62; Scott 1999, 69).

It is also possible to present a selected series of archaeological case studies that either tend to disprove arguments for female infanticide or strongly suggest the presence of male infanticide. Five main archaeological contexts will be examined:

- Paleolithic Europe
- the Bronze Age cemetery at Mokrin
- Roman Ashkelon in modern Israel
- the Phoenician city of Carthage, North Africa
- Moche infant sacrifice in ancient Peru

In three of these contexts—Mokrin, Ashkelon, and Carthage—male infanticide rather than female infanticide is suggested, and it is argued that the assumptions of female infanticide in the Paleolithic are unfounded. The Moche evidence is offered as a telling example of how communities can see infanticide as a means of maintaining the harmony of the universe. The evidence reveals that we can no longer simplistically accept female infanticide as a cultural norm, and we must create more significant discourses about age processes such as infancy and mortuary processes such as infanticide, just as we are striving toward a greater gendered sophistication in academic research.

The Paleolithic

One of the great puzzles of early prehistory is how the population of Paleolithic Europe was kept so low, and why, with the invention of agriculture in the Neolithic period, was there something of a "baby boom" (e.g., Taylor 1996)? A number of commentators have argued for female infanticide as the main mechanism of Paleolithic population control, with Ehrenberg, for example, postulating female infanticide in her widely circulated book *Women in Prehistory* (1989), based on the views of anthropologists such as Birdsell (1968, 239) and Williamson (1978, 66). Yet there is no real evidence for this. Ehrenberg's statements about infanticide are mixed up with discussion of ethnographic observations of the African !Kung hunter-gatherer tribes. Key original work on the !Kung was carried out by anthropologist Lee, who noted that hunter-gatherer women were able somehow to space the births of their children by three to four years, thus ensuring that they did not have more than one infant at a time who needed to be carried, and that population growth was kept very low. But Lee never observed the habitual use of infanticide among the !Kung, let alone preferential female infanticide. His own conclusion was that the women were spacing their pregnancies through extended breastfeeding, with lactation suppressing ovulation (Lee 1980). Other Paleolithic specialists have also pointed out that limited food resources and the prevalence of diseases such as malaria would have been more than enough to have kept Paleolithic population growth in check, and that the body fat content of Paleolithic women was probably low enough to "dampen down" their ovulation/fertility.

But the idea of Paleolithic female infanticide is becoming common currency in the secondary literature, especially among historians. Hoffer and Hull (1984), in their history of maternal infanticide, argue that as many as 50 percent of the newborn females were killed in the Paleolithic (on nonspecified grounds), while Porter (1997) also favors infanticide as a mechanism of Old Stone Age population control in his new medical history of the world.

The Bronze Age

A recent Bronze Age study warranting discussion here is Rega's interpretation of the data from the Mokrin early Bronze Age cemetery north of Bel-
grade in the former Yugoslavia (Rega 1997). The Mokrin mortality profile
suggests that a realistic population is represented in the cemetery, both in
terms of sex and age at death, with two significant exceptions: there is an
absence of neonatal infants in the cemetery, and there are more female older
infants and children than male. The disparity between the numbers of female
and male older infant dead can be best accounted for if there were simply
more female members of the older infant population.

> The statistically significant excess of female children between one and six years may
> be due to the fact that there are greater numbers of females actually alive in this age
> group and, therefore, the pool of those dying is larger. Assuming approximately
> equal numbers of male and females are born, mortality, therefore, may be signifi-
> cantly greater for boys during the first year of life. (Rega 1997, 237)

Rega suggests a number of reasons for this possible case of preferential
male infanticide or neglect, including the idea drawn from ethnographic parallels that the female was highly valued in adult society and thus better cared
for in infancy and childhood than the male. In Jamaica, for example, the fa-
voritism toward female children has been ascribed to the greater role of
women as economic providers and in maintenance of family stability in matrilineal society, and so the consequent higher value of a daughter to the family in general, and to the mother in particular, is apparent (1997, 238). But
value only accrues to females where the prevailing social system dictates that
they will carry their wealth with them through the various stages of their lives
for distribution within their own biological family. Thus, where the practice
of bestowing bride wealth is observed, as with the Mukogodo of Kenya, and
a daughter receives wealth on behalf of her family upon marriage, one sees
preferential treatment of girls in poor families. Conversely, in Greek and
Roman society, and in modern China and India where female infanticide is
known, women did not and do not carry wealth with them throughout their
lives, with dowry systems and other mechanisms operating to transmit the
woman's wealth to the family into which she marries.

The recent history of our own society shows how quickly trends can
change regarding the relative investment of care bestowed on young boys and
girls. Until about the mid-1980s there was still a feeling in some quarters that
the birth of a boy—the "son and heir"—was cause for celebration, and that
girls were some kind of consolation prize for the mother to dress up and fuss
over. However, with the advent of new social practices such as women keep-

ing their own name upon marriage, having their own sources of income, and separate taxation, the investment in the care of girls has improved dramatically, to the extent that in the field of education they now consistently outperform boys at every level and every subject, according to recent U.K. data (discussed in, e.g., Biddulph 1998). Now many parents regard the birth of a girl as a success story in its own right, rather than the disappointment it was once deemed to be. The key point here is that fairly minor shifts in social and economic contexts (for we have not seen any major alteration in the ideology of patriarchy) can have major effects on the perception of infants of either sex. There are therefore specific cultural reasons for the devaluation of female infants, rather than a universal sense of female worthlessness, as in the case of ancient Rome, for example.

Roman Ashkelon

But even the Roman picture is not at all clear. In 1992, Smith and Kahila reported on a large collection of infant bones from a late Roman sewer context at Ashkelon in Israel. They suggested that death was caused by infanticide and they based this on the examination of the long bones that revealed that the infants were all approximately the same age at death (around full term). Infanticide, they argued, is generally carried out immediately after birth. The Ashkelon infants have now been sexed on the basis of DNA by Faerman of Hebrew University (1997; personal communication). She examined the skeletal remains of some 100 neonates that had been discovered in the sewer. Of forty-three left femurs tested, nineteen specimens produced results: fourteen were found to be males and five were females. In other words, if this sample is representative, more males than females were being killed and deposited in the sewer—preferential male infanticide.

This high incidence of male infanticide was explained away by noting that the sewer lay beneath a Roman bathhouse that might have served as a brothel. Pointing out that females could have been saved and reared as prostitutes, the high frequency of males suggests to Faerman the selective preservation of female infants and that the infants may have been the offspring of prostitutes who worked in the bathhouse, thus supporting the idea that it was used as a brothel.

While the empirical data from Ashkelon is undoubtedly fascinating, the interpretation of the meaning of the infant deposits is not entirely unproblematical. We cannot escape from the fact that the first proven example of preferential male infanticide has been conceptualized within the context of female sexual commodification. If the only context of value we can find for female infants is the sexual exploitation of girls, then this appears to be a strangely retrograde step, conceptually speaking, especially given that there is little in-dependent evidence for the use of the bathhouse as a brothel. Further, one suspects that given the quantity of human remains found in the sewer, both it and the baths it served were probably out of use when the deposits were made.

Phoenician Sacrifice

Infant sacrifice is a form of infanticide, but it is also a public performance of beliefs or vows, usually practiced as part of a perceived religious obligation. As a performance, it carries different social connotations than domestic in-fanticide. The identification of infant sacrifice from purely archaeological re-mains is difficult, though a little less problematical than the identification of domestic infanticide. For example, the remains of sacrificed infants have been found in a number of Phoenician cities of the first millennium B.C., such as Carthage in North Africa (Weyl 1968; Brown 1991; Lee 1996; Lee 1997).

This time the texts tell us a story of the killing of the male. A number of Greek and Latin texts dating from the fifth century B.C. to the fifth century A.D. survive that refer to infant sacrifice, and, if the victims are described at all, they are usually said to be one or more of the following: young, male, rich (freeborn, noble), poor, the dedicant's own infant or child, or an infant sold to the dedicant. There are also occasional mentions of the infant being the firstborn male or the best loved, and of being sacrificed singly and in huge numbers, in times of personal crisis and in times of war (Brown 1991, 22). The infants were aged between zero and four years, and they were burned, possibly while drugged, or already dead, and their remains collected and placed in cinerary urns along with small trinkets or pottery provided by the parents (Lee 1996, 67; 1997) "The vessels and other paraphernalia depicted on sacrificial stelae indicate as well that there were rituals associated with killing and burying a child victim that required planning, preparation and, presumably, professional assistance"—and the parents were careful to add their names and genealogies to the markers in order to announce publicly that they had fulfilled their vow to the gods (Brown 1991, 171–72). The infants were buried for the gods beneath the names of their ancestors.

One might feel tempted to ask: infant sacrifice at what price? Were the Phoenician infants given freely to the state and to the gods? Or was there resistance from the parents? Did they feel and think in a grieving way over their loss and their active roles in the deaths of their children? In even asking these questions, and framing them in such a way, we tend to be imposing our own value systems onto these past societies. How can we tell if they thought just like us, especially when we are seeing the practice at least partly through the eyes of the external Greek and Roman critics who left us a written record of the Phoenicians? It is probably, therefore, worth looking at another sacrificial context from a markedly different time and place to see how infant sacrifice actually filled a logical role within a community—the Moche culture of ancient Peru.

Moche Sacrifice: Infanticide as Part of World View

Because the Inka of ancient Peru are known to have sacrificed small children but not infants, it was assumed by many archaeologists that the same conditions probably applied to the earlier Moche culture of the Peruvian north coast (circa A.D. 1–600). It was therefore with some surprise that Steve Bourget and his team uncovered infant remains from the Moche sacrificial temple at Huaca de la Luna during the 1995 and 1996 field seasons. The remains of three infants, aged between one and three years, were discovered in a special plaza of the Huaca de la Luna, one of the principal ceremonial centers of the Moche culture. They were found lying just underneath a series of tortured men captured in battle and killed as sacrifices during spells of torrential rains and flooding known as *el Niño* events. It is significant that the infants form the very first human deposits in this hugely important sacrificial space, breaking the ground with their small bodies and setting in motion a train of ritual at this place that involved the torture and killing of huge numbers of adult male captives. The head of one of the infants was missing.

The infants may well have been buried there because they were perceived as having some special qualities or associations for Moche society. Infants are repeatedly depicted on Moche pottery being held by whistling women, and it is clear from other iconographies, such as those of the hunt and those involving sea creatures, that both the gesture of whistling and the pose of carrying an infant were regarded as part of the sacred lexicon of the Moche's dialogue with ancestors and deities in the fight against the onset of the terrifying and disastrous *el Niño* rains and floods.

If we see the context of these infant deposits not just at the Huaca, but as part of the whole "liturgy" of Moche culture, we can demonstrate the importance of understanding the roles of the infant and infancy within this particular society. Having examined the material culture in detail, including the artistic imagery from pottery, Bourget has convincingly interpreted these infants as having been used to engage with ancestors, contextualizing the deposits within the archaeological evidence of artistic imagery, burials, ritual, and the use of space and dialogue with ancestors and deities. He argues that these young dead form an integral part of the sacrificial apparatus dedicated to the world of the sea and, more particularly, to the control of the cataclysmic *el Niño* events, and that these exceptional rituals form just part of a wider cultural narrative, comprising representations of young children and sacrifices in ritual iconography (Bourget 1997 and 1998; personal communication).

BELIEF

Killing Infants: Birth, Death, Rebirth

Killing a baby in the Western and the Muslim worlds is not sanctioned. In the United States and the United Kingdom, for instance, it is a criminal offence, and the perpetrator is regarded both legally and morally as bad or mad. Indeed, the British legal definition of infanticide, while liberal and accepting of women's experiences, has managed to pathologize motherhood as a state prone to mental disturbance. This is inextricably linked to the patriarchal context within which the legislation was framed and is enforced, that of the Christian ethos where a newborn's life, though tainted with original sin, is nevertheless deemed sacred, and its body and soul unique. But the majority of the world's population is not Christian. More than half believe in reincarnation in some form (Hindus, Jains, and Buddhists, for example), or believe more directly the idea that a person's spirit can leave one body and come back in some form into another body. As Davies points out in his discussion of Indian and Persian souls, "rituals surrounding death are, usually, closely related to basic views of human nature and destiny including the way in which identity is composed, especially in the link between the material body and some energizing spirit"(1997, 81).

And so in Kathiawar, India, for example, British administrators noted a practice whereby female infants were sometimes drowned in milk after a prayer had been offered that they might be reborn as a boy (Reynolds and Tanner 1983, 55).

It is interesting, therefore, to note from a prehistoric context that classical authors identified in the Druidic teaching of Iron Age northwest Europe a belief that deeply affects conceptions of identity, namely, that a person's soul "does not descend to the silent, sunless world of Hades, but becomes reincarnate elsewhere; if they are right, death is merely a point of change in perpetual existence" (Lucan's *Pharsalia*, cited in Green 1997, 51). In other words, the Druids taught that the soul was immortal and underwent an endless cycle of rebirth in different bodies. Caesar comments that such belief encouraged martial bravery because men did not fear death, and Diodorus states that the Gauls believed human souls to be immortal and, at death, went into another body (Green 1997, 51).

Such religions do not set human identity within a historical framework in the same way as do the Western Judeo-Christian religions. Schemes of reincarnation operating under samsara and karma, for example, speak more mythologically and less historically about the passage of time, preferring to emphasize human consciousness, human experience, and various processes of mediation that can be the source of salvation (Davies 1997, 81). Ancient Greek religion had some historical framework, in that there were ideas of creation(s), but it too emphasized human experience within a context of fate and essential divine rights. And, in a review of anthropological evidence for infanticide, Williamson noted two examples that give pause for thought when it comes to interpreting infanticide:

> The Aborigines of Groote Eylandt, Australia, for example, believe that the spirit of a dead infant goes to a store of spirit children to await rebirth, and thus the infant continues to live, though in a different form. . . . Moreover, infanticide is seldom an expression of cruel or violent feeling. . . . It is, as the Japanese term for it indicates, "weeding," like "thinning rice seedlings." (Williamson 1978, 64)

These examples raise some important considerations. The first point is that killed infants may not actually be regarded as dead at all, but simply awaiting rebirth at a more auspicious time. The second point is that concern for fertility is not necessarily incompatible with the practice of infanticide. In addition, one might note the research carried out by Scheper-Hughes (1984) in northeast Brazil, where some 200 out of 1,000 infants do not survive the first year of life. She discovered that there were complex psychological factors affecting a mother's decision to rear or not to rear a particular baby. For example, women depicted the deaths of certain children as a "blessing." Harris, who also had occasion to witness infant death in northeast Brazil during fieldwork there, provides this useful overview of Scheper-Hughes's research data.

> They habitually judged each child on a rough scale of readiness or fitness for life. Children whose mothers perceived them as being quick, sharp, active, and physically well developed received more food and medical attention than their sisters and brothers. Others, whose mothers perceived them to be lethargic, passive, and as having a "ghostlike" or "animallike" appearance, received less food and medical attention and were in fact likely to become ill and die within the first year of life. Mothers spoke of them as children who wanted to die, whose will to live was not sufficiently strong or developed. When children with the fatal stigmata expire, their mothers do not display grief . . . some say that their baby had been called to heaven to become a "little angel." (Harris 1989, 211–12)

The mothers apparently sincerely believed that there was no remedy for the afflictions of their children.

Social Death

One might therefore take on board the important notion, as far as the people being studied are concerned ("emic"), that these neglected and killed babies were never meant for life at all. These may be what we would perceive as violent deaths, as murders, yet because these infants had been marked down for infanticide while still in the womb, or because it was clearly understood that if the emerging infant revealed certain characteristics it would not be allowed to live, there had in fact been a great deal of preparation for the act of infanticide and any psychological consequences. In his discussion of the concept of "social death," Mulkay (1993) notes that many major ethnographies have observed the ways in which the social existence of dying patients is reduced, and sometimes eliminated, owing to other parties' physical, emotional, and communicative withdrawal. Mulkay's work, as do the ethnographies to which he alludes, focuses very much on the care of the dying and the elderly, but I would like here to express my belief that this paradigm has much in it to aid in the understanding of the meanings of infanticidal practices. For example, unwanted pregnancies, where the infanticide of the resulting neonate is more or less inevitable, might be characterized by the parents' lack of initiation of any life sequence or social existence for the fetus/neonate. The death sequence therefore is not prolonged, and there is indeed much physical and emotional withdrawal documented concerning parents and fetuses/neonates.

The known methods of killing the neonate also suggest withdrawal from its bodily existence. Chagnon, in his study of the Yanomamo Indians of South America observed that

> Several techniques are used to kill a newborn child. The most common method is to strangle it with a vine so as not to touch it physically. Another common method is to place a stick across the child's neck and stand on both ends of it until it chokes. In some cases the child is not given the stimulus to breathe and is simply abandoned. Finally, some women throw the child against a tree or on the ground and just abandon it without checking to see if it was killed by the injuries sustained. (Chagnon 1977, 76, quoted by Reynolds and Tanner 1983, 51)

This changes the whole focus of our attention with regard to the status of the infants. They were not "unwanted" in the obvious sense of the word. They simply didn't exist. They were not of the right time, and therefore not for the world at that moment.

The Mortuary Record

The idea of social death and withdrawal should not draw attention away from the fact that social existence may be prolonged well beyond the point of biological termination. "The biologically dead can be experienced and addressed symbolically by the living, and they can influence the conduct of the living. In these respects, the dead may continue to participate in the observable social world as that world is understood by their survivors" (Mulkay 1993, 33). Archaeologists have long understood the mortuary record in these terms and have concerned themselves increasingly with using this record to elucidate relationships between the living and the dead, particularly in terms of dialogue with ancestors.

However, the remarkable thing about the mortuary record for neonates and very young infants (those under one year) is that it barely exists. In Europe, throughout prehistory and antiquity, the exclusion of neonates from cemeteries and burial grounds is common (Scott 1999). Is it that all neonates were denied social existence in order to permit infanticide to be sanctioned when necessary within communities? It should be noted that it is all neonates who are absent, not just female neonates. Therefore, one could suggest that both female and male neonates were devoid of social existence in agricultural and pastoral communities.

Infanticide and Infant Mortality

This raises the very real possibility that all infants, whether deceased through infanticide or natural causes, were treated and possibly regarded in much the same way. Indeed, a blurring of the distinction between infanticide and death through natural causes is known to have been acted out in some social contexts through the practice of neglect/indirect infanticide—where the infant was not directly killed, but was gradually left or "allowed" to die. This may account for the acting out of this practice in extremis through exposure. There are also cultural contexts where infants have been known to have died through deliberate neglect—often starvation—by the parents, but where the parental behavior was justified (by the parents) by arguing that the infant was going to die anyway.

CONCLUSION

This chapter has discussed issues that are part of the dogma of demographic and mortuary archaeology: first, it is routinely held that when we talk of infanticide we are really talking about female infanticide—that infanticide is the story of the killing of the female, and second, that infanticide represents the killing of "unwanted" infants. I have argued that both these beliefs oversimplify a complex situation and confuse data with interpretation. In short, this chapter has concluded that:

- Infanticide was widespread in the past and remains so in some countries.
- The causes, effects, and meanings of infanticide vary from society to society, and within societies.
- Such causes have cultural meanings rather than ecological ones, such as responses to codes of the transmission of wealth across generations.
- Infant boys (elite and nonelite) as well as infant girls (elite and nonelite) were killed. Any overarching theory of infanticide, gender, and eliteness is unlikely to have explanatory power.
- Fathers and mothers variously initiated and practiced infanticide.
- The difficulties of killing neonates was overcome using a number of social strategies, such as believing that the infant would be reborn at a later date and/or by denying the human existence of the newborn infant.
- Such beliefs may account for the virtually complete absence of neonate and infant burials from formal cemeteries in Europe from the Neolithic onward.

We can no longer simplistically accept female infanticide as the cultural norm, and we must create more significant discourses about age processes such as infancy just as we are striving toward a greater gendered sophistication in academic research. However, infanticide was clearly a part of social existence in prehistory and antiquity, as was infant mortality, and the virtual absence of infants from the mortuary record may suggest that in some contexts little distinction was made between what we in the modern West perceive as natural and unnatural deaths. Furthermore, it is a modern construct to consider acts of infanticide as banal and unsophisticated; in fact, acts of infanticide may well link with complex socioreligious beliefs.

I acknowledge that the cross-cultural approach needs very careful handling, but, to turn the argument around somewhat, I suggest that the traditional acceptance of preferential female infanticide in the past is itself a simplistic cross-cultural model. What I have argued here is that an analysis of the data shows a much more complex picture, and one in which male and female infants are killed for all sorts of reasons within all sorts of cultural contexts. That is, we can use ethnographic discourse and mortuary data to demonstrate variety in agency as opposed to some static idea of female "worth." One cannot deny the prevalence of infanticide in the past; but one can and must query the prevailing notion that it represents the killing of the female. One must beware of regarding instances of male infanticide as exceptional, or grounding them in a privileged narrative of power and value while female infanticide is interpreted as the disposal of the powerless and valueless; that infant boys are special sacrifices while infant girls are domestic rubbish. Equally, one must beware a tendency to view a father's killing of the infant as an act of power, but a mother's killing of an infant as an act of desperation. To interpret the evidence thus may well say much more about how we ourselves perceive gender roles and values than it ever would about the realities of past lives and social meanings. The fact that male infanticide tends to be seen as maladaptive and deviant (Weyl 1968; Reynolds and Tanner 1983, 54), whereas female infanticide is seen as adaptive and normal (Freeman 1971), should sound a loud warning note about the theoretical inadequacies of the existing discourse.

On a final note, if we accept that the widespread existence of infanticide in human societies cannot simply be written off as an exercise in mass dowry-avoidance, and that rather than representing the global destruction of "unwanted" female infants, it represents the eradication of both male and female infants, one is left to ponder the implications for some current Darwinian theories. For example, Daly and Wilson, in their infamous treatise on the dangers of being a stepchild in human societies, premise their whole argument on what they call "the profundity of parental love" (1998, 65–66). In this model, they claim that interpersonal attachments, and in particular parental love, are not social constructions, but rather that "There is . . . a strong theoretical rationale for expecting that the evolved human psyche contains safeguards against allowing a mere stepchild, however appealing, easy access to that special mental category occupied by genetic children, the appropriate objects for the most nearly selfless love we know" (65–66). However, the evidence for the commonality of infanticide, and the variety of reasons for infanticide, and the variety of rationales presented to explain the practice indicate that, to the contrary, parental acceptance and love of an infant is contingent on many social factors; and, as Darwinians themselves acknowledge that infancy is an extremely visually attractive stage of development to the human parent, one must consider that the evidence suggests that parental emotional attachment is indeed socially constructed to a very large degree.

ACKNOWLEDGMENTS

I was unable to attend the original conference because of my late stage of pregnancy, but my thanks to Nancy Wicker and Bettina Arnold for encouraging me to provide this chapter for the volume. Nancy and Steve Bourget have been two great sources of inspiration, and I have greatly enjoyed reading their own work on matters pertaining to infancy and culture. Thanks also to Simon Mays and Marina Faerman for being similarly interesting and helpful with regard to the archaeological forensics of infanticide, despite our differences of approach to interpretive narrative. And thanks too, Ken, Madeleine, and Edwin for giving me some time at the keyboard.

REFERENCES

Bates, Daniel G. 1996. *Cultural anthropology*. Needham Heights, Mass.: Allyn & Bacon.

Biddulph, Steve. 1998. *Raising boys*. London: Thorsons (HarperCollins).

Birdsell, Joseph B. 1968. Some predictions for the Pleistocene based on equilibrium systems among hunter-gatherers. In *Man the hunter*. Edited by Richard B. Lee and Irven DeVore, pp. 229–40. Chicago: Aldine and Atherton.

Bourget, Steve. 1997. Too young to die and too old to care: Children and ancestors at Huaca de la Luna. Paper presented at TAG Conference, University of Bournemouth, U.K., 1997.

———. Forthcoming July 2001. Children and ancestors: Ritual practices at the Moche site of Huaca de la Luna, north coast of Peru. In *Ritual sacrifice in ancient Peru: New discoveries and interpretations*. Edited by Elizabeth P. Benson and Anita G. Cook. Austin: University of Texas Press.

British and Foreign Bible Society. 1952. *The Bible Standard Revised Version*. London: W. M. Collins.

Brown, Shelby. 1991. *Late Carthaginian child sacrifice and sacrificial monuments in their Mediterranean context*. Sheffield, U.K.: Sheffield Academic Press.

Chagnon, Napoleon A. 1977. *Yanomamo: The fierce people*. New York: Holt, Rinehart and Winston.

Cheater, Angela P. 1989. *Social anthropology: An alternative introduction*. 2d ed. London: Unwin Hyman.

Daly, Martin, and Margo Wilson. 1998. *The truth about Cinderella: A Darwinian view of parental love*. London: Weidenfeld and Nicolson.

Davies, Douglas J. 1997. *Death, ritual, and belief: The rhetoric of funerary rites*. London: Cassell.

Ehrenberg, Margaret. 1989. *Women in prehistory*. London: British Museum.

Faerman, Marina. 1997. Determining the sex of infanticide victims from the late Roman era through ancient DNA analysis. Abstracts. TAG Conference, University of Bournemouth, U.K., 1997.

Freeman, Milton M. R. 1971. A social and ecological analysis of systematic female infanticide among the Netsilik Eskimo. *American Anthropologist* 73:1011–18.

Frere, Sheppard S. 1978. *Britannia*. Rev. ed. London: Routledge & Kegan Paul.

Green, Miranda J. 1997. *Exploring the world of the Druids*. London: Thames and Hudson.

Harris, Marvin. 1989. *Our kind*. New York: Harper and Row.

Hoffer, Peter C., and N. E. Hull. 1984. *Murdering mothers: Infanticide in England and New England 1558–1803*. New York University School of Law Series in Legal History. Vol 2. Linden Studies in Anglo-American Legal History. New York: New York University Press.

Jones, Peter V., ed. 1984. *The world of Athens: An introduction to classical Athenian culture*. Joint Association of Classical Teachers. Open university edition. Cambridge, U.K.: Cambridge University Press.

Lee, K. Alexandra. 1996. Attitudes and prejudices towards infanticide: Carthage, Rome, and today. *Archaeological Review from Cambridge* 13 (2): 21–34.

―――. 1997. Infant sacrifice at Carthage and the social ideal of the child. Paper presented at TAG Conference, University of Bournemouth, U.K., 1997.

Lee, Richard B. 1980. Lactation, ovulation, infanticide, and women's work: A study of hunter-gatherer population regulation. In *Biosocial mechanisms of population regulation*. Edited by M. N. Cohen, R. S. Malpas, and H. G. Klein, pp. 321–48. New Haven, Conn.: Yale University Press.

McLennan, John Ferguson. [1865] 1970. *Primitive marriage. An inquiry into the origin of the form of capture in marriage ceremonies*. Classics in anthropology series. Reprint, Chicago: University of Chicago Press.

Mulkay, Michael. 1993. Social death in Britain. In *The sociology of death: Theory, culture, practice*. Edited by David Clark, pp. 31–49. Oxford, U.K.: Basil Blackwell.

Porter, Roy. 1997. *The greatest benefit to mankind: A medical history of humanity from antiquity to the present*. London: HarperCollins.

Rasmussen, Knud. 1931. *The Netsilik Eskimos. Report of the fifth Thule expedition 1921–1924*. Copenhagen: Gylendalske Boghandel.

Rega, Elizabeth. 1997. Age, gender, and biological reality in the early Bronze Age cemetery at Mokrin. In *Invisible people and processes: Writing gender and childhood into European archaeology*. Edited by Jenny Moore and Eleanor Scott, pp. 229–47. London: Leicester University Press.

Reynolds, Vernon, and Ralph Tanner. 1983. *The biology of religion*. Harlow, U.K.: Longman.

Scheper-Hughes, Nancy. 1984. Infant mortality and infant care: Cultural and economic constraints on nurturing in northeast Brazil. *Social Science and Medicine* 19 (5): 535–46.

Scott, Eleanor. 1999. *The archaeology of infancy and infant death*. British Archaeological Reports International Series 819. Oxford, U.K.: Archaeopress.

Shelton, Jo-Ann, trans. 1988. Oxyrhynchus Papyri 744 (Select Papyri 105). In *As the Romans did. A source book in Roman history*. Oxford, U.K.: Oxford University Press.

Sherring, M. A. 1872. *Hindu tribes and castes*. Calcutta: Thacker Spink.

Smith, Patricia, and Gila Kahila. 1992. Identification of infanticide in archaeological sites: A case study from the late Roman–early Byzantine periods at Ashkelon, Israel. *Journal of Archaeological Science* 19:667–75.

Taylor, Timothy. 1996. *The prehistory of sex: Four million years of human sexual culture*. London: Fourth Estate.

Weyl, Nathaniel. 1968. Some possible genetic implications of Carthaginian sacrifice. *Perspectives in Biology and Medicine* 12:69–98.

Wicker, Nancy. 1998. Selective female infanticide as partial explanation for the dearth of women in Viking Age Scandinavia. In *Violence and society in the early medieval west: Private, public, and ritual*. Edited by Guy Halsall, pp. 205–22. Woodbridge, Suffolk, U.K.: Boydell Press.

Williamson, Laila. 1978. Infanticide: An anthropological analysis. In *Infanticide and the value of life*. Edited by Marvin Kohl, pp. 61–75. Amherst, N.Y.: Prometheus.

Willshire, W. H. 1895. On the manners etc. of the natives of Central Australia. *Journal of the Anthropological Institute* 24:183–85.

2

Life, Death, and the Longhouse: A Gendered View of Oneota Social Organization

Jodie A. O'Gorman

Mortuary analysis has long been used to examine social structure and to infer social organization (Binford 1971; Brown 1981; Goldstein 1976; Saxe 1970; 1980; and Tainter 1975, 1978). In addition to this social approach, more recent analyses have considered the dynamics of death within economic and political contexts of the living (see Brown 1995). In gender studies of the archaeological record, mortuary analysis in conjunction with other types of data can play a key role in eliciting information about the roles and social dynamics of men and women within a given society.

While there are many reasons for studying gender, one of the most fundamental is that gender is one of the structuring principles of every aspect of culture (Conkey and Gero 1991; Hollimon 1990; Moore 1988; and Wylie 1991). Thus, gender has been an interactive dynamic within every aspect of culture that archaeologists seek to elucidate. All participants in any human society are affected by their culturally constituted gender, and the shape of their social interactions and negotiations for social power are inevitably influenced by gender. Mortuary studies are particularly well suited for examining gender because direct linkages to biological sex can often be made with some degree of assurance.

In this study, which is a condensed version of my dissertation research (O'Gorman 1996), a gender-focused mortuary analysis is used to evaluate and enrich interpretations of social organization by examining how relationships of social inequality are emphasized or de-emphasized in the mortuary program. I juxtapose domestic economics and mortuary behavior, two distinct contexts where social position was negotiated and relationships of social inequality may be visible.

THE ONEOTA TRADITION: CONTEXT FOR THE STUDY
OF THE EMERGENCE OF INEQUALITY

The Oneota Tradition, dating from about A.D. 900 to protohistoric times in the midcontinent of North America, is generally characterized as having a tribal level of sociopolitical organization that is essentially egalitarian in nature. Correlates of complexity such as settlement hierarchies, differential status indicators in mortuary patterns, and craft specialization present in Middle Mississippian culture are largely lacking in Upper Mississippian Oneota (Benn 1989; Hall 1962; and Stevenson 1985). As is the case with many "noncomplex" societies, archaeologists have seldom explored the details and implications of this organization or its social structure (but see Benn 1989, 1995; Hollinger 1993, 1995; and Kreisa 1993).

This chapter examines the possibility for and extent to which Oneota social organization is shaped by social inequality based on and crosscutting gender. I use the notion of social inequality as a measure of differential access to social and subsistence resources (cf. Hayden 1995). The Tremaine Complex, four almost contiguous Oneota sites covering in excess of fifty hectares in southwestern Wisconsin, is the focus of this study. One area in particular at the large Tremaine site, Area H, contained human remains documented in association with at least seven longhouses and an array of storage and processing pits (fig. 1). Recent studies of the development of inequality recognize the household as an important context for the emergence of social inequality (Ames 1995; Blanton 1995). Indeed, the household has long been recognized as an essential scale for the study of social relations of production (Blanton 1994; Goody 1958, 1972; Hammel and Laslett 1974; Hastorf 1993; Laslett 1972; Netting, Wilk, and Arnould 1984; Tringham 1991; and Yanagisako 1979).

What did it mean for Oneota men and women to be "essentially egalitarian"? One way to address this question is to focus on the issue of incipient social inequality. While more formal institutionalized inequality is readily observable in prehistory, the development and nature of incipient social inequality and its links to gender are also important. Before we can understand why inequalities become institutionalized in some societies and not in others, we must more fully understand variations in the bases of social inequalities. As stated by Feinman, "attention must be placed both on those mechanisms in nonstratified societies that have served to level extant inequities before they become institutionalized, as well as on the internal and/or external con-

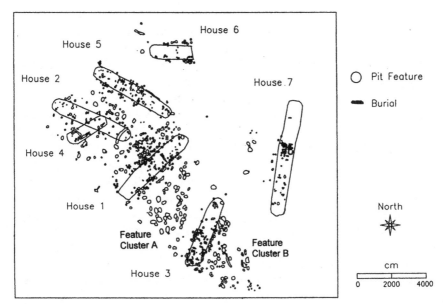

Figure 1. Tremaine Area H.

ditions that work to negate those leveling strategies and sanctions so that existent inequalities are permitted to become more institutionalized" (1995, 262). A structuring principle in social negotiation, gender is thereby a factor in the creation and dynamics of leveling and sanctioning strategies.

My analysis included same-sex/gender and between-sex/gender comparisons at the household, interhousehold, and community levels. While there is a very important distinction between sex (the biological classification) and gender (the social construct), this study assumes an isomorphic relationship between the two. I chose to examine domestic economics (production, distribution, and consumption of subsistence goods within and between households) to identify possible relationships of inequality. I then turned to the mortuary program at Tremaine to view these relationships from another perspective, evaluating to what degree economic relationships of inequality or equality between and among the sexes are reproduced in treatment of the dead.

Ethnographic sources and mortuary data from across the Oneota tradition were used to establish linkages between women and specific resource management activities vital to the success of the Oneota lifeway as represented at Tremaine (see O'Gorman 1996). Ethnographic data can also suggest contexts where the development of social inequalities might be expected. It also offers insight into the rigors of carrying out a successful subsistence strategy that relies on scheduling and planning, detailed knowledge of a wide range of resources, and access to a labor force. The archaeological record demonstrates that the Oneota subsistence strategy in southwestern Wisconsin was intensively diverse (Gallagher and Arzigian 1994). Corn, bean, and squash agriculture along with native cultigen gardening was important. But so too was gathering and managing wild plant crops, particularly wild rice. Ethnographic and traditionwide mortuary data suggest that not only was this crop production the purview of women, but they also fished and harvested many different wetland/riverine species and hunted small mammals. Large-game hunting and warfare was traditionally the domain of men. However, women were frequently active participants in warfare and, although perhaps not directly making bison kills, were integral members of the party for processing (Koehler 1997). In addition to the annual requirements for subsistence, the ethnographic data indicate the need for surplus stores required to engage in socially mandated feasting related to social advancement. This could have fostered competition for increased productivity. Some control over particular subsistence activities by clans occurred historically (Radin 1923; Skinner 1926). Given the evidence for a diverse resource base at Tremaine, a population within the community that is estimated to have reached about 350 people (O'Gorman 1995), and the organizational requirements of tending, harvesting, processing, and storing these diverse resources, there would seem to be a good possibility that some form of social inequality manifested itself between and/or within gender groups.

As Oneota households grew and scalar stress (stresses of large group decision making) increased, mechanisms for dealing with these stresses may have provided contexts for the emergence of social inequality. Using Johnson's (1982) proposed mechanisms for dealing with scalar stress, I suggest that social inequalities emerged at the household level as simultaneous or vertical hierarchies were needed to coordinate and regulate the utilization of some resources. Less permanent, short-term sequential hierarchies probably occurred whereby short-term decisions were made by consensus. However, as some households became more successful at acquiring resources (subsistence or labor), it is possible that social inequalities between households and between women also developed. Surpluses of food and other items may have been used by women to gain and demonstrate social position by providing the necessary provisions and wealth to undertake socially enhancing ventures, such as warfare, hunting, or religious ceremonies.

DOMESTIC ECONOMIC ANALYSIS

Summary and Highlights of the Study

To test my ideas about the presence of social inequalities within and between households, I identified a number of gender-linked archaeological correlates pertinent to the Tremaine data. Use of direct evidence from plant and animal remains to examine differential access within and between households was problematic. Spatial distribution of storage and processing features (defined based on morphology) was used to assess control over access to resources. Spatial distribution of implements used to grow, collect, or process resources could also provide an indication of the nature of women's control over these activities. I also examined the distribution of other portable artifacts with mixed results and only mention the most informative here.

In the domestic economic analysis, which was greatly facilitated by use of a GIS, households were defined spatially using a buffer zone around each house. Two feature clusters were also identified (see fig. 1). Within the households, differential distribution of storage pits was documented. Some portions of these households are completely devoid of storage facilities, an observation that may be related to differential use of space. But even when these areas are omitted from analysis, there are significantly more storage pits in some areas than others. This may be an indication of social inequality whereby some women within the household controlled a greater amount of stored crops.

When only the households are considered, there does not appear to be any significant difference in the amount of storage between houses. Each of the households has a similar amount of storage within a few meters of its walls. However, the storage facilities located in Clusters A and B are considerable. Spatially, the two clusters are more closely associated with Households 1 and 3. It is also possible that these two clusters were, to some degree, communal facilities rather than entirely restricted to one or two households, but their spatial positioning suggests at least partial control by one or two households. Many of the features in Cluster A are distinct in their size and shape—they are the largest and deepest pits at the site, and include a high percentage of processing pits. A total of 41 percent by number and 48.9 percent by volume of all processing pits in the community can be found in Cluster A.

None of the tool groups I examined displayed a spatial distribution pattern that would be consistent with exclusive control over a portion of the domestic economy. However, distributions of several artifact types indicate a greater involvement of one or more households in some activities.

Drills or perforators and projectile points were found in greater abundance within Household 3. Concentration of projectile points, linked primarily to men in traditionwide mortuary data, in this household may be the result of the repeated congregation of men preparing for or engaging in activities related to preparations for warfare or hunting. Ethnographic data suggest that a great deal of men's time was spent planning and preparing for these exploits. Household 3 and Clusters A and B were also associated with a relatively greater number of scapula hoes, but their frequency overall is quite low across the site. Drills and perforators were used by both men and women, and their differential distribution in Household 3 may be related to a greater focus on processing materials procured during hunting.

Because feasting has been documented ethnographically as being an important prerequisite of hunting and warfare, we might expect that Household 3 also would display a greater number of large ceramic vessels. If Cluster B is considered part of Household 3, evidence for this can be found.

I suggest that Household 3 was more involved in hunting and warfare and may even have been the household of a village chief who regulated these activities. Because the household of a village chief would require more surplus to distribute to those in need (Radin 1923), more storage facilities could be expected archaeologically in association with this household. Likewise, if Household 3 was simply more successful or more involved in hunting or warfare, drawing in men from other households to participate in these ventures, we might also expect more storage of surplus to provision and provide the necessary ritual feasting. The association of Household 3 with Cluster A and Cluster B storage and processing pits along with the other artifact data supports the possibility that some type of differential status was associated with this household. Because hunting and warfare are known to have brought elevated status in historic times, we might also expect that both the men and women of this household were involved in creating relationships of social inequality.

ECONOMIC ANALYSIS DISCUSSION

The ability to organize a household's human resources and produce large amounts of storable foodstuffs was especially important in this Oneota community that relied on successful production, storage, and allocation of a diversity of resources. Through the production of surplus that could be used to create obligatory relationships or engage members of the household in status-gaining ventures, Oneota women at Tremaine may have contributed to their own social advancement along with that of their household. Within the households, individual women may have exercised power over these storable resources as the household and community populations grew, and dependence on this important part of the diverse resource base increased. Within the female context of coordinating and making decisions related to the production, procurement, storage, and distribution of these grain crops, which required long-term and skillful decision making, social inequality at the household level emerged.

MORTUARY ANALYSIS

Tremaine Site Burials: Considerations of Time and Space

The most striking aspect of the Tremaine mortuary pattern is spatial. A total of ninety-four individuals is represented within Area H (excluding isolated remains), and individuals are almost always interred within the houses; there are four exceptions (fig. 2). The positioning of four burials outside the houses makes this group spatially distinct, but variation in other characteristics does not appear to be significant. Each house has at least one burial. It is quite possible that not everyone who died during occupation of this village was buried within the houses. In fact, two other burial areas are known within the Tremaine Complex. These areas and their implication for this study are important and are discussed below.

A number of different mortuary practices related to spatial disposition of the dead are known within the Oneota tradition, including cemetery areas within habitation sites, cemetery areas removed from the habitation, intrusive mound burial, and within-house burial (Halverson 1994; Kreisa 1993; O'Gorman 1995; Overstreet 1989, 1995; and Santure 1990). And, as Henning notes, "burials and human bone fragments may be encountered at any location on

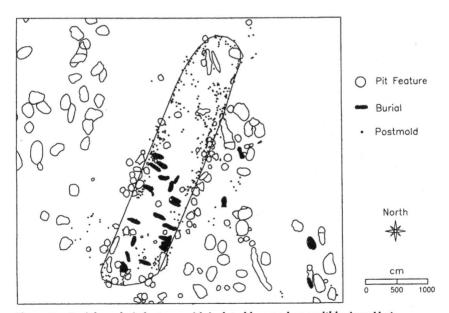

Figure 2. Burials and pit features with isolated human bone within Area H at Tremaine.

an Oneota site" (1970, 141). However, many Oneota burial populations are the result of relatively small-scale excavation, which often precludes an understanding of large-scale context.

At Tremaine, continuity in the reoccupation pattern of houses supports the assumption that households were occupied by the same groups repeatedly over time, with the main occupation of the houses from about A.D. 1400 to 1500 during the Pammel Creek phase (O'Gorman 1995). That these household burials were not all related to a single ritual event is suggested by the superpositioning of some burials over postmolds or into early postmold lines with other groups of burial rows offset nearer the center of the structure, indicative of interment during an earlier episode (fig. 3). The mortuary pattern at Tremaine may have occurred over the total occupation and reoccupation period of the village (A.D. 1300–1650). However, it is assumed that, as a whole, these burials represent mortuary activities of the corporate household primarily dating to circa A.D. 1400 to 1500.

Tremaine Skeletal Population

Skeletal material in the Tremaine Area H population was poorly preserved due to weathering and other taphonomic factors that hampered demographic and pathological determinations (Grauer 1995). A total of eighty-six individ-

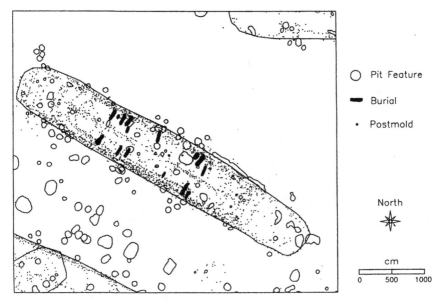

Figure 3.   House 5 showing relationship of burials to post lines.

uals represented by skeletal remains adequately preserved for collection were identified in burial contexts. For this analysis, Grauer's determinations of "probable male" and "probable female" were included within male and female categories (see Grauer 1995 for skeletal data). Another eight child-sized burials were documented in the field, but did not contain bone or contained bone too deteriorated to be recovered (O'Gorman 1995).

Isolated remains (110 elements) found in pit features scattered across the site represent a minimum of five adolescents or adults. Elements represented include fragments of crania, mandibles, dentition, vertebrae, and bone from the arms, hands, legs, feet, and scapula. A minimum of two subadults are represented in these isolated remains, but only by loose dentition (Vradenburg 1993).

While skeletal analyses can offer an excellent opportunity to conduct gender studies of differential health, diet, and activity (Bridges 1989; Cohen and Bennet 1993; Grauer 1991; Hollimon 1990, 1991, 1992; and Wilson 1997), the condition of the Tremaine material precludes much of this kind of analysis. Grauer (1995) notes that inferences based on demographic and pathological determinations in this poorly preserved population must be made with caution. For example, adult females appear to be better represented than males in the population, and females appear to die at younger ages while more males survive to greater age. However, these findings are inconclusive because more adults could not be sexed than males and females combined and a considerable portion of the population cannot be assigned according to age. Pathologies may be underrepresented due to preservation; documented cases include porotic hyperostosis ($N = 6$), and osteoarthritis ($N = 8$) (Grauer 1995). Stable isotope analysis has been conducted for other burials in the Tremaine Complex (discussed below), and future analyses of this kind and perhaps DNA studies of the larger Tremaine population would be valuable.

Attribute Analysis: Physical, Spatial, and Material Dimensions

For each individual, the following physical variables were recorded: age, sex, trauma, articulation, disarticulation, and absence of cranium. Variables related to spatial positioning of the body included disposition, orientation of cranium to the house, orientation of body/grave to the house, disposition of legs, and disposition of arms. Grave goods were coded by an array of variables including presence of sherds; type, content, and position of mortuary vessel; presence of red ochre; counts of the range of artifact types; and number of different artifact types. Univariate and multivariate analyses were conducted. Only the most significant of the results are discussed here.

Many of the cross-tabulation observations were affected by the low frequency of observations. There are also a considerable number of burials in the adult categories that could not be identified as to sex (N = 34). Although the assignment of these individuals by sex would affect the observations, I assume that the sexed individuals are a representative sample of all adult classes and that the preservation factors are independent of sex. Significant observations were made on several variables related to treatment or positioning of the body, demographic characteristics, and some artifact classes.

Secondary Burial

The mortuary pattern at Tremaine consists predominantly of in-house primary burial in linear (possibly family) groupings. Exhumation of the cranium or entire body occasionally occurs, as does secondary burial in about 10 percent of the population. It is unclear whether this secondary processing and related ritual is indicative of multistage mortuary behavior unrelated to social ranking or a correlate of social inequality. The low incidence may indicate the latter. These burials are all adults and include males and females.

Disarticulated burials are more likely to be found in graves containing multiple individuals and in graves that are oriented parallel to the house walls, but are not otherwise spatially differentiated from others buried within the houses. Groups of disarticulated bone and scattered bone were found only in House 7, and one group of disarticulated bone was found outside the houses. Bundle burials were found in Houses 1 and 4 (one case each). An isolated cranium of an adult female buried within its own small but distinct pit in association with another adult female was only observed in one case in House 5.

Disarticulated burials have a slightly higher occurrence of no grave goods (44.44 percent) than primarily articulated burials (26.32 percent), but this may be a function of the number of times any particular burial is exhumed or otherwise moved. Few grave goods were particularly characteristic of disarticulated burials with the exception of the matting remnants with copper and shell fragments found with two of these burials. Mortuary vessels were also restricted within the disarticulated burials. While disarticulated bundle burials may have ceramic fragments, no disarticulated burials had vessels.

Spatial Relationships

Spatial differentiation within households, particularly the orientation of the individual to the house appears to be a significant variable in the mortuary program. Placement of the head toward the center of the house is more common than placement toward the exterior or end walls. I suggest that this spatial variation is related to an individual's social personae and his relationship to others within the household. Males are more restricted in relation to the house. They were primarily buried with their bodies perpendicular to the house side walls, and their heads to the center of the houses. Females were also primarily buried with their bodies perpendicular to the house side walls, but one female was identified in the group of burials outside the houses, and a slightly higher percentage of females were buried parallel to the side walls. Positioning of female crania was more varied between the categories than males (table 1).

Orientation of the cranium toward the exterior wall is related to several other dimensions of the mortuary program. Lack of grave goods is slightly higher within this group (41.2 percent) than it is for the population as a whole (31.5 percent). All three cases of death related to trauma are oriented with the cranium to the outer wall. Positioning of the cranium to the exterior or end walls also offsets the individual from what appear to be family groupings. Those burials with the crania oriented toward the exterior wall are included in some rows, but they are not laid out directly in line with other burials of the row. Rather, they are frequently offset with the crania close to the cranium of another individual in the row. There does not appear to be any restriction by age or sex, but there is a higher percentage of females buried in this orientation.

Variation in position of the body within the grave may also be a socially significant component of mortuary ritual. Women were buried exhibiting more variations from supine than men. Of the four variations—prone, on the left side, on the right side, and semi-reclining—females were documented in each category, and only one male was documented on the right side.

I suggest that this diversity in positioning of the body within the grave and in relationship to the house, coupled with ethnographic data regarding the diversity of women's roles and correlating grave goods discussed below, is linked to women's greater diversity of social relationships. A similar variabil-

Table 1. Percentages of Cranial and Body Positions for Male and Female Burials

Position	Males	Females
Head to center	75	41
Head to exterior side wall	17	91
Head to end wall	8	18
Body perpendicular to side wall	92	70
Body parallel to side wall	8	15

ity in social position has also been suggested in Middle Mississippian society (Wilson 1997).

Grave Goods

There are no obvious symbols of authority or overtly sumptuous goods buried with the dead at Tremaine. Adults are buried with a wide variety of artifacts related to everyday tasks. Mortuary studies drawing on the social approach have demonstrated that the diversity and quantity of grave goods can be related to the social personae and vertical social position of the deceased (Binford 1971; O'Shea 1981). While there are many distinctions between grave goods at Tremaine, it is interesting that households appear to have their own pattern, and two types of data may reveal vertical distinctions of social position. First, there are a few nonlocal items included as grave goods; these are not equally distributed among the households. Second, the number of artifact types interred as grave goods appears to cluster into three groups: those without artifacts, those with one to three, and those with four to seven. The divisions of this variable (number of grave good types) correspond to some extent to age and orientation of the cranium as discussed previously and also to household as explored below.

Cross-tabulation of artifacts, age, and sex confirmed the general impression reported in the preliminary analysis that "artifacts buried with adults tend to be varied and predominantly related to subsistence tasks and everyday activities for both males and females" (O'Gorman 1995, 194). Of the more common tools found in graves, cores and scrapers are found only in the adult-age classes. Less common artifact types, including hoes, sandstone fragments, grinding stones, wedge, drill, and a blade, were only found in the adult-age classes.

Infants (100 percent) and children (66.67 percent) tend to be associated with one type or no grave goods. Adolescents have a high incidence of no grave goods (40 percent), but can also be found with as many as five different types of artifacts. Adult age groups overall have a higher variety of artifact types and a generally lower incidence of no grave goods. There is no significant difference between the number of grave goods for men and women.

Ceramic vessels are present in each of the age groups. The overall occurrence of vessels with burials within the total population is low with adults representing the highest percentage of burials with vessels (9.6 percent). However, when we examine the presence of vessels for each age class, 13 percent of infants have vessels, 44 percent of children, 40 percent of adolescents, 13 percent of young adults, 20 percent of adults, and 75 percent of all old adults have them. The most common type of mortuary vessel is the usually highly decorated and always charred minipot. Five out of twelve minipots contained remnants of shell and bone (sometimes human); all were recovered from adult burials located in Houses 5 and 7.

Variation occurs between households in the number of artifact classes and type of grave goods. House 3 burials were interred with a wider variety of grave goods than individuals in other households. If Houses 4 and 6 with their single burials are omitted, House 3 contains the lowest occurrences of zero to three grave good types and the highest occurrence of four to five items (table 2). Only Houses 5 and 7 contained a single burial each with six or seven types of grave goods documented.

In every house there appears to be a dominant number of artifact types where the occurrence approaches or exceeds 50 percent. In House 1 and House 7, the dominant number of artifact types per grave is zero. No other exclusive similarities between Houses 1 and 7 are observed. Houses 2 and 5 also contain predominantly low numbers of artifact types with one type most common in both houses. There are few other similarities in mortuary patterns or other aspects between these two houses although they are located next to each other and aligned in a similar manner. Use of red ochre is also most common in Houses 2 and 5.

Not all artifact classes were found as mortuary goods in all houses. Copper only occurs in Houses 2, 3, and 7, and in the group outside the houses. Cores were not found with burials in Houses 2, 4, or 6, nor with the burials outside the houses. House 3 burials have higher percentages of scrapers, burials with shell, and burials with river cobbles than the other houses. Catlinite only occurs within two burials, both found in House 3.

Burials without grave goods include males, females, and all age categories with the exception of old adults. The absence of artifacts with burials was most common in the subadult groups, but was only slightly less common in

Table 2. Number of Artifact Types by Percentage in House

No. Grave Goods	H1	H2	H3	H5	H7
0	50.0	14.3	10	12.5	53.9
1	16.7	42.9	10	25.0	28.2
2	0	28.6	10	31.3	7.7
3	16.7	0	0	18.8	7.7
4	16.7	14.3	45	6.3	0
5	0	0	20	0	0
6	0	0	5	0	0
7	0	0	0	6.3	2.6
	100	100	100	100	100

the adult category (table 3). The most interesting distribution of this variable occurs with the placement of the cranium within the houses. As discussed above, orientation of the cranium toward the center of the house is most common. Only 8.1 percent of these burials have no grave goods, while 41.2 percent of those with the crania oriented toward the exterior, and 33.3 percent of those with the crania oriented toward the end of the houses have no grave goods.

Assessing Social Inequality with Mortuary Data

Possible relationships of social inequality were identified in the economic analysis, and implications of that analysis for the mortuary pattern were identified. It was hypothesized that some social inequality may have existed between women within households based on women's involvement with the production and storage of significant wild and domestic crops and the differential distribution of storage pits. I further suggested that the elevated status of some women within households would be emphasized in the mortuary program if this distinction was socially significant. The possibility of social inequality between households among women was more difficult to assess in the economic analysis. Several lines of economic evidence did indicate that individuals in House 3 were involved in activities that may have imparted elevated social status to male and female members of that household. I suggested that individual men of this household may have achieved greater status through their hunting or warfare skills. Furthermore, intrahousehold differences in social status for women may have been more pronounced in this household if there was more emphasis on differential status of the household within the community. Finally, members of Household 3 may have enjoyed an overall higher social position within the community because of their membership in the corporate group. Using the mortuary data, each of these possible relationships of social inequality is explored.

Table 3. Percentage of Each Age Group without Grave Goods

Age Group	Percent	N
Infant	37.5	3
Child	55.6	5
Adolescent	40.0	2
Young Adult	12.5	2
Adult	28.3	13
Old Adult	0	0
Indeterminate Subadult	100.0	2
Indeterminate Age	50.0	0

Relationships of social inequality can be evaluated here, as in the economic analysis, by examining access to resources. The inclusion of some grave goods, particularly trade items, can directly reflect an individual's or his kin's access to those resources. Indirectly, access to these and other types of subsistence and social resources are often related to differential social rank, and the organization of the burial program can reflect these distinctions of social organization.

The first issue defined was whether social inequality between women within households was pronounced enough and maintained within the social structure of the society so that it would be symbolized and reinforced through the mortuary program. This question can be examined by considering the adult female subpopulations from Houses 3, 5, and 7.

Five female burials are identified in House 3, and the results are ambiguous. However, when only the grave goods are considered, there is evidence (albeit limited) to support the hypothesis that some women have higher status than others within this household. Items included with these burials suggest that access and inclusion in the mortuary ritual of nonlocal resources was not equal. Ranking could also be indicated by the female burial with relatively few items (table 4). Most of these burials have a variety of grave goods and the number of different goods is either four or five. The one exception to this is the burial in Feature 309 that only contained red ochre and a small amount of unidentified faunal material. Two of the other four burials contained minipots, and the other two contained nonlocal items; Feature 299 contained three copper cylinders, and Feature 258 contained copper and galena.

The female burials in this house are interesting in their spatial characteristics, but it is difficult to tie these observations to the grave good dimensions. Within the burial area of the house, Features 309, 299, and 429 are clustered at the northern end, while Features 258 and 255 are at the southern end. Feature 429 is an old adult woman, the only individual in the population placed in a prone position. These general areas roughly correspond to clusters of storage pits located within and along the walls of the house. Adults of indeterminate sex and subadults are located between these two clusters of women.

Table 4. Female Burials in House 3 and Associated Artifact Types

Burial	Artifact Type
255	globular pinch pot, flake, core, shell, copper
258	ceramic, flake, shell, galena, copper
299	ceramic, flake, scraper, copper
309	fauna, red ochre
429	ceramic, flake, shell, minivessel

Four female burials were identified in House 5. Observed differences in grave goods and treatment of the body offer some evidence for social inequality. Two women buried along the north side of the structure each have only one grave good. Feature 841, the articulated burial on the south side of the house, contains four kinds of items (table 5). None of the burials have nonlocal items in this house. The isolated cranium in Feature 841a had no associated grave goods. As in the case of the burials discussed above in House 3, if we can assume that the variety of grave goods has some connection to differential access to social or subsistence resources, social inequality may be indicated.

Further possible evidence of differential status between women within House 5 can be argued based on the isolated cranium. It is unclear to me whether this individual was in some way socially significant or that the association of this cranium with the articulated individual is related to the articulated individual's elevated status. In either case, some form of differential treatment is indicated.

Eight female individuals were identified in the House 7 burials. These burials display a wider variety in number of grave goods and treatment of the body than female burials within the other two houses discussed. Most of the excavated burials fall within the midsection of this house. Two other female burials were excavated, one at the northern end and one at the southern end. Eight other burials were documented between the excavated burials in the midsection and the northernmost excavated burial (a female), but these were not excavated (O'Gorman 1995, 179).

Three of the female burials in House 7 contained no grave goods, four contained one or two types of items, and a single burial contained seven (table 6). The nature of these grave goods is different as well. Most notably, the adult female in Feature 938 was buried with seven types of items: a minipot, flakes, scraper, core, retouched tools, a wedge, and shell. The lithic tool kit recovered with this individual was found in excellent context and could indicate a specialized skill of this individual. Of course, specialization does not necessarily connote higher social ranking of a particular individual. As Ar-

Table 5. Female Burials in House 5 and Associated Artifact Types

Burial	Artifact Type
841	ceramic, flake, limestone, river cobble
841a	no grave goods
849	red ochre
850	red ochre

Table 6.   Female Burials in House 7 and Associated Artifact Types

Burial	Artifact Type
904	shell, ceramic
916	grinding stones
930	no grave goods
937	no grave goods
938	flake, shell, scraper, core, retouch flake, minivessel, wedge
940	globular pinch pot
942	no grave goods
950	flake, river cobble

nold (1985) has observed, specialization may occur with increasing population pressure and low agricultural productivity as a nonagricultural subsistence activity. However, I suggest that some social significance is indicated by the unique nature of the assemblage and its inclusion in the burial program within a household that normally did not include many grave goods.

The female burials in House 7 also included an individual with no cranium buried with two grinding stones. As discussed above, it was hypothesized that these burials were part of a mortuary ritual involving ancestor worship and that this woman had gained a special, or at least distinct, status within her household and community.

In summary, support for the hypothesis that some women had achieved a level of social elevation over other women in their respective households may be present, but is ambiguous. When grave goods are considered, distinct differences were found in the number and kind of items interred with females in Houses 5 and 7, and to a lesser degree in House 3. If the burials outside House 3 are associated with the corporate group in House 3, there would appear to be some differential spatial treatment between women as well.

The second issue of inequality, that individuals within House 3 were involved in activities that may have imparted elevated social status to male and female members of that household, has three test implications for the mortuary analysis. First, members of House 3 may have enjoyed an overall higher social position within the community due to their membership in a corporate group that appears to have excelled at or had some control over hunting or warfare. Second, I proposed that relationships between men within House 3 may have been characterized to some extent by social inequality linked to their ability to initiate and successfully lead others in warfare or hunting. The third implication is related to the intrahousehold observations made above for female relationships within the household, and I address it first.

I suggested that intrahousehold differences in social status for women may be more pronounced in House 3. I initially thought that this might be linked to the ability of some women in that household to excel at providing the necessary goods to support the hunting/warfare ventures or their kin ties to powerful men within the group, assuming that this type of inequality would be tolerated by the corporate group. Based on the above observations for female burials within House 3, there is little support for this second hypothesis. In fact, there appears to be less differential treatment between women in this household than in the other two examined.

The second issue, that of social inequality between men within House 3, can be examined by comparing the three male burials. When looking for differential treatment based on the distribution and nature of grave goods, the male burials are much like the female burials. Each contains four or five items and only one contains a nonlocal material. Unlike the female burials, none of the documented male burials contain significantly less variety in grave goods than any other. The types of grave goods are varied between the three burials and may suggest some distinctions in status as one young adult male is found with catlinite, one of the nonlocal materials.

There is no clear spatial indication of differential status between the males in House 3. All three were buried with their crania oriented toward the center of the house. Each of the males is found near or with another individual. The evidence for social inequality between these men is tenuous at best and is based on the presence of a nonlocal grave good.

The third issue, possible indications of status differences between burial populations of the houses, can be evaluated by examining distribution data on nonlocal trade items, the number of artifact types per burial, and other grave good data. Here I examine these variables between males of the different households and between the general burial populations of the households. Women have been compared at the interhousehold level previously. Spatial relationships within the community must also be considered.

Male burials can be compared between Houses 3, 5, and 7. There are no males identified in the burial populations in Houses 1, 2, 4, and 6. Like the females, males in House 3 are generally buried with more types of artifacts than males in Houses 5 and 7 (table 7). The one observation of nonlocal material with a male burial is found in House 3, where this was also observed for females. Male burials in House 7 more frequently have no grave goods than the other houses, which also mirrors the female distribution. The only two male burials with red ochre occur in House 5, where this treatment is common for the burial subpopulation overall.

The number and distribution of grave goods between the overall burial populations in House 3 and the other houses support the notion that this cor-

Table 7. Male Burials in Houses 3, 5, and 7 and Associated Artifact Types

Burial	Artifact Type
House 3	
198	ceramic, flake, limestone, shell
290	scraper, projectile point, minivessel, catlinite
310	shell, sandstone fragment, fauna, river cobble, pipe
House 5	
807	red ochre
812	ceramic, flake, limestone, vessel, scraper, blade, pipe
823	flake, core, red ochre
858	ceramic, flake, retouched flake
House 7	
935	no grave goods
943	crude pinch pot
954	scraper
959	no grave goods
967	globular pinch pot, retouched flake

porate group had achieved a position within the community above that of the other households. House 3 displayed the lowest occurrence of grave goods (three or fewer) and had four to five types of goods more often than any other household. House 3 burials contained a higher percentage of nonlocal items than the other households and were the only burials containing catlinite and galena. Scrapers were more commonly found in association with House 3 in the economic analysis, and this trend is repeated in the mortuary analysis, suggesting that the activity held more importance for the household than simply achieving the task at hand. Through the focus on this and related activities, perhaps members of the household contributed to their overall wealth and status.

In summary, social inequality within the mortuary pattern based on direct and indirect evidence of differential access to social and subsistence resources is found at the community level, and, to differing degrees, within households. Most of these relationships discussed above are based on an interpretation of the variety and nature of grave goods and as such should be viewed with caution. The degree of apparent social inequality based on different frequencies and kinds of artifacts could be related to other social factors. Spatial relationships within the houses reveal some distinctions in social status, but appear to be largely related to significance of the corporate longhouse and individual familial subgroups that make up the larger group.

Intrahousehold social distinctions that may be related to social inequality appear to be more pronounced, at least for women, in Houses 5 and 7. In the larger population of House 7, some women may have been able to gain greater access to resources through special skills, such as those related to management of seed crops or other activities. One indication that women could also specialize in other skills is indicated by the rich tool kit buried with one woman. Whether this specialization imparted elevated status is unclear, but some social distinction can be inferred. In this house we find women who are part of the familial group, part of the corporate group, but have no grave goods while others have significant amounts. The larger population of this household (inferred due to increased size) may have intensified scalar stress related to decision making to ensure adequate stores of vegetal foods, firewood, clothing, and other subsistence needs provided by women. The larger population may have also allowed or prompted other women to specialize in other pursuits to improve their personal or household social position. In the mortuary pattern, the burial of the woman with her two grinding stones with her cranium removed may be related to this increased scalar stress and social inequality. It is possible that those women who had gained control over aspects of decision making in particular subsistence realms became the focus of ancestor worship rituals in death.

Interhousehold relationships of social inequality can be tentatively identified and are based primarily on the variety and type of grave goods associated with each household. The mortuary data suggest that the corporate group in House 3 had greater access to social resources based on its ability to acquire nonlocal goods, and to some subsistence resources based on the elevated occurrence of scrapers. Indirectly, greater access to resources may be indicated by the greater variety of grave goods interred with individuals, which may be an indication of the individual's wealth or position within the corporate group.

Although social inequality may be indicated at both the intra- and interhousehold levels, when the spatial dimension is focused upon, there is an overlying veneer of nondifferentiation. People appear to be buried by their affiliation with a longhouse with some consideration to family group and internal spatial dynamics. However, the interhousehold interpretation of social inequality in the mortuary pattern must be considered incomplete given the likelihood that the entire range of community burials is not represented. Three contemporary burials from the central knoll at the adjacent OT site discussed below demonstrate the existence of a distinct spatial disposal area quite different from that observed in the longhouses. Furthermore, the number and kind of artifacts found with an adolescent on the knoll suggest that this different disposal area may contain individuals from other social groups with higher social rank.

BEYOND THE LONGHOUSE: OTHER CONTEXTS
FOR MORTUARY RITUAL

Two additional areas were found to contain burials within the Tremaine Complex (fig. 4). The southern burial area at OT, located approximately 400 meters southeast of Tremaine, occupies a lowlying portion of the landscape similar to Area H. Their position on the landscape and spatial arrangement in rows (O'Gorman 1993) could suggest that the southern burial area interments are part of a continuation of the Tremaine community pattern (O'Gorman 1995). However, the extremely localized area of excavation (21 square meters) precludes further evaluation of their place within the spatial context of the Tremaine mortuary pattern.

The central knoll burials at the OT site are distinct in their position on the landscape, and I have argued elsewhere (O'Gorman 1995) that their association with a longhouse is unlikely. However, because of the very limited scope of excavation, we cannot assume that these interments are within a cemetery. What we can say about the three individuals recovered from the knoll is: (1) based on radiocarbon dates from multiple levels of grave fill, their interment appears to be contemporary with the main occupation of longhouses at Tremaine during the Pammel Creek phase (A.D. 1400–1500); (2) burial on the knoll was certainly a spatial context distinct from the majority of mortuary treatments; (3) individuals recovered included one adolescent, probably under ten years of age, an adult female thirty to forty years old, and an adult female over forty years in age; and (4) the adolescent was interred with twenty-four triangular projectile points (far more than found with any other individual) and twelve copper cylinders (more than all of the other copper recovered at the Tremaine site in any context).

The clearest evidence for social inequality in this study may be the spatially distinct and topographically elevated burials on the central knoll. Their separateness from the longhouse context and association with relatively abundant and significantly different grave goods is tantalizing. Was the knoll used to symbolically place individuals, families, or clans above and apart from the longhouse community? If so, the status of the adult women buried there is indeed suggestive.

I hesitate to pursue this linkage with the Tremaine community pattern primarily because of the context of radiocarbon dates associated with the burials. Charcoal from grave fill does not necessarily reflect the age of the burial; earlier pit fill or deposits can be incorporated with grave fill. While this problem also exists for the longhouse burials, there we also have better spatial context. Perhaps direct dating of the skeletal material or DNA analyses will help to further link these two populations.

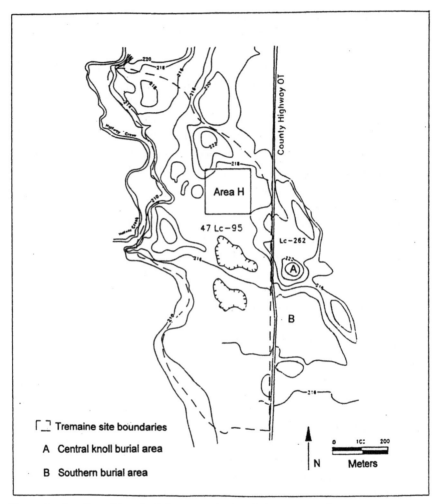

Figure 4. Location of two burial areas at OT in relation to Tremaine.

CONCLUSION

Based on the comparative analysis of domestic economics and mortuary patterns, Oneota social organization at Tremaine included relationships in the households and community that reflect at least incipient social inequality. In the household, the power of some women over production and access to staple crops ensured that each household could supply its own basic subsistence needs. These women probably produced a surplus that could be used to support status-creating ventures within the household, while other women may have produced other goods for the same reasons. In death, the roles of these important women may have been symbolized in the inclusion of hoes or grinding stones or other tools. Their distinct social standing appears to also have been symbolized spatially. However, I would argue that in death their social position is transformed, as it was in life, to benefit the corporate household through a leveling mechanism of interment within the household while recognizing their important social contributions.

The comparative analysis of domestic economics and mortuary patterns at Tremaine suggests that Oneota social organization included a variety of relationships within and between households and the community that reflect some level of social inequality. I propose that particular women within households had control over the production, storage, and access to staple grain crops. Women may have also produced surplus staples to create obligatory relationships or to underwrite status-gaining ventures of the household. I also find some gender-specific evidence for minor degrees of social inequality between and within households in the mortuary program. Perhaps more important, the mortuary analysis also suggests the importance of maintaining equality and transforming social positions of important individuals in life and death to benefit the corporate household.

ACKNOWLEDGMENTS

Tremaine Complex fieldwork and descriptive analyses were funded by the Wisconsin Department of Transportation and carried out under the auspices of the State Historical Society of Wisconsin's Museum Archeology Program.

REFERENCES

Ames, Kenneth M. 1995. Chiefly power and household production on the northwest coast. In *Foundations of social inequality*. Edited by T. Douglas Price and Gary M. Feinman, pp. 155–87. New York: Plenum.

Arnold, Dean E. 1985. *Ceramic theory and cultural process*. Cambridge, U.K.: Cambridge University Press.

Benn, David W. 1989. Hawks, serpents, and bird-men: Emergence of the Oneota mode of production. *Plains Anthropology* 34 (125):233–60.

———. 1995. Woodland people and the roots of the Oneota. In *Oneota archaeology: Past, present, and future*. Edited by William Green, pp. 91–139. Office of the State Archaeologist, Report 20. Iowa City: University of Iowa Press.

Binford, Lewis R. 1971. Mortuary practices: Their study and their potential. In *Approaches to the social dimensions of mortuary practices*. Edited by James A. Brown, pp. 6–29. Washington, D.C.: Memoirs of the Society for American Archaeology.

Blanton, Richard E. 1994. *Houses and households: A comparative study*. New York: Plenum.

———. 1995. Cultural foundations of inequality in households. In *Foundations of social inequality*. Edited by T. Douglas Price and Gary M. Feinman, pp. 105–27. New York: Plenum.

Bridges, Patricia S. 1989. Changes in activities with the shift to agriculture in the southeastern United States. *Current Anthropology* 30:385–94.

Brown, James A. 1981. The search for rank in prehistoric burials. In *The archaeology of death*. Edited by Robert Chapman, Ian Kinnes, and Klavs Randsborg, pp. 25–37. Cambridge, U.K.: Cambridge University Press.

———. 1995. On mortuary analysis—with special reference to the Saxe-Binford Research Program. In *Regional approaches to mortuary analysis*. Edited by Laine A. Beck, pp. 3–26. New York: Plenum.

Cohen, Mark N., and Sharon Bennett. 1993. Skeletal evidence for sex roles and gender hierarchies in prehistory. In *Sex and gender hierarchies*. Edited by Barbara D. Miller, pp. 273–96. Cambridge, U.K.: Cambridge University Press.

Conkey, Margaret W., and Joan M. Gero, eds. 1991. *Engendering archaeology: Women and prehistory*. Oxford, U.K.: Basil Blackwell.

Feinman, Gary M. 1995. The emergence of inequality: A focus on strategies and processes. In *Foundations of social inequality*. Edited by T. Douglas Price and Gary M. Feinman, pp. 255–79. New York: Plenum.

Gallagher, James P., and Constance M. Arzigian. 1994. A new perspective on late prehistoric agricultural intensification in the upper Mississippi River valley. In *Agricultural origins and development in the midcontinent*. Edited by William Green, pp. 171–88. Office of the State Archaeologist Report 19. Iowa City: University of Iowa Press.

Goldstein, Lynne G. 1976. Spatial structure and social organization: Regional manifestations of Mississippian society. Unpublished Ph.D. diss. Department of Anthropology, Northwestern University, Evanston, Ill.

———. 1980. *Mississippian mortuary practices: A case study of two cemeteries in the lower Illinois valley*. Evanston, Ill.: Northwestern University Archaeological Program.

Goody, Jack. 1958. *The developmental cycle in domestic groups*. Cambridge, U.K.: Cambridge University Press.

———. 1972. The evolution of the family. In *Household and family in past time*. Edited by Peter Laslett and Richard Wall, pp. 103–24. Cambridge, U.K.: Cambridge University Press.

Grauer, Ann L. 1991. Life patterns of women from medieval York. In *The archaeology of gender: Proceedings of the twenty-second annual Chacmool conference of the Archaeological Association of the University of Calgary*. Edited by Dale Walde and Noreen D. Willows, pp. 407–13. Calgary: The University of Calgary.

———. 1995. Tremaine skeletal data. In *The Tremaine Site Complex: Oneota occupation in the La Crosse Locality, Wisconsin*. Vol. 3 of *The Tremaine Site (47 Lc-95)*. Edited by Jodie O'Gorman, pp. 409–22. Archaeological Research Series No. 3. Madison: State Historical Society of Wisconsin Museum Archaeology Program.

Hall, Robert L. 1962. *The archaeology of Carcajou Point.* 2 vols. Madison: University of Wisconsin Press.

Halverson, Holly P. 1994. Burials and postmolds. In The Gundersen Site: An Oneota village and cemetery in La Crosse, Wisconsin. *Journal of the Iowa Archeological Society* 41:15–24.

Hammel, Eugene, and Peter Laslett. 1974. Comparing household structure over time and between cultures. *Comparative Studies in Society and History* 16:73–109.

Hastorf, Christine A. 1993. *Agriculture and the onset of political inequality before the Inka.* Cambridge, U.K.: Cambridge University Press.

Hayden, Brian. 1995. Pathways to power: Principles for creating socioeconomic inequalities. In *Foundations of social inequality.* Edited by T. Douglas Price and Gary M. Feinman, pp. 15–86. New York: Plenum.

Henning, Dale R. 1970. Development and interrelationships of Oneota culture in the lower Missouri River valley. *The Missouri Archaeologist* 32:1–180.

Hollimon, Sandra E. 1990. Division of labor and gender roles in Santa Barbara channel area prehistory. Unpublished Ph.D. diss. Santa Barbara: University of California.

———. 1991. Health consequences of divisions of labor among the Chumash Indians of southern California. In *The archaeology of gender: Proceedings of the twenty-second annual Chacmool conference of the Archaeological Association of the University of Calgary.* Edited by Dale Walde and Noreen D. Willows, pp. 462–69. Calgary: The University of Calgary.

———. 1992. Health consequences of sexual division of labor among prehistoric Native Americans: The Chumash of California and the Arikara of the northern Plains. In *Exploring gender through archaeology: Selected papers from the 1991 Boone Conference.* Edited by Cheryl Claassen, pp. 81–88. Madison, Wis.: Prehistory Press.

Hollinger, R. Eric. 1993. Investigating Oneota residence through domestic architecture. Master's thesis, University of Missouri, Columbia.

———. 1995. Residence patterns and Oneota cultural dynamics. In *Oneota archaeology: Past, present, and future.* Edited by William Green, pp. 141–74. Office of the State Archaeologist, Report 20. Iowa City: University of Iowa.

Johnson, Gregory A. 1982. Organizational structure and scalar stress. In *Theory and explanation in archaeology.* Edited by Colin Renfrew, Michael J. Rowlands, and B. A. Segraves, pp. 389–422. New York: Academic Press.

Koehler, Lyle. 1997. Earth mothers, warriors, horticulturalists, artists, and chiefs: Women among the Mississippian and Mississippian-Oneota peoples, A.D. 1211 to 1750. In *Women in prehistory: North America and Mesoamerica.* Edited by Cheryl Claassen and Rosemary A. Joyce, pp. 211–26. Philadelphia: University of Pennsylvania Press.

Kreisa, Paul P. 1993. Oneota burial patterns in eastern Wisconsin. *Midcontinental Journal of Archaeology* 18 (1):35–60.

Laslett, Peter. 1972. Introduction: The history of the family. In *Household and family in past time.* Edited by Peter Laslett and Richard Wall, pp. 1–89. Cambridge, U.K.: Cambridge University Press.

Moore, Henrietta L. 1988. *Feminism and anthropology.* Minneapolis: University of Minnesota Press.

Netting, Robert McC., Richard Wilk, and Eric J. Arnould, eds. 1984. *Households: Comparative and historical studies of the domestic group.* Berkeley: University of California Press.

O'Gorman, Jodie A. 1993. The Tremaine Site Complex: Oneota occupation in the La Crosse locality, Wisconsin. Vol. 1 of *The OT Site (47 Lc-262)*. Archaeology Research Series No. 1. Museum Archaeology Program. Madison: State Historical Society of Wisconsin.

————. 1995. The Tremaine Site Complex: Oneota occupation in the La Crosse locality, Wisconsin, Vol. 3 of *The Tremaine Site (47 Lc-95)*. Archaeology Research Series No. 3. Museum Archaeology Program. Madison: State Historical Society of Wisconsin.

————. 1996. Domestic economics and mortuary practices: A gendered view of Oneota social organization. Ph.D. diss. University of Wisconsin, Milwaukee.

O'Shea, John M. 1981. Social configurations and the archaeological study of mortuary practices: A case study. In *The archaeology of death*. Edited by Robert Chapman, Ian Kinnes, and Klavs Randsborg, pp. 39–52. Cambridge, U.K.: Cambridge University Press.

Overstreet, David F. 1989. *Oneota tradition, culture, history—new data from the Old Spring Site (47Wn350)*. Report of Investigations No. 219. Milwaukee: Great Lakes Archaeological Research Center.

————. 1995. The Eastern Wisconsin Oneota regional continuity. In *Oneota archaeology: Past, present, and future*. Edited by William Green, pp. 33–64. Office of the State Archaeologist, Report 20. Iowa City: The University of Iowa.

Radin, Paul. 1923. The Winnebago tribe. *Bureau of American Ethnology Annual Report* 37:35–560.

Santure, Sharron K. 1990. Norris Farms 36: A Bold Counselor Phase Oneota Cemetery. In *Archaeological investigations at the Morton Village and Norris Farms 36 Cemetery*. Edited by Sharron Santure, Alan Harn, and Duane Esarey, pp. 66–74. Report of Investigation, No. 45. Springfield: Illinois State Museum.

Saxe, Arthur A. 1970. Social dimensions of mortuary practices. Ph.D. diss. Department of Anthropology, University of Michigan, Ann Arbor.

Skinner, Alanson B. 1926. Ethnology of the Ioway Indians. *Bulletin of the Public Museum of the City of Milwaukee* 5 (4):181–354.

Stevenson, Katherine P. 1985. Oneota subsistence-related behavior in the Driftless area: A study of the Valley View Site near La Crosse, Wisconsin. Ph.D. diss. University of Wisconsin, Madison.

Tainter, Joseph A. 1975. Social inference and mortuary practices: An experiment in numerical classification. *World Archaeology* 7 (1):1–15.

————. 1978. Mortuary practices and the study of prehistoric social systems. Vol. 1 of *Advances in archaeological method and theory*. Edited by Michael B. Schiffer, pp. 105–41. New York: Academic Press.

Tringham, Ruth E. 1991. Households with faces: The challenge of gender in prehistoric architectural remains. In *Engendering archaeology: Women and prehistory*. Edited by Margaret Conkey and Joan M. Gero, pp. 93–131. Oxford, U.K.: Basil Blackwell.

Vradenburg, Joseph A. 1993. Skeletal analysis of the Tremaine Site. Manuscript. Museum Archaeology Program of the State Historical Society of Wisconsin, Madison.

Wilson, Diane. 1997. Gender, diet, health, and social status in the Mississippian Powers Phase Turner Cemetery population. In *Women in prehistory: North America and Mesoamerica*. Edited by Cheryl Claassen and Rosemary A. Joyce, pp. 119–35. Philadelphia: University of Pennsylvania Press.

Wylie, Alison. 1991. Gender theory and the archaeological record: Why is there no archaeology of gender? In *Engendering archaeology: Women and prehistory.* Edited by Margaret Conkey and Joan Gero, pp. 31–54. Oxford, U.K.: Basil Blackwell.

Yanagisako, Sylvia Junko. 1979. Family and household: The analysis of domestic groups. *Annual Review of Anthropology* 8:161–205.

3

Gender Studies in Chinese Neolithic Archaeology

Tianlong Jiao

A number of issues related to gender have been consistently discussed in the literature of Chinese prehistoric archaeology since the late 1950s, such as the shifting status between men and women, the relationship between gender role and the lineage system, and the labor division between genders. In the People's Republic of China, these issues have been discussed within a framework of Marxist theory, and therefore have been closely connected with the study of kinship systems and social organizations (Yan 1989).

The late 1980s saw an increasing concern with gender issues in archaeology on a global scale (Preucel and Hodder 1996, 415–26). Having gone through an initial period during which women were the main focus of discussion (Conkey and Gero 1991), today, gender archaeology is actively treating conventional subjects of archaeology, such as the division of labor, trade and exchange, craft specialization, household economy, and even state formation (Preucel and Hodder 1996, 420–22).

In light of the recent theoretical advances in gendered archaeology, this chapter is designed to reanalyze a number of gender concerns in Chinese Neolithic archaeology. Because mortuary practice and iconography are the two major issues that have been regularly employed by Chinese archaeologists to address gender questions, the following discussion will focus on these two aspects. This chapter will make use of the available archaeological discoveries and theoretical constructions to investigate the developmental discourse of gender relationships in Chinese Neolithic society and discuss what Chinese archaeology has contributed and may contribute to gender theory in archaeological interpretation more generally.

51

MORTUARY PRACTICE AND GENDER RELATIONSHIPS

The relationship between genders can be studied in a number of different ways: through analysis of marriage, kinship, or social status patterns. Among the archaeological data, the layout of settlements and the structure of the houses reflect, to a certain extent, the pattern of prehistoric marriage and family configurations. However, they cannot provide specific information about sex identification. Mortuary practices, on the other hand, can tell us the specific sex of individuals, provided the human skeletons are intact and well preserved. In Chinese Neolithic archaeology, two types of burials have been frequently employed to study gender relationships: one is multiple burials, the other is mixed-sex double burials. The following discussion will focus on how Chinese archaeologists have interpreted these mortuary practices and what kind of status between genders can be observed in these burials.

Multiple Burials

The evidence shows that multiple burials were practiced mainly in the Yellow River Valley during the Middle and late Neolithic periods (5000–3500 B.C.). Initially appearing in the Laoguantai Culture (5800–5200 B.C.) and the Beixin Culture (5400–4500 B.C.), this form of mortuary ritual predominated in the early stages of the Yangshao Culture (5000–3000 B.C.) and the early Dawenkou Culture (4300–2400 B.C.), to disappear in later periods.

Multiple burials, in most of which the dead were secondarily buried, can be classified into two types: same-sex burials and mixed-sex burials. It should be pointed out that multiple burial was only one of the various mortuary practices engaged in in Neolithic China. Even at sites where multiple burials were prevalent, a considerable number of single burials existed simultaneously. This sort of phenomenon ought to be considered when we study gender relations.

Same-sex burials are common in the cemeteries of the Dawenkou Culture. For instance, at the Wangyin site, 22 individuals were buried inside Tomb 2240, and all of them were identified as males (SDD 1979). This kind of tomb is also present in the Yangshao Culture. Twenty-eight mutiple burials were found in the Yuanjunmiao cemetery, an important cemetery of the Yangshao Culture that is located in Huaxian County, Shaanxi Province. One of these multiple burials contained three adult males (BU 1983).

However, the majority of the multiple tombs are mixed-sex burials, which usually contain many persons of various ages. In the Yuanjunmiao cemetery, Tomb 405 contained twelve human skeletons, among which were six adult males, three adult females, two children, and one teenager (BU 1983). In many cases, the ratio of males to females in the burials is extremely biased in favor of males. For example, in Tomb 456 at the Yuanjunmiao cemetery, among the seven individuals, six were identified as males, while only one was female. At the Shijia cemetery, another Yangshao culture site, Tomb 6 contained thirty skeletons, twenty-four of which were identified as males, four of which were females and two children (XBB 1978).

Chinese archaeologists commonly attribute this kind of mortuary practice to a lineage society with close blood relations. In this interpretation, the bodies in the same-sex burials were those of brothers, sisters, or other similar blood relatives, whereas those in the mixed-sex burials, based on the distinct quantitative unevenness between males and females, represent the natural state of gender proportions in the household or clan and among blood relatives (Yan 1989).

Nevertheless, there is a wide divergence of opinions on the issue of whether these burials reflect a system of matrilineal or patrilineal descent. Zhang Zhongpei, the scholar who wrote the report of the excavation of the Yuanjunmiao cemetery in Shaanxi Province, maintained that "the Yuanjunmiao cemetery belonged to a tribe which consisted of two clans," and "the community was a matriarchal society"(BU 1983). Based on his analysis of burial structure and the number of funeral offerings, he concluded that women played the leading role in production in the Yuanjunmiao community, and that the "social position of females was generally higher than that of males, with girls generally better treated than boys. Mothers already had the conscious need to distinguish their own daughters and passed their property to them. Moreover, relying on her privileged position, a mother could confer full adult status on the most favoured daughter" (BU 1983).

This interpretation has been challenged by other archaeologists. Wang has argued that this kind of multiple burial is a mortuary practice found in clan societies generally and that it is not limited to matrilineal clan societies. After presenting a great deal of ethnographic evidence, Wang proposed that this kind of burial custom happened both in matrilineal and in patrilineal societies and even in bilineal societies (Wang 1987). Yan has also cautiously pointed out that thus far we lack the evidence to make a conclusive interpretation of the lineage system for the Yangshao community. In Yan's opinion, the earliest society of the Yangshao Culture consisted of nuclear households, extended families, and clans. He argues that the lineage system of the Yangshao Culture was not necessarily matrilineal, although it may have been matrilineal, particularly in the regions where agriculture was fully developed. Yan also believes that the existence of a matrilineal system in some areas does not rule out the possibility that a patrilineal system existed in other areas at the same time (Yan 1989).

The study of the Shijia cemetery by Gao and Lee has shed light on the possibility of reconstructing residential patterns (Gao and Lee 1993). By analyzing the osteological remains, they concluded that this community was patrilocally organized. This result challenges the observations of many Chinese archaeologists who believe that the communities of the early Yangshao Culture were matrilocally arranged. However, this is the only biological study of mortuary remains to date in Chinese prehistoric archaeology, and its applicability needs to be tested against more materials both spatially and temporally.

Obviously, kinship is a very important issue in gender studies. However, it is notoriously difficult, if not impossible, for archaeologists to reconstruct the kinship system of prehistoric societies (Pearson and Underhill 1987). The available data in Chinese archaeology are insufficient to draw any conclusions on this issue at this time. However, if we move beyond kinship to gender status, we do have a lot of information upon which to rely.

Chinese archaeologists have employed a good deal of mortuary evidence to argue that women played a dominant role in early Yangshao society. As described above, Zhang Zhongpei believes that women were more powerful than men in the Yuanjunmiao community. As evidence, he cites Tomb 429 that supposedly contained two female children. These girls were buried in the same manner as the adults, and the quality and quantity of their offerings were outstanding when compared to other graves. For example, 785 bone beads were found inside the tomb (BU 1983). However, as Gao and Lee have pointed out, so far there are no techniques in physical anthropology that allow the identification of the sex of an immature child (Gao and Lee 1993, 269). In fact, the majority of the multiple burials tell us nothing about the overall status of women, because most of the individuals were secondarily buried and generally only few offerings were found. Moreover, there are no obvious indications regarding ownership of these offerings. It may be more appropriate if we interpret them as shared property. In this interpretation, the multiple burials give us an image of an egalitarian society instead of one in which men were controlled by powerful women. Men and women seemed to be partners rather than subordinates and rulers.

This kind of partnership between men and women has also been confirmed by the statistical analysis of the single burials in the Banpo Type cemeteries of the Yangshao Culture (Yan 1989). Based on a large sample of data, Yan elegantly illustrates that there is no clear difference between the amount of offerings for males as compared to females. His analysis also demonstrates that there was no clear labor division between the sexes. Cultivating tools and spindle whorls were found in the burials of both males and females, suggesting that both sexes participated in cultivating activities. The evidence for females as the main contributors to agricultural labor has not been confirmed (Yan 1989).

Mixed-Sex Double Burials

The joint burial of one male and one female is another phenomenon that has been frequently cited by scholars as evidence for a patrilineal society. Many Chinese archaeologists believe that the two persons within the same burial were husband and wife, and therefore that the occurrence of this burial custom was a marker of a patrilineal or patriarchical society (Yan 1989).

However, the available archaeological evidence demonstrates that the mixed-sex double burial is a short-lived mortuary practice that was restricted to certain areas in Chinese prehistory. Such a practice was more common in early and late Dawenkou Culture, but, so far, only about one dozen cases have been reported. It disappeared in the late Longshan Culture (circa 2500–2000 B.C.) in most areas except that of the Qijia Culture in the northwest (circa 2000 to date unknown).

The mixed-sex double burials found in the Dawenkou Culture share an important feature in which the positional arrangement of the man and the woman is interestingly consistent, with males usually buried lying on their left sides while the females are buried lying on their right sides. This intriguing phenomenon has been interpreted in many different ways. Tang has argued that this arrangement indicated the unequal status between the males and the females. "Most of the funeral offerings were placed on the side of the male, which indicates the subordination of the female" (Tang 1975). He further speculates that some women might have been forced to become sacrifices to their patriarchs, making the Dawenkou Culture the first slave society in China. However, this theory has been challenged by others. Cai has argued that the females in joint tombs were not sacrificed to the males. Instead, he believes that middle Dawenkou Culture saw the beginning of the transition from matrilineal to patrilineal clans. Based on this interpretation, Cai has argued that in Dawenkou Culture women's social status had started to decline but they had not yet become slaves to men (Cai 1978). This sort of transitional model was welcomed by some archaeologists, whereas some favored a more abrupt shift from matriarchy to patriarchy (Lu 1976).

However, a comprehensive survey of the archaeological data shows that this observation is not quite convincing. First of all, during the period of the Dawenkou Culture, the mixed-sex double burials constitute only a small proportion of all tombs. Of the 133 burials that were excavated in the Dawenkou cemetery, only four are mixed-sex double tombs (SWG 1974). In Yedian, another cemetery of the Dawenkou Culture, only six tombs containing one male and one female were found among the eighty excavated burials (SB 1985). Clearly, the prevalent mortuary practice was single burials. It is also important to note that all of the large tombs contained only one person, which suggests that the elites of the society were buried individually.

In addition, the placement of offerings in the mixed-sex double tombs are more complex than the above authors have suggested. The placement of offerings in these tombs was not always biased against females. On the contrary, in some of the tombs, more offerings were actually concentrated on the woman's side of the chamber. For instance, in Tomb 31 at Yedian cemetery, forty-two offerings were found on the woman's side, while only one ivory spearhead and one necklace were placed on the side of the man. In fact, it is often very difficult to identify the ownership of these offerings between the male and the female. It would be safer to consider these offerings the shared property of the couple.

By the time of the Middle Dawenkou Culture, the social system had grown more complex. The divisions between groups and individuals became increasingly obvious (Chang 1986). However, the archaeological evidence indicates that the development of a social hierarchy was not necessarily accompanied by a change in gender status. Women's social status did not collapse, nor did the men's power increase. For example, in the Dawenkou cemetery, the deceased in the largest burial, Tomb M10, has been identified as a woman. She was not only provided with an elaborate coffin, but also was furnished with more than 180 funerary goods, including a number of the most exquisite items in the whole cemetery. It would seem reasonable to conclude that she was more powerful than any other individual in her society.

Mixed-sex double burials are also found in the Qijia Culture. A regular pattern of placement of males and females is observed in all excavated tombs of the culture: males were placed in an extended position facing upward, while females were placed on their sides in a flexed position facing the males. This sort of male "dominant" arrangement was eagerly interpreted by many scholars as a manifestation of women's decline in status relative to men, seeming to suggest that women were subordinate to men in this culture in a "typical" patriarchal system (Xie 1984).

This interpretation is also flawed when tested against a comprehensive survey of archaeological data. The mortuary practices of the Qijia Culture were considerably more complex. The prevalent burial custom in the Qijia Culture was the single burial. The mixed-sex double burials constitute the minority of burials in all Qijia cemeteries. Moreover, other kinds of body placement, such as both men and women in extended positions, are also found. In addition to the above burial types, there was another kind of joint burial in which adults were buried with children. A number of multiple burials were also reported. Therefore, we do not see any one institutionalized mortuary practice in the Qijia Culture. Obviously, the practice of mixed-sex double burials should be analyzed in a broader social context.

In addition, the flexed position of the females in some of the tombs cannot be explained simply as a sort of subordination or "enslaving" of women, because flexed burials are quite common in the Qijia Culture. The flexed individuals may be male or female, and many of them were individually buried. Moreover, in many mixed-sex double burials the couples shared their funeral offerings with no sign of a relationship of domination and subordination.

However, during the period of the Qijia Culture, social stratification seems to have increased (Xie 1984; Chang 1986). Human sacrifice was conducted in many communities. In most cases, these victims seem to have been women. In Tomb 76 at the Huangniangniangtai site, a man and a woman were buried together. The skeleton of the man was perfectly preserved, while the skull of the woman was absent, which might indicate that she was decapitated when she was sacrificed to the male individual (GB 1960). In Tomb 314 at Liuwan cemetery, a flexed female was found beside the coffin of a male with her disarticulated left leg under the coffin, which may be an indication of a sacrificial ceremony (ZSK et al. 1984). These sacrificed women were probably slaves or members of the lower class. A hierarchical gender system had probably developed. On the one hand, within members of the same social class, social status between genders seems to have been approximately equal. On the other hand, males of higher social rank appear to have begun enslaving females of lower rank. It is in this regard that we may say that women's status in Qijia Culture declined.

THE WORLD OF THE PREHISTORIC "GODDESS": THE CHINESE "VENUS"

Archaeological data reveal that female icons appeared no later than the Middle Neolithic in China (Jiao 1995). The female figurines found in Middle Neolithic sites are quite similar in shape, showing no obvious differentiation in size or height. Most of them were found in ash pits or in houses, which implies that there were no special shrines built for them. This may indicate that these deities were readily accessible to the common people in their own homes through these figurines (1995). However, by the late Neolithic period, this kind of system had been significantly transformed, as indicated by the discoveries of the Hongshan Culture.

The Hongshan Culture is mainly found in the western Laio River and Daling River regions in northern China. A number of radiocarbon dates place it in the late Neolithic period from 4500 B.C. to 3000 B.C. The most distinguished female icons, temples, and altars of the Hongshan Culture are found at the two important sites of Niuheliang and Dongshanzui (Yang 1989).

The "Goddess Altars" at Dongshanzui

The Dongshanzui site is located in Kezuo County, Liaoning Province. When excavations were carried out at the site by local archaeologists in 1979 and 1982, a group of stone altars that were associated with clay female figurines and fragments of life-sized female icons were recovered (Guo and Zhang 1984). Since this was the first time archaeologists had identified the remains of so-called "goddesses" in China, the discovery evoked much excitement in Chinese scholarship.

The three excavated altars were built roughly along a south–north axis and were formed in three different shapes: round, rectangular, and multicircular. The largest altar consisted of a rectangular stone wall standing from 0.15 to 0.40 meters above the ground and measuring 11.8-by-9.5 meters. Within the rectangular structure were three clusters of rocks and standing stones. The round altar was situated 15 meters north of the rectangular one with a diameter of 2.5 meters and a loess base measuring 0.5 meters high. It was encircled by stone slabs and pebbles. More than twenty fragments of clay human figurines were found near this round altar. Two of them are small, 5 centimeters and 5.8 centimeters tall, respectively, and all of them lack a head and a right arm. One of the figurines depicts a pregnant woman, as evidenced by her round belly. The others are large, about half life-size, but only fragments survived. They depict some sitting human figures who were originally seated on the altar.

The "Goddess Temple" at Niuheliang

Niuheliang is a hilly ridge on the boundary between Lingyuan and Jianping County in Liaoning Province. From 1983 to 1985, archaeologists uncovered more than ten ritual sites and a group of tombs. The most astonishing discovery was the so-called "Goddess Temple." It is an irregular structure containing several rooms. Overall, it measures 18.4-by-6.9 meters. The remains indicate that the wall was built of wattle and daub. Traces of geometric painted designs in red, yellow, white, and other colors were found on the surviving foot of the wall. A number of fragments of human statues as well as animal figurines were uncovered within this structure. The human fragments included a head, arms, shoulder, breasts, and hands belonging to five or six individuals. Conspicuous female features can be observed in the breasts, arms, and shoulders. The life-sized human head is very striking. It has a plump face, long and smoothly contoured ears, and a slightly raised nose. It was painted red, and the eyeballs were represented by inlaid pieces of round jade. Careful observation enabled the excavator to conclude that it was a female head (Sun and Guo 1986).

The size of these fragments indicated that the sizes of the original icons were quite varied. Some of them were about life-sized, others were two or three times life-size. Moreover, they also appeared to differ in age and status. It may be that within this temple, a group of deities was arranged according to some sort of hierarchical system. Some clay fragments of pig's lips and giant bird's claws were also uncovered in association with the human deities. This may indicate that animals were also worshipped by the people at that time.

Thus, if we can associate these figures with deities, then the Goddess Temple in Niuheliang was actually quite a complex pantheon. There is a group of goddesses instead of one, and they all seem to have different statuses or roles. Moreover, there are also animal deities within the temple, which suggests that the religious beliefs of these people may have been very complex.

The female figurines and icons discovered at Niuheliang and Donshanzui have been the subject of much discussion over the past two decades. Many papers have been devoted to the interpretation of these Chinese "Venuses," and often within the context of their significance to the formation of Chinese civilisation (Sun and Guo 1986). Most scholars have recognized the importance of the discovery at Dongshanzui for the study of prehistoric religion. Yu Weichao has proposed that these female figurines were the fertility and agricultural goddesses of the people of Dongshanzui, and that the cluster of standing stones symbolized the "Earth Mother" (ED 1984). Zhang Zhongpei has offered a similar suggestion, but he further proposes that in the Hongshan Culture the worship of goddesses may have been associated with a matriarchal social system (ED 1984). Other scholars have used the data from Niuheliang to develop hypotheses about gender status. Among them is Nelson's analysis of the Goddess Temple at Niuheliang, in which she suggests that women had high social status in Niuheliang society (Nelson 1987, 1991). Many scholars have observed that the main deity in the temple was female. Some believe that this goddess was the legendary ancestor of the Hongshan people and that the temple was actually a shrine of their ancestor (Sun and Guo 1986).

What can these discoveries tell us about gender relations during the Neolithic in northeastern China? As I indicated earlier, the altar at Donshanzui, the temple at Niuheliang, and the actual social life of Hongshan society must be much more complex than originally thought. The different scale and features of Hongshan Culture sites indicate that during this period, the society was hierarchically organized (Yang 1989). The cluster of temples and raised stone circle tombs were conspicuous features of Niuheliang. So far no domestic settlements have been reported near this area, a phenomenon that suggests that Niuheliang was a sacred place to the people in the neighbouring community. A number of raised stone tombs were also found at other sites, however, they were much smaller than those in Niuheliang (Yang 1989). The communities of the Hongshan Culture appear to have been hierarchically organized also. Niuheliang is one of the largest sacred centers in Hongshan Culture, if not the only one.

Unfortunately, very little information about the tombs at Niuheliang has been published, so the gender associations of these tombs are not clear at present. Given what we know about highly ranked societies, however, we may expect to find some sort of gender hierarchy in the Hongshan Culture. However, to date, an appropriate conclusion would be that in the religious system of the Hongshan Culture, the dominant deity or deities were female. This may reflect the fact that women were highly regarded in Hongshan society, yet we need more information to determine if the high status of these "Goddesses" extended to the real world.

CONCLUSION

Archaeological investigations in China over the past seven decades have shown a gradual increase in social complexity during the Neolithic period. This process involved the constant advancement of culture and the continuous evolution of various social relations as well. Archaeological data demonstrate that during the early period of Chinese prehistory, the relationship between men and women was a kind of partnership. The conventional notion among Chinese archaeologists that early prehistoric Chinese society was both matrilocally organized and matriarchally administered cannot be supported by the archaeological data. The change in prehistoric Chinese society from an egalitarian social system to a hierarchical one seems to have occurred during the late Neolithic period (circa 3500 B.C.). However, the emergence of class society and the consequent formation of states (circa 2500–2000 B.C.) were not necessarily accompanied by an overall decline in the social status of women. In these hierarchical societies, an individual's gender status appears to have been closely related to his or her social rank.

The practice of Chinese archaeology has shed light on some general theoretical considerations and methodology of gender archaeology. The subject of gender status can be addressed through the study of mortuary practice and iconography only if the cultural-historical context is clear. However, it should be pointed out that both mortuary practices and iconography were restricted by a number of complex social, economic, and ideological factors that were not only defined by contemporary life, but also strongly influenced by historical tradition. To some degree, they should reflect the contemporary gender relationships as well as other social relations, but they also might give a distorted picture. Therefore, more comprehensive surveys are definitely needed in order to achieve a more scientific analysis of gender in Chinese Neolithic society.

ACKNOWLEDGMENTS

I thank Professor K. C. Chang, Professor Elizabeth Chilton, and Professor Yun K. Lee for their productive comments on the drafts of this chapter. I am grateful to Kit Mallow for her kind help. Needless to say, all the shortcomings of this chapter remain mine. I wish to thank Harvard-Yenching Institute for its generous support that allowed me to attend the Fifth Gender and Archaeology Conference at the University of Wisconsin, Milwaukee in 1998, where I presented the original version of this paper.

REFERENCES

BU (Beijing University). 1983. *The Yangshao Cemetery at Yuanjunmiao.* Beijing: Cultural Relics Publishing House.

Cai, Fengshu. 1978. On the nature of society in the Dawenkou Culture period. *Wen Shi Zhe* Vol. 1.

Chang, Kwang Chih. 1986. *The archaeology of ancient China.* 4th ed.. New Haven, Conn.: Yale University Press.

Conkey, Margaret W., and Joan M. Gero. 1991. Tensions, pluralities and engendering archaeology. In *Engendering archaeology: Women and Prehistory.* Edited by Margaret W. Conkey and Joan M. Gero, pp. 3–30. Oxford, U.K.: Basil Blackwell.

ED (Editorial of *Wenwu*). 1984. A seminar on the Dongshanzui site. *Wenwu* Vol. 11.

Gao, Qiang, and Yun Kun Lee. 1993. A biological perspective on Yangshao kinship. *Journal of Anthropological Archaeology* 12:266–98.

GB (Gansu Museum). 1960. Report of excavations at Huangniangniangtai in Wuwei County, Gansu. *Kaogu Xuebao* 2.

Guo, Dashun, and Keju Zhang. 1984. Brief report of the excavation of the building groups of the Hongshan Culture at Dongshanzui in Kezuo, Liaoning Province. *Wenwu* Vol. 11.

Jiao, Tianlong. 1995. Gender relations in prehistoric Chinese society: Archaeological discoveries. In *The chalice and the blade in Chinese culture: Gender relations and social models.* Edited by Min Jiayin, pp. 91–126. Beijing: China Social Sciences Publishing House.

Lu, Bo. 1976. On the origin of primitive ownership in China in the light of the Dawenkou Culture. *Wenwu* Vol. 7.

Nelson, Sarah M. 1987. The Chinese Neolithic: Recent trends in research. *American Anthropologist* 89:807–22.

———. 1991. The "Goddess Temple" and the status of women at Niuheliang, China. In *The archaeology of gender: Proceedings of the twenty-second annual Chacmool conference of the Archaeological Association of the University of Calgary.* Edited by Dale Walde and Noreen D. Willows. Calgary: University of Calgary.

Pearson, Richard, and Ann Underhill. 1987. The Chinese Neolithic: Recent trends in research. *American Anthropologist* 89:87–122.

Preucel, Robert W., and Ian Hodder, eds. 1996. Understanding sex and gender. In *Contemporary archaeology in theory: A reader.* Pp. 415–30. Oxford, U.K.: Basil Blackwell.

SB (Shandong Provincial Museum). 1985. *Zouxian Yedian.* Beijing: Wenwu Publishing House.

SDD (Shandong Archaeological Team, CASS). 1979. Brief report of excavations at the Wangyin Neolithic site, Yanzhou, Shandong. *Kaogu* Vol. 2.

Sun, Shoudao, and Dashun Guo. 1986. The discovery and study of heads of Hongshan Culture goddess images from Niuheliang. *Wenwu* Vol. 8.

SWG (Shandong Wenwu Guanlichu). 1974. *Bawenkou.* Beijing: Wenwu Publishing House.

Tang, Lan. 1975. The beginning of slave-holding society in China 5000–6000 years ago. In *Collected papers on Dawenkou Culture.* Jinan: Qilu Shushe.

Wang, Ningsheng. 1987. A study of the burial customs and social organisation of Yangshao Culture: A discussion of the theory of Yangshao as a matrilineal society and its methodology. *Wenwu* Vol. 4.

XBB (Xian Banpo Museum). 1978. The Shijia Neolithic site in Weinan County, Shenxi. *Kaogu* Vol. 1.

Xie, Duanjiu. 1984. The Qijia Culture in the upper Yellow River Valley. In *Archaeological discoveries and research in the new China.* Beijing: Cultural Relics Publishing House.

Yan, Wenming. 1989. Burial practices and social systems of Banpo type. In *Studies of Yangshao Culture.* Beijing: Cultural Relics Publishing House.

Yang, Hu. 1989. On the issues of Hongshan Culture. In *Papers in honor of Su Bingqi's fifty-five-year archaeological career.* Beijing: Wenwu Publishing House.

ZSK (Institute of Archaeology, CASS) et al. 1984. *Qinghai Liuwan.* Beijing: Wenwu Publishing House.

Gender and Power

4

Visible Women Made Invisible: Interpreting Varangian Women in Old Russia

Anne Stalsberg

Feminist and gender archaeology developed not least as a reaction against research that did not duly include the female half of humanity or focus on that half in research, analyses, and syntheses. It was, and still is, necessary not only to make women consciously visible in research, but also to understand why women who are clearly visible in the archaeological record could be so neglected by scholars in historical generalizations.

The historiography of the Varangians—the Scandinavians in old Russia (or Old Rus') during the Viking period, is an example of how women who are visible in archaeological material have become surprisingly invisible in the literature, although there have been improvements during recent times. On the basis of the archaeological material, I shall demonstrate how focusing on women's finds influences historical generalizations about the Varangians. I shall also demonstrate how interpreting the grave goods with as little of our own prejudices as possible can lead to new insights into the roles held by women, especially in trade.

BACKGROUND

A chapter in an edited volume such as this one cannot be more than a too-short summary of two and a half centuries of historiography and the voluminous archaeological material on which the discussion is based. As a background, a few details have to be pointed out, at least for the readers who are unfamiliar with this field.

"Varangians" was the term used in early medieval/Viking period Old Rus'ian, Byzantine, and Arab sources for the Scandinavians who went to eastern Europe and Byzantium, and it will be applied in this chapter. The term "Scandinavian" will be used to refer to archaeological finds of Scandinavian origin, Scandinavia, the Scandinavian peoples, and so on. The Finno-Ugric–speaking Saami with their totally different culture then (and now) living in the northern parts of the Scandinavian peninsula are not discussed here. According to the archaeological finds, most of the Varangians came from middle Sweden and, in the later Viking period, also from Gotland. Runic inscriptions on stones in Sweden document Swedes, while the Norse sagas are almost exclusively about Norwegians.

The archaeological finds left by the Varangians have been unearthed mainly in towns along the great rivers Volhov, Dnepr, and the upper Volga in Old Rus' (fig. 1). In addition, there are Scandinavian finds along the rivers emptying into Lake Ladoga from the southeast. It must be kept in mind that there is an important difference between these two areas: the Lake Ladoga area could be reached by seagoing vessels from the Baltic Sea, while the boats had to be hauled through rapids or over portages past the rapids to enter inland Old Rus' and the great river roads farther east and south. Only rivergoing vessels could be used. The Finnic areas southeast of Lake Ladoga came under Old Rus' rule during the tenth century. The Volga Bend area was occupied by Volga Bulgarians. There were Finnic tribes along the upper Volga, Baltic tribes toward the Baltic Sea, nomads on the Pontic steppes, and Slavs in the central parts of what eventually became the powerful and large Old Rus'. For convenience, the whole area discussed here will here be referred to as Old Rus', also because Old Rus' is now in both Russia and the Ukraine.

These finds have direct relevance to the so-called Varangian controversy (or the Norman question) about what role the Varangians played in the origin, early history, and culture of Old Rus' from the ninth to the eleventh century—did they found the first Russian state or was their importance minimal? This is more a political than scholarly question, and it has been most hotly debated in politically tense situations, beginning in 1748 when relations between Russia and Sweden were strained and suggesting that the first Russian state founded by Swedes was unwelcome. It became a political, ideological, and nationalistic issue, first as a reaction in the 1930s to Nazi racism against the Slav *Untermenschen*, and then under the Soviet regime during the Cold War when the only allowed opinion was anti-Normanism that belittled the Varangians' influence and importance. After the fall of the Soviet Union in 1991, the question again became a matter of open scholarly discussion.

The Varangian controversy could not have arisen without *The Russian Primary Chronicle* stating that in the year A.D. 862, there was civil war in north-

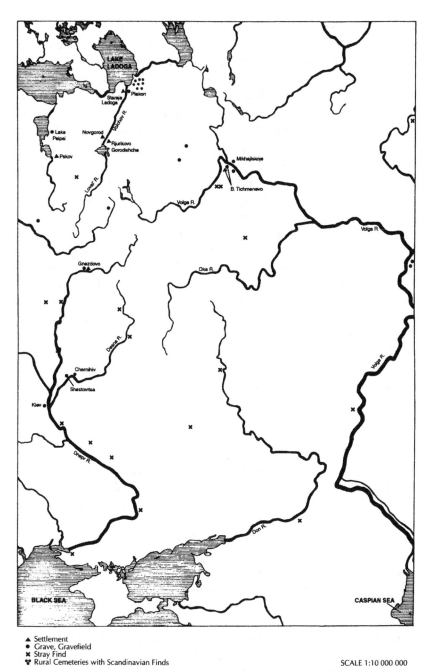

Figure 1.   Locations of Viking Age finds of Scandinavian origin in Old Rus' (redrawn by Annie Chojnacki).

west Old Rus' between the Finnic and Slavic tribes who sent envoys across
the Baltic Sea to the Varangian people in Sweden and invited them to rule
and keep order between the fighting tribes (Sherbowitz-Wetzor 1953). Three
brothers with their kin came to Old Rus', and the Rus'ian land was named
after these Varangians (Sherbowitz-Wetzor, entry for A.D. 862). The term
"rus' " probably means "those who row" and is connected with the name of
the fjord Roslagen at Stockholm. It meant the Varangians in the earliest period, but soon it came to mean the areas in Russia and the Ukraine (cf. Mel'-
nikova and Petruhin 1989).

Medieval written sources—Rus'ian, Arab, Byzantine, Latin, Scandinavian—describe Varangian men, and brave, male activities predominate in the
interpretations of the Varangian activities in Old Rus': conquest, piracy, state
founding, and trade. This is still the case, although it has been known since
the second half of the nineteenth century that there are considerable numbers
of Scandinavian women's finds in Old Rus'. The male interpretations and
sources have been so influential that even scholars aware of the archaeological material have stated, for example, that the Varangians did not take their
women with them into eastern Europe (Talbot Rice 1969, 152). Against this
background, the Scandinavian archaeological finds in Old Rus' are of special
importance because there are more women's than men's finds. Therefore, it
is justifiable to ask why women visible in the archaeological sources have
become invisible in the historical reconstructions and history books.

THE ARCHAEOLOGICAL MATERIAL

Generalizations stressing male activities are in striking contrast to the archaeological material. The ideas on this theme developed in this chapter are based
on collections of Scandinavian Viking age finds in Old Rus' in my master's
thesis (1974), and an unpublished list, updated circa 1990, for my own use.
In total, Scandinavian objects from inland Old Rus' have been found in 107
female graves, 84 male graves, and 36 graves with two or more individuals
regardless of the cultural identity of the grave. Thus, the objects might be
trade goods or gifts. Based on an analysis of the grave goods and the ritual
associated with these graves, 41 female, 18 male, and 21 couples seem to be
Varangian graves (the numbers may not be exact because of difficulties in
ethnic identifications). From the Finnic areas southeast of Lake Ladoga, outside the portages, the corresponding numbers are 31 female, of which 10 are
Varangian; 30 male, of which 16 are Varangian; and 6 couples, of which 3
are Varangian. The striking difference in numbers between men's, women's,
and couples' graves is in reality even larger, because 24 male graves were

included in the material based on the presence of swords. However, it is not clear which swords are actually Scandinavian, which were made on the Continent but ended up in Old Rus' on the belt of a Varangian, or which ones came directly from Frankish areas. These figures cannot in any case be regarded as accurate, since they depend both on the state of the available information and the definition of "Scandinavian" and "Varangian" objects and graves. The numbers are based on my database, which was up to date in 1985; however, as far as I have been able to observe, the ratios between the finds have not been changed substantially by subsequent finds. In any case, these figures demonstrate that there are more women's than men's finds and graves.

Needless to say, we will never know the exact number of Scandinavians who went to Old Rus', nor will we know the correct ratio between the numbers of men and women, since women evidently are overrepresented because of their metal brooches, which are ethnic symbols that have tended to survive in the grave. It is possible that men's costumes signaled ethnicity via perishable materials like textiles in special colors. In reality, there could not have been more women than men; it is hard to imagine an otherwise unknown army of Amazons in Viking society, of which, after all, we are fairly knowledgeable.

The Scandinavian finds in Old Rus' include stray finds as well as those from towns, hoards, and graves. There are objects attributed to women in all categories, but for our purposes, only the graves can be used because only they reflect individuals and thus enable us to compare the number of individuals in cemeteries. I have discussed elsewhere the basic problem of which criteria can be used to identify the deceased as a Varangian (Stalsberg 1988). When found in Scandinavia, such graves with a set of ornaments or other grave goods are regarded by Scandinavian archaeologists as free women—matrons of farms or households. If we accept the Varangian-appearing women in Old Rus' as actually being Varangian, they also were free women.

Further, it is important to bear in mind that women's graves cover the whole period of Varangian presence in the East and at all localities with one exception: Moslem Bulgaria. A pioneer phase without women cannot be excluded since the dating frameworks that I found it possible to apply are too broad to allow such a pioneer period to be recognized if that period was of short duration.

We may now wonder why archaeologists and historians did not include Varangian women in their generalizations in view of their archaeologically attested importance, since the finds have been known since the latter half of the nineteenth century. It is too simple to claim that it is because these scholars were men, since they were not all men; it is, rather, a result of their backgrounds. As Kehoe argued in her excellent article "Shackles of Tradition," male American anthropologists who had grown up in bourgeois, Victorian Europe were unable to correctly evaluate positions held by women in North American Indian tribes (Kehoe 1983). The Victorian ideal was *Kinder, Kirche, Küche* (children, church, kitchen), and women were regarded as being too frail for education and responsibility. These inequities have been kept alive in the literature at least partly by the scholarly system of references to earlier literature (Stalsberg 1991a, 1991b). Much of the same argumentation can also be applied to ninth- through eleventh-century Christian and Moslem authors, the only contemporary sources who might have mentioned the Varangian women. Their theology had fixed ideas about the proper place of women and, perhaps, therefore did not mention women in responsible positions among the heathen Scandinavians. (The Scandinavian and Russian sources were written 100 to 200 years after the Viking Age.)

In short, the important point is that the fact that there were quite a few women among the Varangians and that they were in no way invisible in the archaeological record cannot be explained away. In fact, they were so many that their numbers must have consequences for the general understanding of Varangians in the East.

GENERAL INTERPRETATIONS AND WOMEN'S FINDS

Different interpretations have been presented over the years since the first controversy of 1748 (for further discussion of the material and references, see Stalsberg 1982; 1987). The Vikings are famous for piracy, which is documented also in eastern Europe along the coast of the east Baltic Sea and in the Caspian Sea, which the Vikings most probably reached from the Black Sea and the Mediterranean. Since the pirates' route to Old Rus' and the river system on the east European plain from the Baltic Sea was so complicated, they could not arrive unexpectedly, pillage, and leave unhindered—in any case, not repeatedly. Further, Varangian graves are dispersed among other graves in the burial grounds, which were mainly near towns. In addition, there were women and families, which is confirmed by three children's graves. It does not fit, with repeated piracy, that Varangian men and women were allowed into the sacred burial grounds for a period of 150 to 200 years. It is probable that the burial grounds reflected the population they served, and we may therefore conclude that the Varangians were accepted in the towns (though not necessarily integrated—e.g., the Hanseatic traders who were not fully integrated into the towns but were fully accepted in the towns where they had merchants).

Although it has been surmised that colonization or agricultural settlement in Old Rus' ran parallel to the Vikings on the British and Atlantic isles, archaeology does not seem to support colonization in Old Rus' inside the portages and rapids, since the finds are concentrated in the towns. The Scandinavian finds and Varangian graves in the Finnic areas southeast of Lake Ladoga are spread in rural settlements along rivers more directly accessible from Lake Ladoga and, accordingly, the Baltic Sea. Along the smaller rivers between Novgorod and Volga, there also are Scandinavian finds from smaller cemeteries. There is not necessarily any parallel between Danish and Norwegian settlement on the British and Atlantic islands, and Swedes in Old Rus'. One reason Norwegians and Danes left their homelands seems to have been the lack of free land to cultivate. There still were unsettled areas in northern Sweden and also in coastal Finland where Swedes could and did settle. However, the presence of women and children would support the idea of settlers and life on farms.

The foundation of the Old Rus' state by the Varangians is the first and classic theory of the Varangian controversy. It is based on *The Russian Primary Chronicle*, according to which the first Rus'ian dynasty was of Swedish descent (see above). This has been hotly debated since 1748, because it touched the national pride of the Russians. Today, many Russian scholars believe that the Od Rus' princes really were invited to rule, and I agree. These scholars hold that the foreign princes were hired by the tribes in northwest Old Rus' to govern as neutral rulers according to the Old Rus' law to stop the civil war (Yanin 1992, 83, 91). Archaeology cannot contribute to this discussion.

Written sources also refer to hired Varangian officials and mercenaries serving the Old Rus' princes. Mercenaries do not easily become involved in loyalty conflicts in civil wars and wars between tribes. The treaties with Byzantium in A.D. 907 and 945 were signed by many Scandinavians on behalf of the Old Rus' princes, and they accordingly served as high-level officials. *The Russian Primary Chronicle* mentions trouble with the mercenaries, but, on the whole, the relation between the rulers of the state and the servants appears to have been orderly and quiet (Sherbowitz-Wetzor 1953). Those servants who served abroad for long periods might very well have brought their families or married natives, as suggested by a few grave finds indicating mixed marriages. It is natural to connect the officials with some well-equipped graves outside Staraja Ladoga, Gnëzdovo, Kiyv, and Eernihiv—all important towns in Old Rus'. There are more women's than men's graves among them, which, as I have argued, is a false picture since there could not have been such a majority of women among the Varangians. It is typical to find graves that might be connected with mercenaries and officials in the cemeteries of the towns, which had to be both controlled and protected by the prince's men.

Two other activities, trade and crafts, are archaeologically directly attested to by weighing equipment in graves and by finds in the cultural layers of towns including Scandinavian-style ornaments that were unfinished or broken during production. Certain details in the style of some objects (e.g., two swords) seem to indicate that the makers were either not first-generation Varangians or were non-Varangian craftsmen working for Varangians and according to the latter's tastes. Trade is by nature a peaceful or voluntary activity, incompatible with hostility and piracy. One can easily suppose that Varangian traders and craftsmen (women?) lived in Old Rus' towns with their families. Traders and their facilities may have remained in Old Rus', or they may have returned to Scandinavia after some years of service for the organization or the prince.

As seen above, the women's finds alone are not sufficient to know which conclusions are probable; they must be seen in context with the other sources, such as topography, and so forth. The women's finds (and the few children's graves) have special importance by indicating the existence of Varangian families abroad, which is more compatible with orderly and peaceful life rather than hostile relations. It also indicates that the societies in Old Rus' were able to accept and safeguard aliens. The probable fact that Varangian families, not only men, went abroad, has importance also for a discussion of how Varangian trade and other activities were organized (see Stalsberg 1996).

AN ALTERNATIVE EXPLANATION

The argumentation above is based on the assumption that the women who were buried dressed as Varangian women actually were free Varangian women, that is, women who either had come from Scandinavia or were of early generations and had their cultural (ethnic) identity intact. Nevertheless, it might be that this is all or partially wrong, that at least some of these women were in fact Slavic wives of Varangian men, dressed up and buried like Varangians, or perhaps even thralls or concubines, buried according to their masters' burial rituals. Thus, the Varangian-looking women, instead of identifying Varangian women, indicate Varangian men, their masters. However, even this explanation indicates organized conditions and a stable relationship between the Varangians and the other peoples in Old Rus', and hence does not alter the general interpretations discussed above.

TRADING WOMEN

Naturally, women's finds are the main sources for studying women's roles, ranks, and positions in prehistory and early history. It has long been known that weighing equipment is often found in Scandinavian women's graves of the Viking Age. I have done a preliminary analysis of part of the material, enough to draw some conclusions about women taking part in that portion of the trade of their family or economic unit (Stalsberg 1991b). The results are promising for a further study of the organization of trade during the Viking Age, both in Scandinavia and perhaps especially in Old Rus'. I can so far only present a sketch of this problem, since much more investigation of sources and theories is needed.

The Archaeological Material

The weighing equipment consisted of small folding balance scales and the weights to be used with them (fig. 2). They were used to weigh valuables, especially silver. One scale from a grave on the Volga has the Arab inscription "toll" or "tax" (Fehner and Janina 1978). They are dated to the late ninth to early eleventh centuries (Jondell 1974:10; cf. Callmer 1980, 207; Graham-Campbell 1980, 88). This weighing equipment has usually been regarded as belonging to male tradesmen. However, these "men's tools" have frequently been found with women who were buried during the Viking Age. I have checked only the graves containing Scandinavian finds in Old Rus', not the complete material. Weighing tools have been found in 37 of these graves—22 percent of them women's graves, or 25 percent if we count only the graves that I have defined as actually being Varangian. At Birka, the Viking Age town at the Swedish end of the route that extended eastward toward Old Rus', such tools have been found in 132 graves—32 percent women's, 28 percent men's, 3 percent couples', and 37 percent of unknown gender. These comprise both weights and scales. My information for Norway is about scales only: from a total of 63 graves, 17 percent are women's, 81 percent men's, and 2 percent couples'. The material is too modest for real statistical analysis, but one can trust that from 17 to 32 percent of the weighing equipment was found in women's graves. The survey of the finds is not complete but is sufficient to draw some basic conclusions.

Some of the women's graves at Birka are, in fact, girls' graves, which in Gräslund's opinion (in this book) might suggest another meaning than actually serving weighing purposes. However, as a parallel to "child-sized" axes and wooden toy swords in towns such as Trondheim (Norway), Staraja Ladoga, and Novgorod, these weights and scales can be understood as prepara-

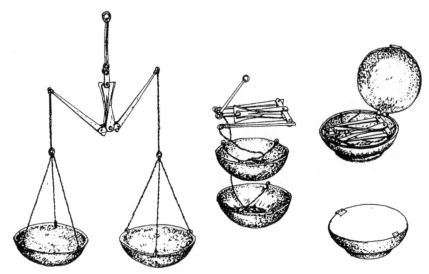

Figure 2.   Folding scale, showing how it was folded (drawn by Sigmund Alsaker after Åke Gustavsson).

tion for the children's future positions as warriors and matrons. Therefore, I have included these finds in the material.

Explanations

Different explanations have been suggested, such as, that a woman with weighing equipment was a tradesman's widow buried with his tools, or that she died when in charge of the household and his tools in his absence (Blindheim 1981, 91; Dommasnes 1982, 83; Ellmers 1984, 178). If women's graves with weighing equipment were exceptions, such explanations might be reasonable. But as the figures show, from one-fifth to one-third of the weighing equipment is found in women's graves. Further, these explanations are not in accordance with the basic postulate for analyzing grave goods, namely, that there is a strong connection between the dead and the grave goods. Without this assumption, archaeology could say nothing about the buried person. Based on this premise, the women had a right to be buried with the weighing equipment. I think they constitute the tools of women's economic unit, household, or family—not specifically the property of the female (or male) deceased person. This must mean that the matron took part in the work of the trading family, and that the notions of tradesman and tradeswoman are not apt; tradesfamily is better.

However, why could a woman be buried with equipment that was so closely connected with the public sphere where trade took place, since women had their domain "inside the threshold," according to the Norse laws (Virtanen 1981, 565)? Men and women were not equal, but they were indispensable members of their economic micro-unit (i.e., their family), but with sharply separated tasks. It seems reasonable that the matron who ranked higher in her husband's absence or death was buried with the family weighing equipment, but it may also be that it was because of her role in the family trading. Further study of trade organization may shed some light on this question.

For the Varangians at an outpost in Old Rus', it might have been appropriate for both matron and husband to take part in the trading. A unit in which more than the tradesman himself took care of the trading was not as vulnerable as a unit in which the trade depended on one person, because it would always be operative. Such an organization would be effective in the outposts in the towns in Old Rus' since the economic or trading unit would always be present at the market even when the man was traveling (for it must have been easier for a man than for a woman to travel for trade). This point needs further elaboration before any more conclusions may be drawn.

Comparable Positions

The idea of women taking part in trade has proved provocative—to my surprise. However, it is not a radical thought for Scandinavian women of the early Middle Ages and the Viking Age. I have compared the position of the matron of the trading families with that of the matron on farms. From slightly later medieval Scandinavian laws, we know that she was in charge of the work inside the threshold, *innanstokks*, as the legal term was, and that she had the legal right to the keys of the farm, a right that is archaeologically confirmed to have existed during the Viking Age (cf. Stalsberg 1991b, 49). She controlled what was valuable enough to be kept locked away. Recent studies by Steinsland, historian of religion, have found that women had central positions in the heathen cult on farms, more so than admitted to by early Christian sources (Steinsland and Sörensen 1994, 214). Thus, women could have responsible, independent positions in their households—even if these households were represented in the public sphere mainly by men but also by widows. The position of a woman was secured by her remaining legally a member of her own family after marrying into another family, and thus still under the protection of her own relatives (Steinsland and Sörensen 1994, 120).

The position of matron of a farm is reflected also by such women being buried with a boat just as frequently as men were in Norway during the Viking Age. These are boats that two, three, or four persons could row and sail—most likely the farm boat. A ship needing a professional crew is something else, and such vessels were more often buried with men. Without boats, it was impossible to live along the greater part of the Norwegian coast; farms would be isolated, on islands or on fjords, with high mountains that were difficult to cross. A boat was also necessary for exploiting vital marine resources. I do not have any explanation for why the matron rather than the husband was given the farm's boat for use in the burial ritual, but a detailed study might reveal some pattern (Nilsen 1997; Stalsberg 1998, 1999).

I would suggest that a woman who had the responsible position of a matron of a farm and had the right to be buried with the farm's boat could also take part in the trade of her economic unit, that is, the family or household. Since such a view has proved to be controversial (as the comments from other archaeologists indicate), it is important to keep in mind—and accept—what L. P. Hartley said about the past being a different country where things are done differently (Hartley quoted in Lowenthal 1993, xvi).

CONCLUSION

Viking period women in Scandinavia are clearly visible in historical reconstructions thanks to the Norse sagas and laws as well as the many women's graves. Among the latter, there are many rich graves, and the richest of all Scandinavian graves, the Oseberg burial in Norway, may have been the grave of a woman with her thrall (discussed by Ingstad 1992). In the reconstructions of Varangian activities in Old Rus', however, women have not played any great role. The first major point made above demonstrates how focusing on women's finds shows that the Varangians were not only warriors, conquerors, officials, tradesmen, and princes, as mentioned in the written sources, but that there were men, women, and as a natural consequence, children, that is, families, among the Varangians who lived in or visited Old Rus'. Varangians with families among them reflect different activities than purely male groups. As demonstrated, the noticeable presence of women influences our understanding of the character of Varangian activities (fig. 3).

The second point made above demonstrates that accepting that a conspicuous number of women were buried with weighing equipment confirms that things were done differently in the past. The fact that a woman in a society otherwise unequal with regard to gender had the right to be buried with her family's weighing equipment adds an aspect to her person and thus to our understanding of the society, for example, how Varangian trade may have

Figure 3. **The trading family through the eyes of an archaeologist (drawn by Geir Helgen).**

been organized. Finally, the noticeable presence of women among the Varangians and the number of women with weighing equipment further stress the difference between the evidence of the archaeological material and the written sources of this period. It is well known that chroniclers, like journalists, wrote down what they deemed important and what served either their purposes or those of their masters. Arab sources mention women among the Varangians, but neither Norse, Russian, nor Latin sources mention them since these sources were political rather than ethnographic. It is a good example of how written and archaeological sources supplement each other, as is natural, since they are left by the same society. It is understandable that chroniclers and historians have left out women in writings about politics, but it is less understandable how women who are so visible in the archaeological record have been overlooked to a surprisingly large extent in both archaeological and historical reconstructions over the years.

REFERENCES

Blindheim, Charlotte. 1981. Gravenes innhold. Sammenfatning. In *Kaupangfunnene*. Norske Oldfunn, 11. Pp. 91–92. Oslo: Universitetets Oldsaksamling.

Callmer, Johan. 1980. Numismatics and archaeology: Some problems of the Viking Age. *Fornvännen* 75:203–12.

Dommasnes, Liv Helga. 1982. Late Iron Age in western Norway. Female roles and ranks as deduced from an analysis of burial customs. *Norwegian Archaeological Review* 15:70–84.

Ellmers, Dettlev. 1984. *Frühmittelalterliche Handelsschiffahrt in Mittel-und Nord-Europa*. 2d ed. Offa-Bücher 28. Neumünster: Wachholtz.

Fehner, M. V., and S. A. Janina. 1978. Vesy s arabskoj nadpisju iz Timereva. *Voprosy sredenvekovoj arheologii Vostoènoj Evropy*. Pp. 184–92. Moscow: Nauka.

Graham Campbell, James. 1980. *Viking artefacts. A select catalogue*. London: British Museum.

Ingstad, Anne Stine. 1992. Oseberg-dronningen—hvem var hun? In *Osebergdronningens grav*. Edited by Arne Emil Christensen, Anne Stine Ingstad, and Bjorn Myhre, pp. 224–57. Oslo: Schibsted.

Jondell, Erik. 1974. Vikingatida balansvågar i Norge. C1-uppsats i arkeologi. Uppsala: Uppsala universitet.

Kehoe, Alice B. 1983. The shackles of tradition. In *The hidden half: Studies of Plains Indian women*. Edited by Patricia Albers and Beatrice Medicine, pp. 53–73. Lanham, Md.: University Press of America.

Lowenthal, David. 1993. *The past is a foreign country*. Cambridge, U.K.: Cambridge University Press.

Mel'nikova Elena A., and V. Ja. Petruhin. 1989. Nazvanie "rus' " v etnokul'turnoj istorii drevnerusskogo gosudarstva (IX–X vv). *Voprosy istorii* (8):24–38.

Nilsen, Rut Helene Langebrekke. 1997. *Båtgravskikk?* Master's thesis, Trondheim: Norwegian University of Technology and Science.

Sherbowitz-Wetzor, O. P., trans. 1953. *The Russian primary chronicle*. Vol. 60. Cambridge, Mass.: Medieval Academy of America.

Stalsberg, Anne. 1974. Dei skandinaviske vikingtidsfunna i Rus'-riket. Master's thesis, University of Oslo.

———. 1982. Scandinavian relations with northwestern Russia during the Viking Age: The archaeological evidence. *Journal of Baltic Studies* 13 (3):267–95.

———. 1987. The implications of women's finds for an understanding of the activities of the Scandinavians in Rus' during the Viking Age. *KAN (Kvinner i arkeologi i Norge)* 5:33–49.

———. 1988. The Scandinavian Viking Age finds in Rus'. *Bericht der Römisch-Germanischen Kommission* 69:448–71.

———. 1991a. Women as actors in north European Viking Age trade. In *Social approaches to Viking studies*. Edited by Ross Samson, pp. 75–83. Glasgow: Cruithne Press.

———. 1991b. Tradeswomen during the Viking Age. In *Nordic Tag. Proceedings of the second Nordic TAG conference*, Umeå, 1987. Archaeology and Environment. Vol 11. Pp. 45–52. Umeå: University of Umeå.

————. 1996. Varangian women in Old Rus': Who were they? *KAN (Kvinner i arkeologi i Norge)* 21:83–101.

————. 1998. O skandinavskih pogrebenijah s lodkami epohi vikingov na territorii Drevnej Rusi. *Istorièeskaja arheologija. Tradicii i perspektivy, K 80-letiju so dnja rozhdenija Daniila Antonoviea Avdusina.* Edited by A. E. Leontev, T. A. Pukina, A. S. Horosev, Ju. L. Sapova, V. L. Janin, pp. 277–87. Moskva. Pamjatniki istorièeskoj mysli. Moskow: Moskovskij gos, universitet im. Lomonosova.

————. 1999. *Skandinavske båtgraver fra vikingetiden i Rus'-riket: oversikt og tolkning.* AmS-Rapport 12 B. Stavanger: Arkeologisk museum i Stavanger.

Steinsland, Gro, and Preben Meulengracht Sörensen. 1994. *Menneske og makter i vikingenes verden.* Oslo: Univeresitetsforlaget.

Talbot Rice, Tamara. 1969. The crucible of peoples. In *The Dark Ages.* Edited by David Talbot Rice, pp. 149–56. London: Thames and Hudson.

Virtanen, E. A. 1981. Kvinnearbeid. In *Kulturhistorisk leksikon for nordisk middelalder.* Vol. 9. Pp. 565–71.Copenhagen: Rosenkilde og Bagger.

Yanin, V. L. 1992. The archaeological study of Novgorod: An historical perspective. In *The archaeology of Novgorod, Russia.* Edited by Mark A. Brisbane, pp. 67–106. Society for Medieval Archaeology, Monograph 13. Lincoln, U.K.: Society for Medieval Archaeology.

5

The Position of Iron Age Scandinavian Women: Evidence from Graves and Rune Stones

Anne-Sofie Gräslund

Feminist historians commonly state that archaeological source material conceals the existence of women; however, in my opinion, given the archaeological evidence, this is not true. Women are not invisible in archaeology; in fact, they have been present in archaeological research right from the beginning. Swedish archaeologist Oscar Montelius (1843–1921) is an extraordinary example of an early scholar working on the position of women in prehistory (Arwill-Nordbladh 1991); in his private life he was interested in women's rights and he supported the fight for female suffrage (Gräslund 1999, 162). Many other archaeologists acknowledged the presence of women in prehistory, even if they did not reflect on their conditions. The fact that women are not invisible is certainly due to the archaeological source material, which is so different from the historical sources. However, if you look for women, they are present in works written by early medieval historians from the Continent and Britain, as will be discussed below.

Archaeological material is more concrete and literally comprehensible than textual evidence. Women are often manifested at common prehistoric sites such as graves and settlements. This observation may reflect that I am an archaeologist who works with the archaeological record of the first millennium A.D. In Scandinavia, the border between prehistory and the Middle Ages is circa 1050 to 1100. For this time period, there is often no doubt that an excavated grave is that of a woman. Jewelry may be found in a grave or in the excavation of a burned-down house, loom weights may be found alongside the wall, indicating the location of the loom where it is assumed that women of the farm worked. In Stone Age archaeology, however, the difficulty of finding women's material remains on settlement sites has been pointed out (cf. e.g., Thomas 1983, commented upon in Gero 1991).

Archaeological evidence is left by both men and women, whereas historical documents have been written mostly by men. This is probably one reason why women appear so seldom in early medieval Scandinavian written records. Another reason may be the context of historical records, which is often public, perceived as being the male sphere. From the nineteenth century when the science of archaeology began, its purpose was to study the conditions of daily life, simply because evidence guides interpretations in that direction. Of course, this emphasis gives a greater possibility of a fairly comprehensive representation of social activity including both men's and women's daily life.

It has often been argued that women's history is the invisible history and that our aim should be to make women visible. These concepts of "visible" or "making visible" can either refer to the source material—women are visible in archaeology since they are represented—or it can refer to interpretation. In that case, "visibility" is not always so apparent. However, the evidence is there, even if our interpretations may be wrong.

Two current areas of research on the second half of the first millennium A.D. in Europe for both archaeologists and historians are the creation of kingdoms and formation of states. Very little (if any) information on women is found in publications devoted to such research. What about kings from this period of time—did they not have wives with some influence? In short, where are all the queens when the topic is royal power? The old saying, "Behind every successful man there is a woman," comes to mind. This means, of course, that women play an important role in helping men to become successful—not that they stand behind them.

Today, a gender perspective is needed in much of archaeological research, and to study the relations between men and women really adds important dimensions to interpretation. Sometimes it may be reasonable to study distinctively male topics, and certainly women cannot be visible everywhere, but in my opinion, there must also be some space for women in the world of power structures. Such a statement may appear contradictory to the aims of feminist archaeology, which places interpersonal relations in the forefront, replacing more conventional concepts of power politics, governance, and authority, but in fact, it is complementary (Conkey and Gero 1991, 15).

Judging from several classic feminist archaeological works, gender roles of modern times with women acting in the private sphere and men in the public seem to have been strongly established already by the first millennium A.D. (and long before, probably beginning in the Neolithic). Thus, one can hardly expect direct public and political power for women. That does not, however, mean that they lacked influence. Besides, the significance of this public/private sphere division may be questioned for much of our earlier history, while what is today considered private certainly had much more public importance at that time.

HISTORICAL EVIDENCE: EXAMPLES OF POWERFUL WOMEN IN THE EARLY MIDDLE AGES

A classic institution to examine in a feminist approach to history is marriage. It is well known from history that royal marriages served a political purpose; ties between different royal families meant peaceful and important relations between countries as well as creating a larger territorial power. In many of these marriages, women were not "passive objects of exchange"; on the contrary, they often took an active part in political affairs as in the case of Eleanor (1124–1204), heiress of Aquitaine, first married to King Louis VII of France, then wife of Henry II of England and mother of Richard the Lionheart (Georges Duby 1997, 5–20.) It is also well known that some princesses and queens had a very strong influence on their husbands and, therefore, within the arena of public power. One example can be seen in a letter from Theodoric the Great concerning the wedding of his niece Amalaberga and a Thuringian king. The letter says that Amalaberga was expected to become a loyal and comforting counselor to the king. After referring to some additional examples, Norr concludes: "It is obvious that any analysis portraying noble and royal women as passive pawns in a system of exchange between rulers and families, alongside precious gifts like swords and good horses, fails to do justice to the German-speaking peoples and, particularly, its women" (Norr 1998, 124). Expectations of maintaining peace and friendship between families as well as increasing territorial power were certainly not only relevant on a royal level; Viking Age farmers and chieftains probably counted on the possibility of making new and advantageous family ties, just as farmers and landowners did in later times.

Poems written by Venantius Fortunatus in the sixth century for the wedding of the Merovingian King Sigibert and the Visigothic Princess Brynhilde from Spain in the year 566 portray the king and the queen as ideal creatures of classic perfection, but they also show a mixture of the classical and Germanic virtues of a monarch and his queen as the primary nuclear family of the kingdom (Herschend 1996, 287). At the same time, these poems emphasize the parallel between German pagan wedding traditions and Christian ideology. A change in the power balance between kings and queens is observed during the period A.D. 600 to 800, due to the economic and demographic crises affecting royal power. This is reflected in *Beowulf*, as the kings become weaker and the queens stronger (Herschend 1996, 298–99).

A wedding poem written considerably later may be seen as a counter-weight to the Sigibert-Brynhilde poem, with its clear ideological and mytho-logical background. It was written for the wedding of King Erik Magnusson and Princess Margareta, the daughter of Scottish King Alexander III, in the year 1281 in Bergen, Norway (Bagge 1980). The joy over the alliance and the peace between the two countries are the principal themes. Queen Marga-reta died in 1283 and left a daughter with the same name, called the Maid of Norway by the Scots. She was the only direct heir to the Scottish crown and died in 1290 in the Orkneys while on her way to Scotland to claim her heri-tage when she was nine years old at the most. This happened not more than 200 years after the late Viking Age, when marriage alliances may have been made for similar reasons.

Concrete visibility, that is, demonstration, must be the first step in the pro-cedure of finding women in history, and the next step is to investigate their conditions. As an example, I present my own research on rune stones (fig. 1). In 1989, I published an article on women and rune stones in Sweden for the purpose of tracing the Viking Age family pattern in the social group erecting rune stones (Gräslund 1989). To a fairly high degree, women figure in the runic inscriptions in the Mälar area of central Sweden. In Uppland, the prov-ince in this region that is richest in rune stones, women are mentioned in 39 percent of the inscriptions either as the erector of the stone or commemorated by it, alone or together with men (fig. 2). The family pattern showed that up to six sons were mentioned but not more than two daughters. (There are very few exceptions: three daughters are mentioned once in Uppland and twice in the contiguous province of Södermanland). My hypothesis is that this is due to the fact that female infanticide was practiced in the Mälar area at this time.

Five years later, returning to the subject of women of the rune stones, I was not satisfied by only showing that they existed in the texts—I wanted to know how they were mentioned (Gräslund 1995). A very special inscription was chosen as a starting point (fig. 3). The Hassmyra stone (Jansson 1964) in Väst-manland says: "The good farmer Holmgöt had the stone set up in memory of Odendisa, his wife. There will not come to Hassmyra a better housewife who runs the farm. Balle the Red cut these runes. To Sigmund, Odendisa was a good sister." The phrase "who runs the farm" (in Swedish, *som råder för gården*) is remarkable and indicates the importance of the housewife for the household and for the farm. It has been compared to the oldest provincial law of the region (written down in the thirteenth century but probably much older, at least in parts), which states in the inheritance section that the woman should be given in marriage to the man "for honor and as wife, sharing his bed, for lock and keys and for right of inheritance of a third of the property,

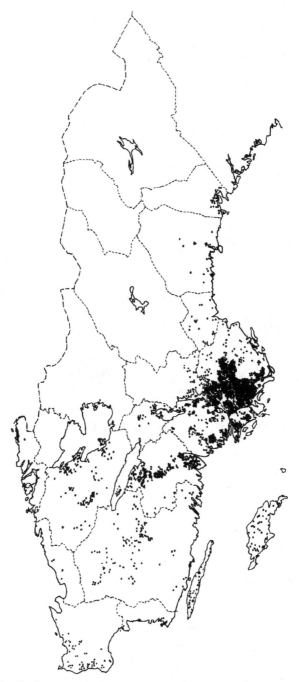

Figure 1. Distribution map of Viking Age rune stones in Sweden (after Jansson 1987).

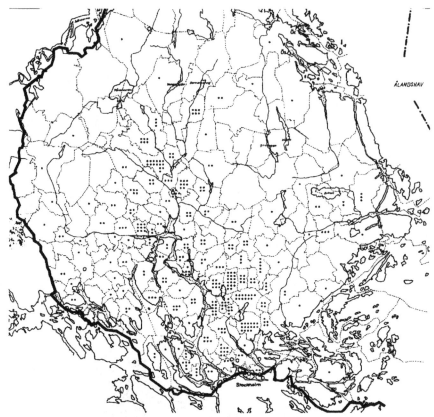

Figure 2.   The distribution of Uppland rune stones with inscriptions that mention women.

including all his personal property and for all his acquisitions" (Jansson 1964, 76).

The Hassmyra stone is datable on stylistic grounds to the last quarter of the eleventh century (Gräslund 1994). It contains information about the virtues of both the erector and the person being commemorated, as well as a verse—two unusual traits. Good men are frequently mentioned in runic inscriptions, but good women are very rare. The same is true regarding the recording of deeds and the manner of death; we often find this information about men but extremely rarely about women, a fact that may be explained by gender roles. Judging from Old Norse literature, the division of labor was normally strictly divided into male and female chores. The border was the threshold of the house—women worked indoors, men outdoors. If women mainly lived, worked, and died at home on the farm, it seems quite natural

Figure 3.   The rune stone Vs 24, Hassmyra, Västmanland (after Jansson 1964).

that it was not necessary to mention it. In light of the paucity of information about women's deeds, it is notable that they so often had runic memorials made and bridges built. When their activity deviates from the traditional female roles in these exceptional ways, it suggests a contradiction between the ideology of labor separation and the reality of overlapping spheres. Both men and women had rune stones raised and bridges built, certainly acts of prestige and therefore worth mentioning. As rune stones and bridges begin around Christianization, women's actions in these cases have special significance, an interesting combination along with other testimonies to their active role in the conversion to Christianity.

Women with considerable power are often found in written sources concerning conversion (Gräslund 1997). Women were often the first ones to accept the new faith and frequently influenced their husbands to follow suit. Many examples of this common pattern can be found in Bede's work on seventh-century England, in the work of Paul the Deacon on the Langobards, and in the work of Gregory of Tours on the Franks. These examples almost always concern royal families. Information of the same kind is given by Saxo Grammaticus about the tenth-century pagan Danish King Gorm and his wife, the Christian English Princess Thyra, and by Thietmar of Merseburg about the tenth-century pagan Polish King Mieszko who wanted to marry the Christian Bohemian princess, Dubrovka. The modern history of missionization shows many similar examples that women were the first of their families to accept Christianity and thereafter influence their husbands, for example, from India, Nigeria, and Greenland (Lennemyr 1989, 27; Hermansson 1991, 170; Lidegaard 1991, 66).

Several examples of royal women playing an important role in the foundation of communities as well as acting as powerful abbesses are found in the history of early monasticism. Originally, they could, in fact, be the head of double communities, that is, both a monastery and a nunnery (Bagge 1992, 371–72), for example, Theodochilde, Abbess of Jouarre, east of Paris, in the middle of the seventh century (Müller-Wille 1996, 218). Women also acted as church founders. In many early medieval churches, women's graves have been excavated in locations that support the idea that they were the church founders (for Scandinavia, see Stiesdal 1983, 7; for the Continent, see Stein 1967, 162, and Theune-Grosskopf 1989, 284; cf. Borgolte 1985, 27).

Two power centers in early medieval kingdoms on the Continent have been pointed out by Bagge: the army and the household. The army was a male field; the household, however, gave women a key role, partly because they controlled the economic resources of the farm in storehouses (cf. the husband's assessment of Odendisa, in the runic inscription mentioned above), and partly because feasts, which were politically important, were their responsibility (Bagge 1992, 341–42). The household was a unit much larger than in later times, and the royal household was a large part of the total economy.

Returning to the powerful women of the Viking Age in Scandinavia, the fact that all known examples of family hall buildings have very similar architecture and furnishings is essential. When a daughter from one hall married into another—women tied the aristocratic network together—she knew how it all worked and could therefore immediately act as the housewife (Herschend 1998, 151–52). This was similar to the farming society of later times with its complementary education, in which boys learned certain skills and girls other skills, thus ensuring that the future couple should be able to run a farm together.

In this connection it is important to point out that there are innumerable examples from medieval as well as the later Scandinavian peasant society that women's work was absolutely indispensable. A farm was like a firm, run by husband and wife together, in which the work of both partners was of equal importance although different and complementary. A result was the need for the above-mentioned distinct training of boys and girls. The boys were trained by their fathers as they followed them in their work, and the girls were trained by their mothers.

Finally, it should be mentioned that in the Icelandic sagas, written down in the thirteenth century but describing Viking Age society, the women usually stayed at the farm but acted through the men in circumstances far outside the female sphere. Women could not easily exceed the borders of space literally but they could compensate for it through speech: "The men had the sword, the women had their tongue" (Breisch 1994, 84).

ARCHAEOLOGICAL EVIDENCE: GRAVES OF POWERFUL WOMEN

A gendered perspective on the archaeological evidence of graves implies methods for sex determination. Three methods are used for this matter, one osteological, a second archaeological according to grave finds, and a third based upon morphological criteria of the external shape of the grave.

An osteological determination may be used if the bones are reasonably well preserved; unfortunately they often are not. In addition, for best results, osteologists prefer to analyze skeletons in situ, which is impossible for previous excavations. Another problem is that cremation was a very frequent method of burial in the first millennium A.D. in Scandinavia. Cremated bones are considerably more difficult to analyze and the uncertainty of sex determination is greater, partly because the bones are normally crushed into small pieces and partly because often only a small portion of the bones are present in the grave; consequently some of the characteristically sex-related bones may be missing. Great hopes are now set on future DNA analyses, but the method is under development and the sources of error are still numerous.

The most common method used is so-called archaeological sex determination, based on the finds of objects in the grave. For every single period of the first millennium A.D. (circa 0–150, early Roman Iron Age; circa 150–375, late Roman Iron Age; circa 375–550, Migration Period; circa 550–800, Vendel period (Sweden) or Merovingian Period (Denmark and Norway); and 800–1050 to 1100, Viking Age), there are suggestions about which objects indicate women and men, based on osteologically analyzed graves. Generally, weapons are seen as related to male graves and most jewelry is associated with female graves (see for example Petré 1993). One or two beads may occur in a male grave, but more than three beads are regarded as indicating women's graves. Tools and utensils may be sex neutral or in certain periods may indicate sex, sometimes male and sometimes female. An important difference between osteological and archaeological sex determination is that, in the first case, the question is obviously about biological sex, but in the second case, it may be the biological or the social sex. As Danish archaeologist Damm puts it: "We must ask ourselves if we should give primacy to the assumed sex of the dead or to the artifacts found with them. The question is whether the female gender was allowed to adopt the warrior role, or were people who were sexually female able to take on male gender roles? Here we face another basic question in gender archaeology: the relation between sex and gender" (Damm 1991, 132).

Certain morphological elements in the external shape of graves have also been used as sex indicators. For example, raised stones are usually assumed to indicate men's graves while so-called grave balls—large round stones, sometimes with ornamentation—mark women's graves.

Since archaeological sex determination in its simplest form—weapons interpreted as grave goods in men's graves, and jewelry as grave goods in women's graves—is a very elementary and obvious method, it is quite natural that women have been visible in grave finds since the beginning of archaeology. There are, however, rather few examples of research on burials that apply what can be called a gender perspective, and most of them are recent.

Richly equipped women's graves from the Roman Iron Age in the area north of the large Mälar lake in central Sweden can be taken as an example (Andersson 1998). These high-status burials are inhumation graves in cemeteries with both cremations and inhumations; however, the difference between the burial methods seems not to be sex specific. They indicate the same burial custom as the so-called aristocratic graves of Lübsow type (Gebühr

1974). Scandinavian examples are the well-known rich graves from Juellinge, Denmark (Müller 1911), and Store Dal and Hunn, Norway (Petersen 1916; Resi 1986). The rich female graves from the Mälar area have been interpreted in earlier research as graves of the wives of chieftains and other wealthy men. In a article by Andersson, these graves are discussed with regard to status and dating. Using a fine chronology for artifacts from the Roman Iron Age, Andersson has been able to show that the richest graves belong to a very short period of time, the first half of the second century A.D. (phase B2b), only one, or at most, two generations. His interpretation is that they are an expression of a social change, expressed by newcomers from outside establishing themselves as political leaders and therefore needing to make an impressive display. Therefore, they are seen not as material manifestations but rather as ideological ones, using funerals to legitimize the growth of a new local elite at this time. The title of the article is "Rich or Poor—Aware or Unaware?" and the conclusion is that these women were neither rich nor aware, but rather used as pieces in a political game (Andersson 1998).

When reading Gilchrist's criticism of Mytum's view about women in early Christian Ireland, one gets the impression that he had drawn a similar conclusion about women as objects: "imported spindle whorls recovered from archaeological contexts may indicate the movement of women upon marriage. Such approaches imply that women are objects of exchange, without the possibility of their own agency. These models are unsatisfactory because they are incomplete: they have failed to consider women's strategies for maintaining some control over their role in economic production and their place in kinship networks" (Gilchrist 1997, 46–47).

However, what Mytum writes in fact is: "some spindle whorls are of nonlocal materials, and were probably traded or exchanged as finished products. Documentary evidence shows that spinning was a female activity, and it may be that nonlocal spindle whorls indicate movement of women on marriage, as suggested by Clarke for the Iron Age at Glastonbury" (Mytum 1992, 236). As far as I understand it, nothing at all is said by Mytum about women's conditions in marriage. In my opinion, a woman bringing her own spindle whorl from the home of her childhood may well have become a very powerful housewife in her new home and attained an important place in kinship networks.

Gilchrist criticizes Richard Hodges (1989) as well for neglecting the role of women in building political analyses and initiating cultural change in his writing about Anglo-Saxon and Frankish women. He treats all women as a single group, regardless of age, social position, or ethnicity, and he does not consider the power that their reproductive value would have given them (Gilchrist 1997, 46–47).

The view expressed by Hodges according to Gilchrist, as well as Andersson's conclusions concerning the Roman Iron Age graves in the Mälar area, coincide with the opinion held by many feminist archaeologists that women have always been subordinated in archaeological studies. However, I ask myself if this is not an anachronism, influenced by the circumstances of the last two centuries, when women of the bourgeoisie really have been subordinate. In historic times in peasant society as well as in artisan families, women's work played an important economic role and therefore led to high status for women, a situation that with all probability harks to Scandinavian prehistoric society of the first millennium A.D. For that reason, I much prefer Gilchrist's statements on women with a possibility for their own agency over the view of totally powerless women, victims of other people's will.

Norwegian archaeologist Dommasnes has applied a gender perspective to west-Norwegian grave material from the second half of the first millennium A.D. from an early stage in feminist archaeology (Dommasnes 1979). She looks for differences in social status between men and women to get information about the division of labor between the sexes. Her analysis of grave goods, especially tools and utensils, reveals wealthy and powerful housewives working with textile production and periodically taking part in the outdoor work at the farm, especially during harvest time. Men are distinguished by weapons and by tools for hunting and craftsmanship, such as tools of the carpenter and smith (Dommasnes 1979, 107).

In connection with the Celtic luxury grave of Vix in France, dated to the fifth century B.C., where a woman was buried with all signs of very high status, including a gold torc, Arnold discusses the phenomenon of "the honorary male syndrome," where in a patriarchal society women can sometimes be given certain male signs of status. Her conclusion is that the Celtic princely women's graves represent high-status women as women rather than high-status women as men, primarily because they lack weapons (Arnold 1996, 165).

The boat-grave cemeteries of the second half of the first millennium A.D. in Svealand in Sweden are often described as a purely male matter. Within Svealand in the Upplandic cemeteries of Vendel and Valsgärde, the custom of burial in boat graves is completely confined to men. In Tuna in Badelunda, Västmanland (also in Svealand), however, the boat graves were exclusively made for women, while in Tuna in Alsike and in the vicarage of Old Uppsala in Uppland, both sexes are buried in boats. However, in two of these boat-grave cemeteries there were also cremation graves. At Tuna in Badelunda, the cremation graves contained both men and women; there were probably six women's and fifteen men's graves (Nordahl 1994, 83). At Valsgärde, about fifty cremation graves were excavated, most of them women's graves (Schönbäck 1983, 128). These cover a long period of time, at least from the Migration period until the middle Viking Age. Many of these cremations contain nothing more than combs, ceramics, and burned bones, but some of them seem to be the remains of very rich funerals.

As early as 1934, the findings from a rich grave from the eighth century was published under the title "The Grave of a Noble Woman in the Valsgärde Cemetery" (my translation) by Lindqvist (1934, 138–42), who stressed above all the location of the grave at the highest point of the cemetery as well as the skillful use of the terrain to create an illusion of a mound, considerably larger than it was in actual fact. The monument clearly demonstrates that this woman was really honored. The grave goods consisted of jewelry and a key handle, which is an important detail that shows the woman's power over the resources of the farm.

There are also some Viking Age female graves at Valsgärde, where the grave goods indicate powerful status for the buried women. In a tenth-century woman's grave, a richly decorated animal's head carved from walrus ivory with eyes of carnelian was found (fig. 4), a unique object interpreted as the upper part of an animal-headed staff (Lindqvist 1956, 19). Such an object seems to indicate very high status, reminiscent of the animal head poles from the boat burial at Oseberg in Norway (Schetelig 1920, 199), with a suggested magic/religious function (Grieg 1928, 65). A wood carving of a small animal's head with very distinct eyes and teeth from the Oseberg find seems to be an especially good parallel to this object (fig. 5). As the buried woman in the Oseberg ship has been interpreted as a priestess in a fertility cult (Ingstad 1992), and the animal-headed staffs are seen as having a religious function, a similar interpretation may be considered also for this Valsgärde woman.

Another tenth-century grave at Valsgärde contained a so-called whip handle that gives an impression of dignity when compared, for example, to the scepter found in the aristocratic Högom grave in northern Sweden (Gräslund 1998). In two of the women's graves, drinking-horn mounts were found. This is interesting with regard to ritual drinking, often emphasized as a very important component of late Iron Age aristocratic feasting hall culture during the second half of the first millennium A.D. (Norr 1998, 125; concerning connections between political power and the pagan cult including ritual drinking, see Meulengracht Sørensen 1991, 237). A comparison can be made with the Birka grave, Bj 523, also in Svealand (Arbman 1943, 157), a chamber grave of a woman richly equipped with jewelry (fig. 6), two drinking horns with silver mounts, a bronze bowl, a wooden bucket, two wooden bowls, gaming pieces of glass, and a small wooden sculpture of an animal's head (fig. 7). The animal's head sculpture is an extremely rare object, and the parallels with the Valsgärde grave mentioned above are clear.

Figure 4. Animal head from Valsgärde Grave 85 (photo Allan Fridell).

To return to Arnold's definitions, the evidence speaks in favor of the Valsgärde high-status women as women. The high-status men at Valsgärde were no doubt buried in boat graves, but what about the Tuna women in their boat graves? Probably they were also high-status women as women. They lacked weapons, which were important elements of male high-status equipment. Power, however, involves more than the mere display of weapons. Consequently, rich women's graves such as those discussed above do not necessar-

Figure 5. Animal head from Oseberg (after Schetelig 1920).

ily give rise to the conclusion that those women were only the wives of powerful men. There is every reason to accept the possibility that they were powerful themselves.

The question of prehistoric women's visibility depends upon the capability of the archaeologist and the desire to acknowledge or identify women and to understand the whole context. In my opinion, it is anachronistic to think, for

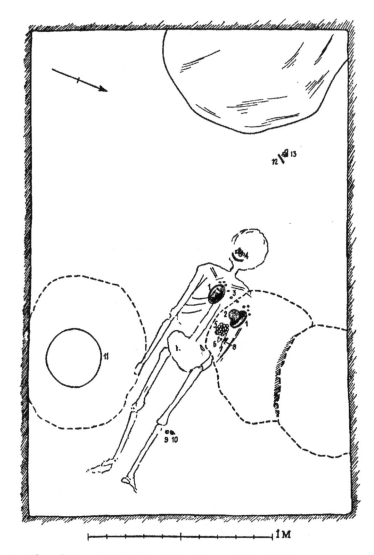

Figure 6.   Plan of Grave Bj 523, Birka (after Arbman 1940–1943).

example, that sewing needles devalue women. Embroidering may have another meaning for us today as we have heard so much about "wasted female
work," as was commonly said by female politicians in Sweden in the 1970s
in connection with women's liberation. In earlier times, one of women's main
tasks was to produce textiles needed on the farm, which was absolutely cru-

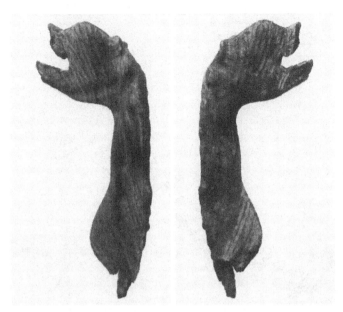

Figure 7.   Animal head from Grave Bj 523, Birka (after Arbman 1940–1943).

cial work. Aristocratic and royal women, however, did not participate in cloth weaving or the making of clothing, but were initiators and supervisors of the work, and they themselves worked with embroidery and tapestry weaving. In this connection, Koch's work on the hierarchy of Merovingian women's graves in southern Germany is highly interesting. At the cemetery of Pleidels-heim, three different family groups of different social levels have been discerned. In each group, there is a clear hierarchy of the women's graves. Tools for textile work differentiate the real housewife from the rest of the farmer's group. Only one woman in each generation, the one with the richest jewelry, was buried with a spindle whorl, interpreted as a symbol of her power over the textile supplies of the farm (Koch 1996, 36). In the more aristocratic groups, textile tools are found either in the grave of the noble housewife or in that of her "lady-in-waiting" (Koch 1996, 39–40). Take the Bayeux Tapestry as another example (Wilson 1985). According to tradition, Queen Mathilde of Normandy, wife of William the Conqueror, and her court ladies were the artisans who made the tapestry, ordered by Bishop Odo. Even if this tradition is not fully reliable, the tapestry was probably designed by a man who saw the battle, whether or not it was embroidered by women. It certainly conveys a message as political and tendentious as the one conveyed by a male historian.

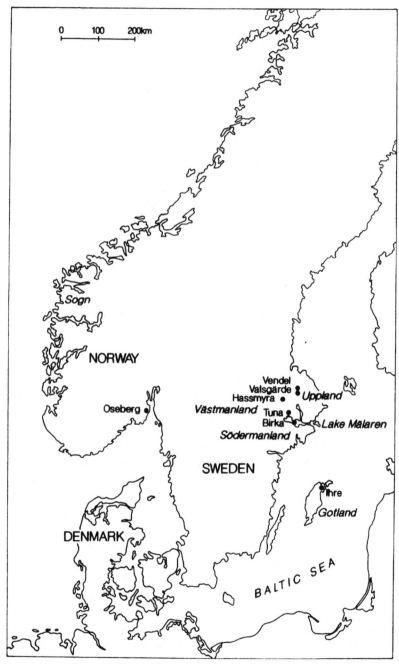

Figure 8. Map of Scandinavia showing sites mentioned in the text (illustration Alicja Grenberger).

CONCLUSION

Keys found in the graves of Scandinavian women of the first millennium A.D. not only express that the place of women was mostly indoors and that women did not take part in what today is called official life, but they also show a role transformed into power, as responsibility for the household economy and feasts made women powerful. It is uncertain whether the official sphere was more important than the domestic, as they often intermingled. The hall can be regarded as an excellent example of this—in the hall, female and male meet and official meets private as well, an interesting conjunction where commonly used boundaries dissolve.

In this chapter, I have presented some archaeological and documentary evidence concerning women and their conditions/position in society. For the Scandinavian Viking Age, the written evidence is very rare, but there are contemporary runic inscriptions, in some cases very informative. As analogies, I have also used literary evidence from Germanic Europe and from the British Isles. The archaeological evidence used consists of grave material. Both these source categories illustrate women with considerable power and possibilities for their own agency.

REFERENCES

Medieval Sources:

Bede. 1994. *The ecclesiastical history of the English people.* Edited by Judith McClure and Roger Collins. Oxford, U.K.: Oxford University Press.

Gregory of Tours. 1951. *Gregorii Episcopi Toronensis,* Vol. 1 of *Libri Historiarum.* 10th ed. Edited by Bruno Krusch and Wilhelm Levison. Scriptores rerum Merovingicarum. Hannoverae: Impensis Bibliopolii Hahniani.

———. 1974. *History of the Franks.* Translated by Lewis Thorpe. Hammondsworth, Middlesex, U.K.: Penguin.

Paul the Deacon. 1907. *History of the Langobards.* Translated by William Dudley Foulke. Philadelphia: University of Pennsylvania Press.

Saxo Grammaticus. 1979–1980. *The history of the Danes.* 2 vols. Translated by Peter Fisher, and edited by Hilda Ellis Davidson. Totowa, N.J.: Rowman & Littlefield.

Thietmar of Merseburg. 1957. *Chronik.* Edited by Werner Trillmich. Ausgewählte Quellen zur Deutschen Geschichte des Mittelalters 9. Darmstadt: Wissenschaftliche Buchgesellschaft.

Modern Sources:

Andersson, Kent. 1998. Rik eller fattig—medveten eller omedveten. Kvinnan i Uppland och Västmanland under romersk järnålder. In *"Suionum hinc civitates." Nya undersök-*

ningar kring norra Mälardalens äldre järnålder. Occasional papers in archaeology, 19. Edited by Kent Andersson, pp. 59–88. Uppsala: Institutionen för arkeologi och antik historia.

Arbman, Holger. 1943. *Birka. I. Die Gräber. Text*. Uppsala: Almqvist & Wiksell.

Arnold, Bettina. 1996. "Honorary males" or women of substance? Gender, status, and power in Iron-Age Europe. *Journal of European Archaeology* 3 (2):153–68.

Arwill-Nordbladh, Elisabeth. 1991. Det emancipatoriska arvet efter Oscar Montelius. *KAN (Kvinner i Arkeologi i Norge)* 12:9–15.

Bagge, Sverre, trans. 1980. *En kongelig bryllupssang/A song for the royal wedding in Bergen* A.D. 1281. Bergen: Håkonshallens Venner.

———. 1992. Europe 300–1200. In *Cappelens Kvinnehistorie*. Vol. 1 of *Urtid, Oldtid, Middelalder til ca 1500*. Edited by Ida Blom, pp. 317–77. Oslo: Cappelen.

Borgolte, Michael. 1985. Stiftergrab und Eigenkirche. Ein Begriffspaar der Mittelalterarchäologie in historischer Kritik. *Zeitschrift für Archäologie des Mittelalters* 13:27–38.

Breisch, Agneta. 1994. *Frid och fredlöshet. Sociala band och utanförskap på Island under äldre medeltid*. Acta Universitatis Upsaliensis. Studia historica Upsaliensia, 174. Stockholm: Almqvist & Wiksell.

Conkey, Margaret W., and Joan M. Gero. 1991. Tensions, pluralities, and engendering archaeology: An introduction to women and prehistory. In *Engendering archaeology: Women and prehistory*. Edited by Margaret W. Conkey and Joan M. Gero, pp. 3–30. Oxford, U.K.: Basil Blackwell.

Damm, Charlotte. 1991. From burials to gender roles: Problems and potentials in postprocessual archaeology. In *The archaeology of gender: Proceedings of the twenty-second annual Chacmool conference of the Archaeological Association of the University of Calgary*. Edited by Dale Walde and Noreen D. Willow, pp. 130–35. Calgary: University of Calgary.

Dommasnes, Liv Helga. 1979. Et gravmateriale fra yngre jernalder brukt til å belyse kvinners stilling. *Viking* 42:95–114.

Duby, Georges. 1997. *Eleanor of Aquitaine and six others*. Vol. 1 of *Women of the twelfth century*. Cambridge, U.K.: Polity Press.

Gebühr, Michael. 1974. Zur Definition älterkaiserzeitlicher Fürstengräber vom Lübsow-Typ. *Praehistorische Zeitschrift* 49 (1):82–128.

Gero, Joan M. 1991. Genderlithics: Women's roles in stone tool production. In *Engendering archaeology: Women and prehistory*. Edited by Margaret W. Conkey and Joan M. Gero, pp. 163–93. Oxford, U.K.: Basil Blackwell.

Gilchrist, Roberta. 1997. Ambivalent bodies: Gender and medieval archaeology. In *Invisible people and processes: Writing gender and childhood into European archaeology*. Edited by Jenny Moore and Eleanor Scott, pp. 42–58. London: Leicester University Press.

Grieg, Sigurd. 1928. *Kongsgaarden. Osebergsfundet II*. Oslo: Den Norske Stat.

Gräslund, Anne-Sofie. 1989. "Gud hjälpe nu väl hennes själ." Om runstenskvinnorna, deras roll vid kristnandet och deras plats i familj och samhälle. *Tor 22* (1988–1989): 223–44.

———. 1994. Rune stones—on ornamentation and chronology. In *Developments around the Baltic and the North Sea in the Viking Age. The Twelfth Viking Congress*. Birka Studies 3. B. Edited by Björn Ambrosiani and Helen Clarke, pp. 117–31. Stockholm: Riksantikieambtet and Statens Historiska Museer.

————. 1995. Runstenskvinnorna ännu en gång. *Tor* 27:459–74.

————. 1997. The christianization of Scandinavia from a female perspective. In *Rom und Byzans im Norden. Mission und Glaubenswechsel im Ostseeraum während des 8.–14. Jahrhunderts.* Edited by Michael Müller-Wille, pp. 313–29. Mainz: Akademie der Wissenschaften und der Literatur.

————. 1998. A princely child in Birka. In *Studien zur Archäologie des Ostseeraumes. Von der Eisenzeit zum Mittelalter. Festschrift für Michael Müller-Wille.* Edited by Anke Wesse, pp. 281–89. Neumünster: Wachholtz.

Gräslund, Bo. 1999. Gustaf Oscar Augustin Montelius. In "The great archaeologists." Encyclopedia of archaeology, 1. Edited by Tim Murray, pp. 155–63. Santa Barbara, Calif.: ABC-Clio.

Hermansson, Karin. 1991. "Cherubim and Seraphim" och kvinnorna. In *Det mångreligiösa Jos. Om kyrkoliv och kristen-muslimska relationer i Nigeria. En fältstudierapport.* Edited by Christopher Steed, pp. 191–222. Uppsala: Uppsala Universitet, Teologiska Institutionen.

Herschend, Frands. 1996. A note on late Iron Age kingship mythology. *Tor* 28:283–303.

————. 1998. *The idea of the good in late Iron Age society.* Occasional Papers in Archaeology 15. Uppsala: Institutionen för arkeologi och antik historia.

Hodges, Richard. 1989. *The Anglo-Saxon achievement: Archaeology and the beginnings of English society.* London: Duckworth.

Ingstad, Anne-Stine. 1992. Oseberg-dronningen—hvem var hun? In *Oseberg-dronningens grav: vår arkeologiske nasjonalskatt i nytt lys.* Edited by Axel E. Christensen, Anne-Stine Ingstad, and Bjorn Myhre, pp. 224–57. Oslo: Schibsted.

Jansson, Sven B. F. 1964. *Västmanlands runinskrifter,* granskade och tolkade av S. B. F. Jansson. Sveriges Runinskrifter 13. Stockholm: Almqvist & Wiksell.

Koch, Ursula. 1996. Die Hierarchie der Frauen in merowingischer Zeit, beobachtet in Pleidelsheim (Kr. Ludwigsburg) und Klepsau (Hohenlohekreis). In *Königin, Klosterfrau, Bäuerin, Frauen in Frühmittelalter.* Bericht zur 3. Tagung des Netzwerks archäologisch arbeitender Frauen 19.–22. oktober 1995 in Kiel. Edited by Helga Brandt and Julia K. Koch, pp. 29–54. Münster: Agenda.

Lennemyr, Maria. 1989. Kristna kvinnors identitet i Indien. En "case study" från Dornakalstiftet i Sydindiaen. In *Vilket Indien!? Rapport från ett missionsvetenskapligt fältstudium våren 1989.* Edited by Hans Kvarnström, pp. 17–44. Uppsala: Uppsala Universitet, Teologiska Institutionen.

Lidegaard, Mads. 1991. Kristendommen og den eskimoiske kultur. *Tidsskriftet Gronland* (3):61–76 (1991).

Lindqvist, Sune. 1934. En förnäm kvinnas grav på Valsgärde gravbacke. *Finska fornminnesföreningens tidskrift* 40:138–42.

————. 1956. *Från Upplands forntid. Kort vägledning genom Uppsala universitets museum för nordiska fornsaker jämte några ord om runstenarna i Universitetsparken.* 3d ed. Uppsala: Almqvist & Wiksell.

Meulengracht Sørensen, Preben. 1991. Håkon den gode og guderne. Nogle bemærkninger om religion og centralmagt i det tiende århundrede—og om religionshistorie og kildekritik. In *Fra Stamme til Stat i Danmark, 2. Hovdingesamfund og Kongemagt.* Jysk Arkæologisk Selskabs Skrifter 22:2. Edited by Peder Mortensen and Birgit M. Rasmussen, pp. 235–44. Århus: Universtetsforlag.

Müller, Sophus. 1911. *Juellinge-fundet og den romerske periode*. Nordiske fortidsminder 2:1. Kjøbenhavn: Gyldendalske Boghandel.

Müller-Wille, Michael. 1996. Königtum und Adel im Spiegel der Grabfunde. In *Die Franken-Wegbereiter Europas. Vor 1500 Jahren: König Chlodwig und seine Erben*. Edited by Alfred Wieczorek et al., pp. 206–21. Mainz: Verlag Philipp von Zabern.

Mytum, Harald C. 1992. *The origins of early Christian Ireland*. London: Routledge.

Nordahl, Else. 1994. Kort kommentar till brandgravarna. In *Tuna i Badelunda. Guld, kvinnor, båtar*. Vol. 2. Edited by Erik Nylén and Bengt Schönbäck, pp. 83–86. Västerås: Västerås Kulturnämnd.

Norr, Svante. 1998. *To rede and to rown: Expressions of kingship in the Scandinavian late Iron Age*. Occasional Papers in Archaeology, 13. Uppsala: Institutionen för arkeologi och antik historia.

Petersen, Jan. 1916. Gravplassen fra Store-Dal i Skjeberg. *Norske Oldfund* 1. Kristiania: Universitetets Oldsaksamling.

Petré, Bo. 1993. Male and female finds and symbols in Germanic Iron Age graves. *Current Swedish Archaeology* 1:149–154.

Resi, Heid Gjosten. 1986. *Gravplassen Hunn i Østfold*. Norske Oldfunn 12. Oslo: Universitetets Oldsaksamling.

Schetelig, Haakon. 1920. *Vestfoldskolen. Osebergfundet III*. Oslo: Den Norske Stat.

Schönbäck, Bengt. 1983. The custom of burial in boats. In *Vendel period studies. Transactions of the Boat-Grave Symposium in Stockholm, February, 2–3, 1981*. Studies 2. Edited by Jan Peder Lamm and Hans-Åke Nordström, pp. 123–32. Stockholm: The Museum of National Antiquities Stockholm.

Stein, Frauke. 1967. *Adelsgräber des achten Jahrhunderts in Deutschland. Text und Tafeln*. Germanische Denkmäler der Völkerwanderungszeit, Serie A, 9. Berlin: de Gruyter.

Stiesdal, Hans. 1983. Grave i tidlige vesttårne. Nogle nyereiakttagelser. *Hikuin* 9:7–38.

Theune-Grosskopf, Barbara. 1989. Ein frühmittelalterlicher Kirchenbau mit "Gründergrab" in Cognin, Savoyen? *Archäologisches Korrespondenzblatt* 19:283–96.

Thomas, David Hurst. 1983. *Gatecliff Shelter*. Anthropological papers of the American Museum of Natural History 59, pt. 1. New York: American Museum of Natural History.

Wilson, David M. 1985. *The Bayeux tapestry: The complete tapestry in colour*. London: Thames and Hudson.

Gender Roles and the
Ambiguity of Signification

6

Gender and Mortuary Analysis:
What Can Grave Goods Really Tell Us?

Barbara A. Crass

Burials have been described as containing more information per cubic meter than other archaeological features. Since human remains can often be sexed, burials can provide important clues to the identification of genders, assuming that gender roles were signaled in a mortuary context. But is it really that straightforward? Special considerations must be taken into account, especially with portable items associated with burials, such as grave goods.

Three topics are addressed in this chapter. The first concerns the implications and considerations of mortuary analysis in indigenous cultures. Restrictions on the excavation of burials should not discourage scholars from doing mortuary analyses as a tremendous amount of documentary material may be available from previous excavations. The second is an overview of gender differentiation and ideology in traditional Inuit society, based on the observations of native and nonnative sources. This includes a discussion of the Inuit concept of an individual compared to the Western concept. Third, challenges associated with using grave goods to identify gender roles are examined by comparing the ethnographic record with archaeologic data on pre-Christian Inuit cairn burials in Canada and Greenland. Practices such as borrowing, replenishing, and exchanging goods are discussed.

In summary, this chapter demonstrates how data from previously excavated graves supplemented by early ethnographic data and folklore can be used to provide a plausible view of gender roles and ideology in traditional Inuit society. Grave goods can provide important clues to the identification of gender roles among the Inuit, as this study demonstrates.

This chapter also contains a brief discussion of problems I experienced in collecting burial data from previously excavated burials for my dissertation. Also included is a discussion of gender ideology and attribution in traditional Inuit societies. In addition, the ethnographic record will be compared with the archaeologically recovered material from cairn burials in the eastern Canadian Arctic and Greenland.

Since the term "Eskimo" is viewed by some as derogatory, in this chapter I will use Inuit as defined by the Inuit Circumpolar Conference Charter adopted in Barrow, Alaska, on June 15, 1977. This term encompasses all regional groups including the Siberian Yupik of Siberia and Alaska, the Central Yupik, the Alluttiq and the Inupiat of Alaska, the Inuvialuit of Canada, and the Kalaallit of Greenland.

The Inuit range has at various times covered the coastal areas of the Chukchi Peninsula in Siberia, the northern interior and coast of Alaska as far south as Kodiak Island and Prince William Sound, the northern coast and interior of Canada, including the shores of Hudson Bay, and the coast of Greenland (fig. 1). With the exception of a few of the more southerly areas below the tree line that have rich salmon runs, the Inuit depend on arctic sea mammals and inland caribou herds for their livelihood. An extremely short growing season provides little flora for gathering. The Inuit use some berries, herbs, and even tiny roots harvested from lemming caches.

This chapter is based on research for my dissertation, a project that entailed the gathering of Inuit burial data from multiple sources (Crass 1998). Although no one had previously done a comprehensive analysis of mortuary practices of the Inuit, their burials had been excavated and plundered for more than a century, sometimes in the name of science. The first step was gathering information on the burials, the associated goods, and the skeletal remains.

Translating the literature and tracking down lost or misplaced artifacts in museum collections posed one set of problems. The Native American Graves Protection and Repatriation Act (NAGPRA) offered additional challenges. I was not excavating burials, and I was not interested in personally examining human remains. All I wanted was the reports on previously excavated burials and the associated analyses of human remains and burial goods. I was alarmed to discover that, for various reasons, some human remains had been housed for decades in museums without being analyzed, even for basic data such as age and sex. Literally hundreds of burials were excavated but never published in sources made readily available to other scholars. With the repatriation of many of these burial goods and human remains, the information has been lost. Some museum curators were so protective, or perhaps frightened, because of NAGPRA, that I was not even allowed access to museum records, field notes, or other documentation dealing with burial excavations.

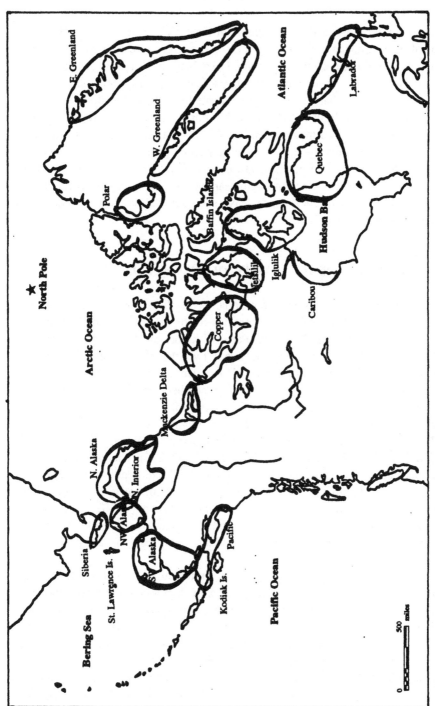

Figure 1. Distribution of Inuit groups. (Adapted from Damas, ed. 1984, ix.)

I encountered most of these problems in the United States, but repatriation has affected Canada and Greenland also. However, access to written documentation in the museums in Canada, Greenland, or Denmark (where much of the Greenlandic documentation is housed) proved less problematic.

I mention these challenges here to indicate that although Native American burials are currently avoided if possible during excavations today, a vast storehouse of recorded information is available in archives, government documents, and other literature. This is an important consideration since burials are a "primary source of potential attribution of sex" (Conkey 1991, 59) and are therefore a logical place to begin searching for clues to gender ideology in any culture. At the moment at least, such sources are still available for study and should be utilized.

GENDER DIFFERENTIATION IN TRADITIONAL INUIT SOCIETY

Fixed gender differentiation is not apparent in all aspects of Inuit society. This stems in part from Inuit conceptions of the afterlife and the continued role of the dead among the living. Personal names are considered an aspect of one of the souls (most groups believe in two) the Inuit possess. Names are viewed as containing part of a person's essence, or *inua*. When the name of a recently deceased relative or community member is given to a newborn, the infant is believed to acquire some of the wisdom, skills, and traits of the deceased. The child becomes a living representative of the deceased person, who is often viewed as being partially reincarnated (Nuttall 1994; Saladin d'Anglure 1977; Wachtmeister 1956; Weyer 1932, 293). This procedure may be repeated, resulting in the child assuming multiple gender roles and extended kin relationships with members of the community in an accretive manner, irrespective of the child's sex or age. Throughout life, as a person acquires more names, the number of gender roles and extended kin relationships increase, as can the multiple gender identities (Saladin d'Anglure 1994).

Stefansson (1926, 401) described an Inuit couple he knew who had a seven-year-old son, "whose father called him stepmother and whose mother called him aunt, for those were their respective relationships to the woman whose soul was the boy's guardian." The use of kinship terms, such as aunt instead of son, indicates that the nature of the relationship is more important than the sex of the individual (Giffen 1930, 58). Since the individual Inuk usually has multiple gender roles, the absence of gender-specific pronouns in Eskimo languages is easy to understand (Barker 1995; Birket-Smith 1928; Fortescue 1984). This stands in contradiction to the ordered and highly complex gender-specific aspects of European languages such as German or Spanish.

This lack of fixed gender differentiation is not only found in language and personal pronouns, but also in activity patterns. An attentive reading of early ethnographies discloses that activities such as hunting and domestic chores are not strictly sex specific. Jenness, as well as others, noted that the division of labor was fluid and flexible (cf. Brower cited in Blackman 1992, 205–6; Jenness 1957, 177; Nansen 1893, 125; Rae cited in Boas 1888, 485; Rainey 1947, 253; Ray 1885, 44; Thalbitzer 1941, 599, 602). Both men who cooked and mended their clothes and women who hunted, stalked seals on the ice, and were members of whaling crews are described. Perhaps more important, Jenness claimed "The Eskimos seemed to consider this all natural" (1957, 177). These activities seem to be based primarily on need and not on gender attribution.

Certain ethnographically attested gender attributions do exist, however. Clothing often differs in design, trim, and cut, depending on gender. Outer parkas differ between males and females throughout the Inuit range. A woman's parka has deep armholes and huge shoulders and is cut high at the hip for functional reasons. Rounded flaps are at the front and back, with the back flap extended to various lengths. The hood, or *amaat*, is designed specifically for carrying an infant. A woman's marital status and the number of children she has borne are indicated by variations in these aspects of the woman's parka (Chaussonnet 1988; Carpenter 1997; Bahnson 1997; Hall, Oakes, and Qimmiu'naaq 1994). A man's parka has the sleeves sewn to the body at right angles, either a straight bottom or short rounded flaps, and, in some areas, an animal tail is left hanging from the back (Bahnson 1997; Foote 1992). The shape of the hoods and the pattern of white fur insets on children's parkas identifies boys and girls (Hall, Oakes, and Qimmiu'naaq 1994).

Although gender is often indicated by clothing styles, this may not always reflect the biological sex of the individual. Among the Caribou Inuit, a child given the name of a deceased relative of the opposite sex wore the clothing of that sex (Hall, Oakes, and Qimmiu'naaq 1994). Transvestism is also employed by adults, especially shamans, as a means of protecting a person from evil spirits (Chaussonnet 1988, 216). Inuit shamans are traditionally viewed as having androgynous features, occupying a shifting position between male and female. Their clothing could combine the characteristic features of both sexes (Hall, Oakes, and Qimmiu'naaq 1994, 52).

Other gender transformers are found in the ethnographic record. Occasional gender transformation is found in the *Mitârneq*, an annual ritual that takes place in Greenland on New Year's Eve. Some archaeological evidence exists to indicate this custom has ancient roots (Kleivan 1960, 7). Participants

of all ages dress as members of the opposite sex. The clothing is usually extremely sexual with the "male" costume having an artificial penis, often of
exaggerated size, attached at the crotch. The "female" costume usually has
pendulant breasts or a pregnant stomach. One unique "female" costume was
described as having an open-mouthed catfish attached between the legs to
represent a pudendum (Nellemann 1960, 111).

Many ethnographers described adult gender transformers from most of the
Inuit groups. According to Bogoras, Siberian shamans could change their
gender to varying degrees, and become a "soft man being" where biological
males became "similar to woman" and biological females became "similar
to man" (1904–1909, 449). These changes are marked by a range of attributes, from just changing the hairstyle or dress to a complete gender transformation where they "transformed" into a member of the opposite sex. Some
informants claimed shamans could even acquire the appropriate genitalia
with the spirits' aid, thereby changing their biological sex.

Similarly, biological males who dressed, worked, and lived as females are
described among the Inuit of Kodiak Island (Black 1977, 99; Dall cited in
Thalbitzer 1914, 603; Davydov 1977, 166; and Sarychev [1790] cited in
Holmberg 1985, 52). No female-to-male gender transformers are reported
from Kodiak Island. Often these transformers were shamans, but all gender
transformers were influential (Davydov 1977, 166). Some of them were
males raised as females since infancy, either because of their "feminine" appearance or a desire of the parents to have a daughter. Parents could designate
a male child to become a shaman at birth and raise that child as a female
(Iosaf in Black 1977, 99).

Gender transformers may have been overlooked by or been invisible to
naive ethnographers. Nansen (1893, 125) had an opportunity to observe two
female gender transformers in east Greenland in the 1890s, but could not distinguish them from the men. They were both good sealers and clever at wom-
en's work (Holm 1914, 67 n. 1; Thalbitzer 1941, 602).

Gender transformation is still a part of traditional Inuit life. Recently,
Stewart (1998) described a boy in Pelly Bay, Canada, who was *kipijuituq*, a
taboo state declared by the child's grandparents at birth. As a *kipijuituq* the
boy was dressed and treated as a girl until he killed a prescribed animal upon
reaching adolescence as a rite of passage. After a ceremony, the boy was
dressed and treated as a male. Stewart admits to some confusion regarding
female infants being *kipijuituq*.

The *sipiniit* is another type of gender transformation that has been rarely
mentioned. An infant who changes sex at birth due to human negligence,
complications of delivery, or the will of the dead is a *sipiniq*. One description
of the process is from the Ammassalik of east Greenland.

All foetuses have a penis. This foetus is like a boy. When he starts to move and he is still very little, he grabs his penis and only lets go at his birth, if he wants to remain a boy. If he wants to be a girl, at the moment he begins to move he does not grab his penis. His penis therefore transforms little by little into a vulva and a girl will be born. (Robbe 1981, 74, cited in Saladin d'Anglure 1994, 86)

In east Greenland, the practice of children of one biological sex being raised and trained as though they were of the opposite sex is currently used to remedy an unequal sex ratio within a family. A family with several daughters may decide to raise the next female infant as a male, or vice versa. The existence of female hunters is mentioned for this area in the early ethnographies, so the practice may have traditionally filled a role played by infanticide elsewhere (Robert-Lamblin 1981).

These and other observations demonstrate fluidity in the concepts of sex and gender in Inuit society. Recently, the traditional roles of men and women in Inuit society have been described not as a "sexual division of labor" but as two complementary forms of one function (Bodenhorn 1990; Kawagley 1995, 20). Given the fluidity of gender attributions during life, firm gender differentiation in Inuit burial assemblages would not be expected. This is substantiated and has been presented elsewhere (Crass 1998, 2000). Only five of 147 burial good categories (3.4 percent) were found to have a statistically significant association with one sex, but none were found exclusively with one sex, although possibly with one gender. The finding of these few items, *ulus* (knives) and mattocks with females, and snow knives, arrowheads, and harpoon heads with males, is consistent with the ethnographic evidence for gender fluidity and transformation. In a fluid model, any so called sex-specific items would be expected to be found associated with some individuals of the opposite sex.

ARCHAEOLOGICAL RECOVERY OF BURIAL MATERIAL

How much of the burial material is recoverable by an archaeologist? This question brings us to the final part of this chapter, a comparison of the ethnographic descriptions with the archaeological recovery of material. To do this, I will use cairn burials as an example. These aboveground burials are the most common type of burial found in Greenland and Canada.

The ethnographic observations and archaeological data are divided into six groups based on geographic and cultural criteria. The Canadian groups are the Central Inuit, comprising the Copper, Netsilik, and Iglulik Inuit groups of central Canada; the Baffin Inuit from Baffin Island; the Labrador (or Lab) Inuit of Labrador; and the Quebec Inuit of northern Quebec. The two groups from Greenland are the west Greenland Inuit and the east Greenland Inuit. The data presented in tables 1 through 4 use these divisions, although for cases where no data are available for Quebec, the category is deleted.

Seven hundred ninety-seven burial cairns were examined: 637 single burials, 140 multiple burials, and 20 cenotaphs, yielding 1,067 individuals. A portion of the human remains were sexed; 276 were identified as female, and 201 as male. None of the human remains in west Greenland had been sexed.

A frequent burial good category found throughout the area was containers. Several historic observers and ethnographers claimed cooking pots and cups were placed in or on burial cairns, especially female cairns (Graah 1837, 67; Hawkes 1916, 120; Kroeber 1900, 31; Lyon 1825, 371; Peary 1898, 506; Rasmussen 1929b, 200). In Labrador, Hawkes (1916, 90) reported all pots deposited in cairns were either broken or had holes bored in them (table 1). Similar practices were occasionally noted in Greenland (Schultz-Lorentzen 1928, 245). According to data on material recovered archaeologically from cairns, some type of container was found in at least half the cairns in Labrador, and 67 percent ($N = 18$) of the containers were broken. A significant percentage of cairns in west Greenland also had containers. Of the nineteen (37 percent) cairns with containers, six (32 percent) were broken. An association of containers with females cannot be demonstrated from the archaeological data. In the few cases where the sex of the individual was known, an almost equal number of males and females had containers.

Lamps and sewing implements, including needles, needle cases, or thimble holders, were also claimed by ethnographers to have been left on or in female cairns (Boas 1888, 613; Cardno n.d.; Crantz 1767, 237; Egede 1818, 153; Graah 1837, 67; Hawkes 1916, 120; Hayes 1867, 294; Kroeber 1900, 31; Peary 1898, 506; Rasmussen 1929a, 200). Only a few cairns were found archaeologically that contained lamps or sewing implements ($N = 2\text{--}7$) (table 2); the highest percentage was found in west Greenland with 14 percent for both lamps and sewing tools. For the sexed human remains, the association between males and females and lamps is fairly even: two lamps were associated with females, one with a male, and one with a male and female in a

Table 1.   Containers (by percentage)

	Central	Baffin	Laborador	Quebec	W. Greenland	E. Greenland
Cairns	7.0	0	52.0	20	37.0	18.0
Broken	86.0	0	67.0	—	32.0	33.0
Female	38.5	0	29.9	—	0	0
Male	30.8	0	29.9	—	0	0
Unknown	30.8	0	48.2	—	100	100

multiple burial. The burial of multiple individuals in one cairn, as was the case in Labrador, complicates the interpretation when a male and a female are buried together. A few more females than males were found to have sewing implements, but the numbers were small (N = 5 for females, N = 1 for males).

Early ethnographers claimed kayaks and sleds were left on or beside male cairns (Bessel 1884, 877; Bilby 1923, 166; Crantz 1767, 237; Egede 1818, 153; Graah 1837, 67; Hawkes 1916, 120; Kroeber 1900, 31; Peary 1898, 506; Rasmussen 1929a, 200; 1908, 114). A whole or a partial kayak was found on or near only seven cairns (n = 1–3) (table 3). All the sexed individuals associated with a kayak are males. With the exception of Quebec, where sleds were associated with all ten cairns, whole or partial sleds were found on or near a slightly higher percentage of cairns (from 2 to 14 percent [N = 1–7]) than were kayaks. Sleds were found in association with two females and two children. The archaeological data and the statement from Ryder (1895) that sleds were "commonly" found associated with cairns both imply that sleds were associated with males and females, as well as children.

Most ethnographers claimed weapons were usually left on or near cairns, especially those containing males. But according to the archaeological data, only 15 to 40 percent (N = 3–75) of the cairns contained a weapon of any type (table 4). Weapons were not found preferentially with males; they were associated with individuals regardless of age or sex. Weapons were found in the burials of children, females and children, females alone, females and males together, and males alone.

The ethnographic and archaeological data show some concordance but not complete agreement here. The earliest ethnographic information consists primarily of descriptions of what different individuals observed. These men came from varied backgrounds, usually with little understanding of the native language. This early record of Inuit mortuary practices was collected by people whose primary goals in the Arctic were economic, political, or religious. The scope of their experiences was limited by these primary missions. A cur-

Table 2. Lamps and Sewing Tools (by percentage)

	Central	Baffin	Labrador	W. Greenland	E. Greenland
Lamp	1.0	0	4	14	8
Female	50.0	0	100	0	0
Male	50.0	0	50	0	0
Sewing	2.0	0	8	14	4
Female	66.7	0	50	0	50
Unknown	33.3	0	0	0	0

Table 3.   Kayaks and Sleds (by percentage)

	Central	Baffin	Labrador	Quebec	W. Greenland	E. Greenland
Kayak	1.0	0	6	—	2	2.0
Males	50.0	0	67+	—	0	0
Sled	2.0	5	10	100	14	6.0
Female	33.3	0	20	—	0	0
Male	33.3	100	40	—	0	0
Child	0	0	0	—	0	66.7

sory exploration of the area in which their ships are wintering does not constitute a survey of the surrounding area for the range of mortuary practices.

The archaeological data also contain gaps and inconsistencies. Sites have been excavated over the past seventy years by Danish, Canadian, and American archaeologists. Theoretical backgrounds of researchers, excavation and analytical techniques, and research goals have changed throughout the years. Improved transportation has provided the means for a wider diversity of specimens and samples to be removed from the field for laboratory analysis.

The passage of time is a factor both in the methods of excavation and in the degree of preservation of the material remains. Preservation of different materials varies greatly, even in the Arctic. Wooden or skin containers placed in a cairn may appear as nothing more than an organic stain. Items can be disturbed or removed from a cairn by humans, animals, wind, and weather during the course of centuries. People have gathered the remains of kayaks or sleds from cairns for use as firewood. In 1631, Captain Luke Foxe and his crew were in the Roes Welcome area and claimed "we rob'd their graves to build our fires, and brought a whole boate's loading of fire-wood on board" (Christy 1894, 320).

The ravages of time in the Arctic include people removing "desirable" things and sometimes adding items. Cairns were not only opened and items

Table 4.   Weapons (by percentage)

	Central	Baffin	Labrador	W. Greenland	E. Greenland
Cairns	40	15.0	29.0	25	20
Child	8	33.3	0.0	0	10
F and child	1	0	13.3	23	10
F only	27	33.3	20.0	0	10
M only	41	33.3	26.7	0	0
F and M	0	0	33.3	0	0
Unknown	23	0	6.7	77	70

removed by collectors and archaeologists in the more recent past, but items were also taken or replaced by natives. Rasmussen (1908, 73, 114) replaced items he took from a burial with tea, matches, and some meat. This activity was viewed as perfectly acceptable. According to Kumlien (1879, 28), on Baffin Island, items could be taken from burials and reused after one year had passed. In Labrador, burial cairns still serve as a sort of hardware store for "hard times." Items may be put into the cairns during prosperous times and removed during hard times (William Fitzhugh, personal communication, December 7, 1998).

What I have described is a very complex gender ideology that is best described as fluid. This fluidity is expressed in the archaeological record by the absence of any gender-specific burial goods. A few trends do exist, though. *Ulus*, or women's knives, and mattocks are associated more often with female than male burials. Snow knives, arrowheads, and harpoon heads are associated more often with male burials. However, all these items are also found in some burials of members of the opposite sex.

Can gender be accurately determined or described from analyses of Inuit burial goods? This is not as easily done as one might initially expect. In some ways this is unfortunate, for in the absence of ethnographic information, the burial goods have little inherent meaning in regard to gender. Or to state this another way, the significance of the Inuit burial goods can only reliably be interpreted within their ethnographic context. When the problems of determining sex or gender from burial goods for this group are compounded by incomplete preservation, replacement or exchange of goods by the society, and subsequent looting, the clues are difficult to discern. The rich ethnographic record is required to provide the framework to interpret the clues that remain. The archaeological data alone provide an incomplete picture of Inuit prehistory. To use an analogy, if the archaeological data are a few dozen pieces from a jigsaw puzzle, you may not be able to determine what the completed puzzle represented with just the pieces. However, if you had an idea what the picture might represent (via the ethnographic record) you could place some of the pieces and might be able to say a great deal about a few of them.

REFERENCES

Bahnson, Anne. 1997. Ancient skin clothing passing through Copenhagen. In *Fifty years of Arctic research. Anthropological studies from Greenland to Siberia.* Edited by Rolf Gilberg and Hans Christian Gulløv, pp. 47–56. Copenhagen: Department of Ethnography, The National Museum of Denmark.

Barker, Robin. 1995. Seeing wisely, crying wolf: A cautionary tale on the Euro-Yup'ik border. In *When our words return: Writing, hearing, and remembering oral traditions of Alaska and the Yukon.* Edited by Phyllis Morrow and William Sneider, pp. 79–97. Logan: Utah State University Press.

Bessel, Emil. 1884. The northernmost inhabitants of the earth. *American Naturalist* 18:861–82.

Bilby, Julian William. 1923. *Among unknown Eskimo: An account of twelve years intimate relations with the primitive Eskimo of ice-bound Baffin Land, with a description of their ways of living, hunting customs, and beliefs.* Philadelphia: J. B. Lippincott.

Birket-Smith, Kaj. 1928. *Five hundred Eskimo words, a complete vocabulary from Greenland and central Eskimo dialects.* Copenhagen: Gyldendalske Boghandel, Nordisk Forlag.

Black, Lydia T., trans., ed. 1977. The Konyag (the inhabitants of the island of Kodiak) by Iosaf [Bolotov] (1794–1799) and by Gideon (1804–1807). *Arctic Anthropology* 14 (2): 79–108.

Blackman, Margaret B. 1992. *Sadie Brower Neakok. An Iñupiaq Woman.* Seattle: University of Washington Press.

Boas, Franz. 1888. The central Eskimo. *Sixth annual report of the Bureau of American Ethnology, 1884–1885.* Washington, D.C.: Government Printing Office.

Bodenhorn, Barbara. 1990. "I'm not the great hunter, my wife is": Iñupiat and anthropological models of gender. *Études/Inuit Studies* 14 (1–2):55–74.

Bogoras, Waldemar. 1904–1909. The Chukchee. In *The Jesup north Pacific expedition.* Edited by Franz Boas. Vol. 7 (1–3). *Memoirs of the American Museum of Natural History* 11. New York: American Museum of Natural History.

Cardno, David. n.d. *Journals of arctic whaling and sealing voyages, 1866–1924.* SPRI MS 1200. Scott Polar Research Institute. Cambridge, U.K.: Cambridge University.

Carpenter, Edmund S. 1997. Nineteenth-century Aivilik Iglulik drawings. In *Fifty years of Arctic research. Anthropological studies from Greenland to Siberia.* Edited by Rolf Gilberg and Hans Christian Gulløv, pp. 71–92. Copenhagen: Department of Ethnography, National Museum of Denmark.

Chaussonnet, Valérie. 1988. Needles and animals: Women's magic. In *Crossroads of continents: Cultures of Siberia and Alaska.* Edited by William W. Fitzhugh and Aron Crowell, pp. 209–26. Washington, D.C.: Smithsonian Institution Press.

Christy, Miller. 1894. *The voyages of Captain Luke Foxe of Hull and Captain Thomas James of Bristol in search of a northwest passage in 1631–1632.* London: Hakluyt Society.

Conkey, Margaret W. 1991. Contexts of action, contexts of power: Material culture and gender in the Magdalenian. In *Engendering archaeology: Women and prehistory.* Edited by Joan M. Gero and Margaret W. Conkey, pp. 57–92. Oxford: Basil Blackwell.

Crantz, David. 1767. *The history of Greenland: Containing a description of the country, and its inhabitants: and particularly, a relation of the mission, carried on for above thefe thirty years of the Unitas Fratrum, at New Herrnhuth and Lichtenfels, in that country.* 2 vols. London: Brethren's Society.

Crass, Barbara A. 1998. Pre-Christian Inuit mortuary practices: A compendium of archaeological and ethnographic sources. Ph.D. diss. Department of Anthropology, University of Wisconsin, Milwaukee.

————. 2000. Material and symbolism associated with gender in Inuit burial practices. In *Reading the body: Representations and remains in the archaeological record*. Edited by Alison E. Rautman, pp. 68–76. Philadelphia: University of Pennsylvania Press.

Davydov, Gavrill Ivanovich. 1977. *Two voyages to Russian America, 1802–1807*. Translated by Colin Bearne. Kingston, Ontario: Limestone Press.

Egede, Hans P. 1818. *A description of Greenland by Hans Egede, who was a missionary in that country for twenty-five years*. London: T. and J. Allman.

Foote, Berit Arnestad. 1992. *The Tigara Eskimos and their environment*. Point Hope, Alaska: North Slope Borough Commission on Iñupiat History, Language, and Culture.

Fortescue, Michael. 1984. *West Greenlandic*. London: Croom Helm.

Giffen, Naomi M. 1930. *The rôles of men and women in Eskimo culture*. Chicago: University of Chicago Press.

Graah, Wilhelm A. 1837. *Narrative of an expedition to the east coast of Greenland, sent by order of the King of Denmark, in search of the lost colonies*. 2d ed. Translated by G. G. Macdougall. London: John W. Parker.

Hall, Judy, Jill Oakes, and Sally Webster Qimmiu'naaq. 1994. *Sanatujut. Pride in women's work. Copper and Caribou Inuit clothing traditions*. Ottawa: Canadian Museum of Civilization.

Hawkes, Ernest William. 1916. *The Labrador Eskimo*. Canada Department of Mines, Geological Survey Memoir 91, Anthropological Series 14. Ottawa: Government Printing Bureau.

Hayes, Isaac I. 1867. *The open polar sea: A narrative of a voyage of discovery towards the North Pole, in the schooner "United States."* New York: Hurd and Houghton.

Holm, Gustav F. 1914. Ethnographical sketch of the Angmagsalik Eskimo. *Meddelelser om Grønland*. Vol. 39 (1).

Holmberg, Heinrich Johan. 1985. The Koniags. In *Holmberg's ethnographic sketches*. Translated by Fritz Jaensch, and edited by Marvin W. Falk, pp. 35–61. Rasmusson Library Historical Translation Series I. Fairbanks: University of Alaska Press.

Jenness, Diamond. 1957. *Dawn in Arctic Alaska*. Chicago: University of Chicago Press.

Kawagley, A. Oscar. 1995. *A Yupik worldview, a pathway to ecology and spirit*. Prospect Heights, Ill.: Waveland Press.

Kleivan, Inge. 1960. Mitârtut. Vestiges of the Eskimo sea-woman cult in west Greenland. *Meddelelser om Grønland* 161 (5):1–29.

Kroeber, Alfred L. 1900. The Eskimos of Smith Sound. *Bulletin of the American Museum of Natural History* 12. New York: American Museum of Natural History.

Kumlien, Ludwig, ed. 1879. *Contributions to the natural history of Arctic America, made in connection with the Howgate polar expedition, 1877–1878*. United States National Museum Bulletin 15. Washington, D.C.: United States Government Printing Office.

Lyon, George Francis. 1825. *The private journal of Captain G. F. Lyon, of H.M.S. Hecla, during the recent voyage of discovery under Captain Parry*. 2d ed. London: J. Murray.

Nansen, Fridtjof. 1893. *Eskimo life*. Translated by William Archer. London: Longmans, Green, & Company.

Nellemann, George. 1960. Mitârneq: A west Greenland winter ceremony. *Folk* 2:99–113.

Nuttall, Mark. 1994. The name never dies: Greenland Inuit ideas of the person. In *Amerindian rebirth: Reincarnation belief among North American Indians and Inuit*. Edited by Antonia Mills and Richard Slobodin, pp. 123–35. Toronto: University of Toronto Press.

Peary, Robert E. 1898. *Northward over the "Great Ice": A narrative of life and work along the shores and upon the interior ice-cap of northern Greenland in the years 1886 and 1891–1897.* 2 vols. New York: Frederick A. Stokes.

Rainey, Froelich. 1947. The whale hunters of Tigara. *Anthropological papers of the American Museum of Natural History* 41 (2):231–83. New York: American Museum of Natural History.

Rasmussen, Knud. 1908. *People of the polar north: A record.* Compiled from the Danish originals: I. The new people: Polar Eskimo; II. The west Greenlanders; III. The east Greenlanders. Edited by G. Herring. London: Kegan Paul, Trench, Trübner, and Co.

———. 1929a. Intellectual culture of the Iglulik Eskimos. *Report of the fifth Thule expedition, 1921–1924* 7 (1). Copenhagen: Gyldendalske Boghandel, Nordisk Forlag.

———. 1929b. Intellectual culture of the Iglulik Eskimos. *Report of the fifth Thule expedition, 1921–1924* 7 (2). Copenhagen: Gyldendalske Boghandel, Nordisk Forlag.

Ray, Lt. Patrick H. 1885. Ethnographical sketch of the natives of Point Barrow. In *Report of the international polar expedition to Point Barrow, Alaska, in response to the resolution of the House of Representatives of December 11, 1884.* 48th Cong., 2d sess., House Executive Document 44, pt. 3. Washington, D.C.: Government Printing Office.

Robert-Lamblin, Joëlle. 1981. "Changement de sexe" de certains enfants d'Ammassalik (Est Groenland): Un Rééquilibrage du *sex ratio* familial? *Études/Inuit Studies* 5 (1): 117–20.

Ryder, Carl. 1895. Om den tidligere eskimoske Bebyggelse af Scorecby Sund. *Meddelelser om Grønland* 17 (6). Copenhagen: C. A. Reitzels Forlag.

Saladin d'Anglure, Bernard. 1977. Iqallijuq ou les reminiscences d'une âme-nom Inuit. *Études/Inuit Studies* 1 (1): 33–63.

———. 1994. From foetus to shaman: The construction of an Inuit third sex. In: *Amerindian rebirth: Reincarnation belief among North American Indians and Inuit.* Edited by Antonia Mills and Richard Slobodin, pp. 82–106. Toronto: University of Toronto Press.

Schultz-Lorentzen, C. W. 1928. Intellectual culture of the Greenlanders. In *Greenland: The present and past population.* Edited by Martin Vahl, George C. Amdrup, Louis Bobé, and Adolf S. Jensen, pp. 209–70. Copenhagen: C. A. Reitzels Forlag.

Stefansson, Vilhjalmur. 1926. *My life with the Eskimo.* New York: Macmillan.

Stewart, Henry. 1998. The " Kipijuituq" in Netsilik society. Changing patterns of gender and patterns of changing gender. Paper presented at the Approaches to Gender in the Arctic Symposium at the Alaska Anthropological Association meetings, March 19–21, 1998, Anchorage, Alaska.

Thalbitzer, William, ed. 1914. Ethnographical collections from east Greenland (Angmagsalik and Nualik) made by Gustav Holm, George Amdrup, and Jan Petersen and described by William Thalbitzer. In *The Ammassalik Eskimo: Contributions to the ethnology of the east Greenland natives.* Pt. 1. *Meddelelser om Grønland* 39 (7):321–755. Copenhagen: C.A. Reitzels Forlag.

———. 1941. Social customs and mutual aid. In *The Ammassalik Eskimo: Contributions to the ethnology of the east Greenland natives.* Pt. 2. *Meddelelser om Grønland* 40 (4):565–716. Copenhagen: C. A. Reitzels Forlag.

Wachtmeister, Arvid. 1956. Naming and reincarnation among the Eskimos. *Ethnos* 1–2:130–42.

Weyer, Edward M. Jr. 1932. *The Eskimos. Their environment and folkways.* New Haven, Conn.: Yale University Press.

7

Sharing the Load: Gender and Task Division at the Windover Site

Christine Hamlin

In 1982, an early Archaic period mortuary pond was discovered near Titusville, Florida, during construction activities for a housing subdivision. Named after the subdivision whose entrance it graces, the Windover archaeological site (8BR246) is remarkable in several respects. The recovery of a *Lagenaria siceraria* gourd dated to 7,290 ± 120 years B.P., for instance, is the earliest evidence of bottle gourds north of Mexico (Doran, Dickel, and Newsom 1990). The fiber arts assemblage from Windover is one of the largest such collections in the New World (Doran and Dickel 1988). The human skeletal material recovered at the site, similarly, makes up one of the largest New World populations from this period (Doran 1986). Materials rarely recovered at sites of this age were found at Windover and these have contributed to research on myriad topics. Biocultural adaptation has been studied through osteological analysis, population and microevolutionary studies have used mitochondrial DNA from the site, population polymorphisms and diet have been studied via bone protein analysis, and floral and faunal studies have aided in the refinement of models for environmental reconstruction (Doran and Dickel 1988).

The materials recovered at the site also provide ample data for those interested in gender studies. The excellent preservation of cultural materials, in association with a skeletal population with balanced demographic representation, provides evidence that may enable a better understanding of social organization in a period for which little physical evidence remains. This evidence suggests that the generalizations typically made regarding gendered task divisions at conventional prehistoric sites may be in need of reevaluation, with labor division not as rigidly systematized as is typically assumed. A master's thesis written under the direction of Professor Glen H. Doran at Florida State University in 1998 provided the groundwork for this study, which represents the first attempt to provide a perspective on gender configurations at Windover, based upon an analysis of the entire artifact assemblage.

THE WINDOVER SITE

The Windover site is located on the eastern coast of Florida, approximately eight kilometers west of the Kennedy Space Center (fig. 1). Radiocarbon dating indicates that the site was inhabited between 8120 ± 70 years B.P. and 6990 ± 70 years B.P. (Dickel and Doran 1988), which corresponds to the early Archaic period in the southeastern United States. Windover is one of four known mortuary pond sites. The others—Bay West (8CR200), Republic Groves (8HR4), and Little Salt Spring (8SO18)—are, like Windover, in Florida. These sites are slightly later in date, having been inhabited in the middle Archaic period. Windover is the only one of the sites that was systematically excavated.

The remains of 169 individuals were recovered at Windover. Those recovered ranged from neonatal or newborn to approximately seventy-five years of age, and included forty-seven females, forty-eight males, and seventy-four persons of undetermined sex. Sixty-nine of these "sex-unknown" were subadults (under age seventeen). Subadults survive less frequently in the archaeological record because of the relative softness of their bone (Gordon and Buikstra 1981, 569), and to find them in these numbers is unusual. The concentration of sex-unknown individuals in the younger age range is due to the fact that subadults cannot be sexed as reliably as adults (table 1).

The anaerobic matrix of Windover pond preserved a tremendous amount of information regarding the funerary rites of those using the site. Bodies of the deceased were placed in the pond within forty-eight hours of death (Doran 1992), as shown by the absence of decompositional gas vacuoles in brain tissue recovered from crania at the site (Dickel 1988; Hauswirth et al. 1991). These vacuoles appear within forty-eight hours after death, when the brain begins to break down structurally. Burials were typically in flexion, with 92 percent of individuals for whom these data were available ($N = 63$) ranging from semi-flexed to tightly-flexed (using Ubelaker 1978 criteria). Fifty-one percent of those for whom position information ($N = 55$) was available were placed in the pond on their left sides, 33 percent on their right side, and 16 percent were prone.

Thirty-three percent of those for whom orientation data were available

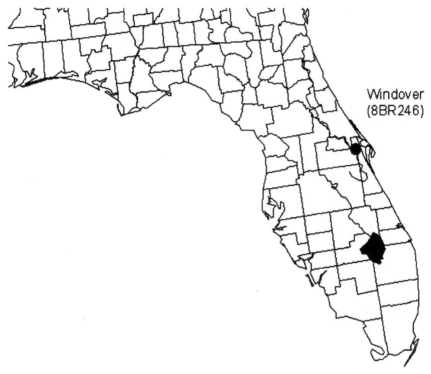

Figure 1. Map of Florida with Windover site pinpointed. (courtesy of Glen H. Doran)

(N = 64) were buried with their heads oriented toward the west, and 22 percent toward the southwest. Nineteen percent were oriented toward the east, and 8 percent toward the southeast. Mixed orientations account for the remaining burials.

Textiles recovered at Windover suggest that some of the deceased were wrapped in matting or cloth prior to being placed in the pond. The majority of textiles recovered at the site appear to be the remains of shrouds, blankets, capes, or togalike garments (Andrews, Adovasio, and Harding 1988). The presence of fine-gauged fabrics and what appears to be a cap or hood on one cranium suggests that some individuals, at least, were buried clothed (Andrews, Adovasio, and Harding 1988). Two baglike textile artifacts were also recovered at the site. One contained the skeletal remains of a neonate or newborn, recovered from between the legs of a mature female (fig. 2).

Wooden stakes were associated with a number of burials at Windover. These were either pushed through the shroud or matting in which the deceased was buried to "pin" the individual to the soft pond floor (Doran 1992),

Table 1. Demographic Data for Windover Population

Age Group	Total	Females	Males	Sex-Unknown
0 to 1 year of age	14	0	0	14
2 to 5 years of age	17	0	0	17
6 to 10 years of age	19	0	0	19
11 to 15 years of age	15	0	0	15
16 to 20 years of age	10	6	0	4
21 to 25 years of age	14	10	4	0
26 to 30 years of age	5	0	5	0
31 to 35 years of age	5	2	2	1
36 to 40 years of age	10	3	7	0
41 to 45 years of age	10	4	6	0
46 to 50 years of age	15	7	8	0
51 to 55 years of age	3	2	1	0
56 to 60 years of age	7	2	4	1
61 to 65 years of age	10	3	7	0
66 to 70 years of age	2	2	0	0
71 to 75 years of age	1	0	1	0
Age Unknown	12	6	3	3
Total	169	47	48	74

or were used to outline individual graves or grave clusters (Newsom 1998). Unmodified wood was also sometimes stacked in an inverted cone over burials.

Analysis of stomach contents of individuals recovered at the site indicates that the types of plants and fruits ingested matured between July and October, suggesting that Windover was seasonally inhabited (Doran 1988). Growth-ring analysis of wooden stakes recovered at the site supports a late summer/ early fall usage (Newsom 1998).

Because of the excellent preservation of the materials recovered, it is possible to reconstruct with some certainty the physical and material components of the funerary rites of those using the Windover pond. The evidence suggests that those within the group who died during the late summer or early fall were brought to the Windover pond within forty-eight hours of death. The majority of the deceased were placed in a flexed position on their left sides, with their heads oriented toward the west. The dead may have been interred in clothing, and/or wrapped in a shroud or mat, and had grave goods deposited with them. A shallow depression was made in the pond bottom, and the individual was placed therein. Wooden stakes appear to have been used to secure the individual in position; the stakes may, alternatively, have been used to designate or mark the grave or clusters of graves. Unmodified

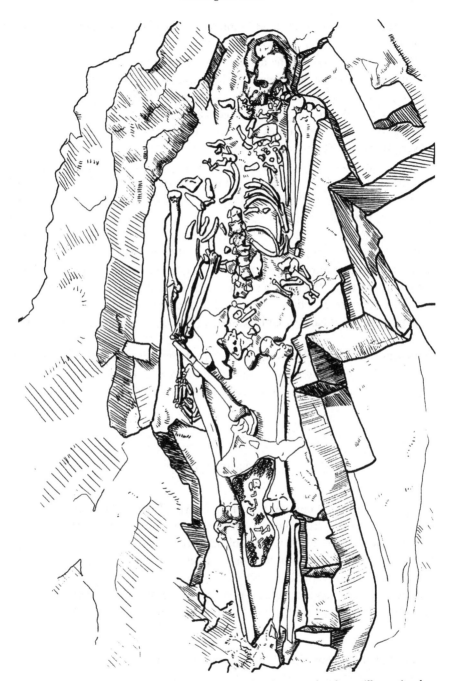

Figure 2. **Female burial with neonate in textile bag between her legs. (illustration by Christine A. Beetow)**

wood was also sometimes piled in an apex over graves to secure their position, to deter scavengers, or both.

What cannot, of course, be determined from the materials recovered at the site is the ideological component of these traditions—what they represented to the people of Windover. It has been suggested that water may have been used as a burial medium because it acts as a barrier to the souls of the deceased (Hall 1976; Beriault et al. 1981), an interpretation based on historic descriptions of Native American behavior by early European settlers. The wooden stakes associated with early Archaic burials have been interpreted (cf. Beriault et al. 1981, 55) as an attempt to ensure that "troublesome spirits [did] not break free of their water barriers." It is not possible to know if this is, in fact, the motivation behind the mortuary customs in evidence at Windover. Caution should be used in the application of motivations from historic Native American groups to peoples who lived thousands of years ago, especially when no cultural or genetic relationship has been demonstrated between the groups. DNA analyses conducted on the Windover population indicate that they are genetically unrelated to modern Native American groups living in the southeastern United States (Doran, personal communication 1999).

Having briefly detailed what is known about the mortuary behaviors of those at Windover, our attention now turns to an examination of grave goods distribution patterning and the evidence it provides for a study of gender roles.

METHODOLOGY

A database listing all cultural materials recovered at Windover was prepared using information from Doran (personal communication 1998), Dickel (1988), and Penders (1997). All tool descriptions are from Penders (1997). Chi-square (X^2), a statistical test that evaluates the relationship between two nominal or ordinal variables, was used by the author to determine differences between the actual and expected artifact quantities for the comparison of data regarding subadult-to-adult distribution patterns and distribution by gender.

Artifact Distribution: General Population Data

Of the 169 individuals recovered at Windover, 82 were recovered in association with cultural materials, 63 had no associated materials, and 24 were commingled. Commingled status indicates that the remains of two or more individuals were recovered together and that any artifacts in association with this skeletal material could not be attributed to a given individual with certainty. The effective sample size for an examination of artifact distribution, then, is 145 (table 2). This number includes eighty-nine adults and fifty-six subadults; by sex, forty females, forty-six males, and fifty-nine individuals of undetermined sex. The eighty-two individuals recovered in association with artifacts included twenty-three females, twenty-nine males, and thirty individuals of unknown sex. Of the latter, twenty-nine were subadult (table 3).

There were no statistically significant differences in the general distribution of cultural materials between subadults and adults at Windover [$X^2 = 0.84$, $p < .36$]. Nor were there statistically significant differences between females and males at the site [$X^2 = 0.27$, $p < .60$]. The general distribution of artifacts at Windover does not appear, then, to have been based on the age or sex of the deceased buried at the site.

Population Data for Function Categories

Rothschild (1990) and others have shown that an effective means of examining gender roles in the archaeological record is an examination of the artifact assemblage using functional categorizations. The types of tools consistently associated with a given gender are considered to suggest that members of said gender were responsible for a given task. The author used the following functional categories in the analysis of the Windover artifact assemblage: Domestic, Fabricating and Processing, Hunting-Related and Weaponry, Ornaments, Other, and Unmodified Materials. A brief discussion and illustration of each category follows.

Function Category: Domestic

Domestic artifacts are those items used in the performance of duties related to food preparation and clothing or textile manufacture. Domestic artifacts

Table 2. Summary Distribution of Sample by Age and Sex

	number of individuals (N =)
Effective Sample	145
Adults	89
Subadults	56
Females	40
Males	46
Sex-Unknown	59

Table 3. Distribution of Cultural Materials by Age and Sex

Age At Death	Total	Females with Artifacts	Females without Artifacts	Males with Artifacts	Males without Artifacts	Sex-Unkn. with Artifacts	Sex-Unkn. without Artifacts
0 to 1	9					4	5
2 to 5	15					8	7
6 to 10	15					8	7
11 to 15	14					6	8
16 to 20	6	1	2	0	0	3	0
21 to 25	13	5	4	1	3	0	0
26 to 30	5	0	0	3	2	0	0
31 to 35	3	0	0	2	0	0	1
36 to 40	10	3	0	3	4	0	0
41 to 45	9	3	0	5	1	0	0
46 to 50	15	6	1	6	2	0	0
51 to 55	3	1	1	1	0	0	0
56 to 60	6	1	1	2	1	1	0
61 to 65	10	1	2	4	3	0	0
66 to 70	2	2	0	0	0	0	0
71 to 75	1	0	0	1	0	0	0
Age Unkn.	9	0	6	1	1	0	1
Total	145	23	17	29	17	30	29

recovered at Windover include turtle-shell containers, a wooden bowl, a wooden pestle, and textiles of three types: cordage, fine-gauge woven fabric, and matting. Also included in this artifact category is a *Lagenaria* species gourd that had been modified for use as a container, a process whereby the gourd was desiccated, and the peduncle and seeds were removed (Newsom 1998).

Forty individuals at the site were associated with domestic artifacts. This number includes eleven females, nine males, and twenty individuals of un-known sex, nineteen of whom were subadult. Females were recovered with two domestic category artifact types—textiles and turtle-shell containers—while males were associated with textiles alone. All five of the artifact types in the domestic category are seen in association with the sex-unknown individuals.

No statistically significant differences between subadults and adults or fe-males and males were found when comparing the distribution of domestic items among the entire sample of 145. Considering the distribution of domes-tic artifacts among those individuals who received artifacts of any type, how-ever, there was a statistically significant difference between subadults and adults ($X^2 = 2.29$, $p < .02$). A possible explanation for this finding is presented in the discussion of distributional patterning that follows the general presentation of results.

Function Category: Fabricating and Processing Tools

This artifact category includes all the implements needed to manufacture the goods and items necessary for daily life, such as antler perforator/punches, an antler shaft straightener, awls of various types, deer ulna gouge/butchering tools, and deer ulna gouge/burnishing tools. A faunal bone needle, mammal canine graver/burnishers, antler pressure flakers, and shark-tooth drills were also recovered, as were a number of the multipurpose pin/awl/battens, a chert biface knife/scraper, and shark-tooth graver/scrapers. A single chert flake recovered at the site is included herein since it is the byproduct of a fabrication process (lithic projectile point manufacture).

Seventeen of the sample 145 burials included artifacts of this classificatory category. This includes two females, twelve males, and three individuals of undetermined sex, all of whom were subadults. Females were associated with five artifact types within this category and males with ten. Of these, only females were recovered with shark-tooth graver/scrapers, while only males were recovered with antler perforator/punches, a bone needle, mammal canine graver/burnishers, hollow-point awls, and shark-tooth drills. No statistically significant differences were evident between subadults and adults when considering the sample of 145, though differences were clearly present between females and males ($X^2 = 6.63$, p $< .01$).

Considering the distribution of fabricating and processing artifacts among only those individuals who received artifacts reinforces these results. Twenty-three of the forty sample females were recovered in association with some category of artifact. Two of these twenty-three, or 8.70 percent of the females with associated artifacts at the site, had artifacts classified as fabricating and processing tools. Twenty-nine of the forty-six sample males were recovered in association with some type of artifact. Twelve of these, or 41.38 percent of the males with associated artifacts at Windover, had these materials. These differences are unambiguous and statistically significant ($X^2 = 5.41$, p $< .01$). Fabricating and processing artifacts are, then, clearly associated with males.

Function Category: Hunting-Related and Weaponry

Artifacts termed "hunting-related and weaponry" include atlatl components such as cup/hooks, a dart shaft, and weights, as well as projectile points of antler and stone, and a snare trigger. These items were predominantly used in the procurement of nonvegetable food (Tuross et al. 1994), though evidence suggesting that interpersonal conflict was not unknown to these people was also recovered at the site (Dickel et al. 1989).

Fifteen individuals were found in association with artifacts classed as "hunting-related/weaponry." This number includes two females, eleven males, and two individuals of unknown sex, both of whom were subadults. Antler projectile points of two types (antler tine and barbed antler) were recovered with females, while males were associated with a wider variety of hunting-related/weaponry artifacts. These included three types of projectile points (antler tine, Florida Archaic point [lithic], Kirk-like point [lithic]) and antler atlatl components (atlatl cup/hooks, a dart shaft, and atlatl weights). Individuals for whom sex was undetermined were recovered with antler tine projectile points and a snare trigger.

Statistically significant differences were found within the sample of 145 individuals in the distribution of artifacts from this function category between subadults and adults, with adults disproportionately represented with these goods ($X^2 = 4.71$, p < .03). Males, too, were disproportionately represented with hunting-related/weaponry artifacts ($X^2 = 6.63$, p < .01). An examination of the distribution of artifacts from this category among only those who were recovered with some type of cultural material affirms these findings. Hunting-related/weaponry category artifacts seem, then, to be conclusively associated with males when compared with females, and with adults when compared with subadults.

Function Category: Ornaments

Necklaces are the only type of artifact recovered at Windover that appears to have been strictly ornamental. Beads for necklaces were manufactured of four different materials—antler, fish vertebrae, Sabal palmetto seeds, and shell. Five individuals were recovered with associated necklaces. This number includes two females and three individuals of unknown sex (all subadults). The application of chi-square to those who received this artifact category is not possible because of small sample size (N = 5). Indeed, only 3.45 percent of the sample 145 were found in association with ornamental items. When one factors out those in the sample without grave goods, the three subadults represent 10.34 percent of the twenty-nine subadults with associated goods, while the two females represent 8.70 percent of the twenty-three females with associated goods. This does not appear to be a significant distributional difference. The fact that only females and subadults were recovered in association with necklaces at the site may be significant, as it suggests that these may have been items not associated with males in this population.

Function Category: Other

The catch-all "other" category includes all those items that do not neatly fit in the other artifact categories. To explain their inclusion in this category, a short description of each artifact type is included.

Bird bone tubes recovered at Windover are believed to have been used as either beads for ornamentation or as smoking tubes (Penders 1997, 121–22). Butchered faunal bones are likely food remains that then would have been used in the manufacture of tools, as in the case of the miscellaneous modified antler and modified deer metapodials recovered at the site. Seed caches appear, in some cases, to be stomach contents, and in others, food remains placed with the deceased. An intact *Opuntia* species, or prickly pear, pad was also likely a food offering; *Opuntia* seeds were not uncommon inclusions in stomach contents recovered at Windover. Finally, the wooden stakes that are a frequent feature of Archaic period mortuary wet sites are included in this artifact category.

Because of the disparate nature of the artifact types included in this function category and the possibility that some of the inclusions are likely stomach contents (i.e., unintentional inclusions), results based simply on presence or absence provide little substantive information. Chi-square, therefore, was not performed on this artifact category. It is interesting to note, however, that only females and subadults were recovered in association with butchered faunal bone and bird bone tubes.

Function Category: Unmodified Material

The "unmodified material" recovered at the site was of two types: faunal bone and shell. These materials may have been included with the deceased for utilization in the manufacture of tools or ornaments in the afterlife, or may have been intended as food offerings.

Unmodified material was found in association with fifteen individuals at Windover. This number includes five females, five males, and five individuals of unknown sex, all of whom were subadult. Both faunal bone and shell were found with females, while only faunal bone was recovered with males. This is, interestingly, consistent with the findings discussed in the section on artifacts classed as "ornaments"; no males at Windover were found in association with artifacts manufactured from shell. Individuals of undetermined sex were recovered in association with only faunal bone.

Unmodified materials do not show statistically significant differences in their distribution between subadults and adults or between females and males when considering the sample of 145 individuals. The inclusion of these materials among those with other artifact types also shows no statistically significant differences between subadults and adults or between females and males. There appears, then, to be no pattern in the distribution of this artifact category that cannot be explained by random chance.

DISCUSSION

An examination of distributional patterning in the artifact assemblage recovered at Windover by functional category indicates that statistically significant differences were present when comparing subadults to adults and females to males. Nonrandom patterns in the distribution of hunting-related and weaponry category artifacts based upon age were apparent in the sample of 145 individuals. When considering only those individuals recovered in association with cultural materials, nonrandom distribution of artifacts by age is also evident in the domestic category.

If, as is typically suggested in mortuary studies, distribution of grave goods represents actual usage patterns, how does one explain the fact that subadults show a nonrandom distribution for domestic category items? Interestingly, all nontextile domestic-category inclusions with subadults were containers—a gourd container, a turtle-shell container, a wooden bowl—or items used with containers, such as a wooden pestle. A possible explanation for the inclusion of these items with subadults lies in a consideration of care-giving strategies. If females at Windover were the primary care providers, perhaps the children were expected to "help out," to participate in the activities in which their mothers were engaged, until they could assume other age- or gender-appropriate tasks. A consideration of artifact types at the site that were exclusive to a single sex shows that subadults occur more often with "female-only" artifact types than with "male-only" ones (table 4). Seven of the eight "female-only" artifact types were recovered in association with subadults at the site, compared with only two of the nine "male-only" artifact types. This may explain *why* the domestic-category artifacts were included with subadults, but it does not address why they would have been included disproportionately.

Nonrandom distribution of artifacts based upon gender was also found at Windover. The disproportionate distribution of materials from the fabricating

Table 4. Artifact Types Associated with a Single Sex at Windover

Females (number of artifacts)	Males (number of artifacts)
barbed antler projectile point (2)	antler perforator/punch (2)
bird-bone tube (4)	atlatl components [cup/hook, weight] (10)
butchered faunal bone (quantity unknown)	bone needle (1)
Opuntia (prickly pear) pad (1)	deer ulna gouge/burnishing tool (2)
shark-tooth graver/scraper (1)	hollow-point awl (6)
shell necklace (2)	lithic projectile point (2)
textile bag/container (1)	Mammal canine graver/burnisher (3)
turtle-shell container (4)	misc. modified antler (1)
	shark-tooth drill (2)

and processing and hunting-related and weaponry categories in favor of males suggests that they may have been primarily responsible for these duties. The general nature of these findings, however, reveals little about the actual division of tasks within the Windover community. An examination of distribution by artifact type provides a clearer picture of these divisions.

Both sexes were recovered in association with antler-tine projectile points from the hunting-related and weaponry category. Only females, however, were recovered with barbed antler projectile points and only males with lithic projectile points. Atlatl components were also recovered only in association with males. Penders (1997) suggested that antler points may have been used in the procurement of small mammals, reptiles, and fish, while implements such as lithic points and atlatls were likely used for hunting large terrestrial and marine mammals. Males, then, may have been responsible for hunting big game, while both sexes may have hunted small game and speared fish. Use-wear analysis suggests that the male-only hollow-point awls may have been used in the manufacture of fishing nets; if so, males were likely responsible for this task.

A number of artifact types from the fabricating-and-processing category were used by both sexes. Since most of the tools of the Windover population had more than one use, though, it is unknown if the tools were used by both sexes for the same task. Use-wear studies show that antler pressure flakers, for instance, may have been used to modify stone and/or shell. Since lithic artifacts were only recovered with males, and shell artifacts only with females, perhaps both genders used the same tool for similar tasks, but on different materials. The association with males and females of beveled-tipped burnisher/awls used for working fiber materials and wood, and modified deer metapodials used for tool manufacture suggests that both genders participated in these tasks.

The exclusive recovery of bird-bone tubes and turtle-shell containers with females may indicate that females were responsible for the preparation of plant medicines. If the hypothesis regarding the association of primarily female artifact types with subadults is correct, the wooden pestle and wooden bowl recovered at the site with subadults were also "female artifacts," suggesting that females may indeed have performed this role. The two textile net bags recovered at Windover were in association with a female and a subadult. This may indicate that females participated in gathering activities, though the small number of bags recovered at the site suggests that one should not assume that females were primarily responsible for this duty. The gathering of materials that could not be held in a textile bag—thus necessitating the use of the more rigid turtle-shell containers—may also have been performed by females. These containers may also have been used for the preparation of nonvegetative foodstuffs, as shown by the fact that only females and subadults were associated with butchered faunal bone.

The use of functional categories for the examination of gender roles at Windover, then, suggests that males were primarily responsible for the processing of faunal materials for the fabrication of tools, as well as for the procurement of nonvegetative foodstuffs. A more detailed picture, available through the discussion of artifact types, suggests that while males were more likely to have tools related to these tasks, they were not the exclusive holders of these materials. It appears likely that females hunted small mammals, speared fish, gathered and prepared foodstuffs and possibly plant medicines, while males netted fish and hunted larger terrestrial and marine mammals. Butchering animals and filleting fish appear to have been tasks both genders performed, as evidenced by the presence of deer ulna gouge/butchering tools with both sexes. Textile manufacture, too, seems to have been a nongendered task based on the association of pin/awls and beveled-tipped ulna burnisher/awls with both genders, though the type of textile produced may have differed by sex.

CONCLUSION

Analysis of the distribution of artifacts by function and type suggests that the division of labor at Windover was not a rigid one in the sense that there are few male-only or female-only tasks. Both males and females, it appears, engaged in hunting and fishing, though the method, equipment used and end product may have differed by gender. Textile manufacture, similarly, may have been a task shared by males and females, with males primarily responsible for the production of fishing nets. The exclusive association of females with shell at Windover suggests that they collected shellfish, or perhaps both sexes collected shellfish, but only females chose to adorn themselves with ornaments manufactured from shell. The intentional placement of food remains with females may indicate that the preparation of at least some types of food was a female task, especially in light of the fact that no containers were recovered at Windover in association with males. Females, finally, may also have been responsible for the preparation and administration of plant medicines.

Well-preserved sites like Windover indicate that the generalizations made regarding task divisions at conventional terrestrial prehistoric sites may need reevaluation. This study suggests that labor division is likely not as rigidly systematized as it is typically portrayed, with tasks often being shared rather than being strongly gender-specific. Without the extraordinary preservation of organic materials, this population too would have exhibited the common pattern—males with lithic materials—instead of serving as a rich illustration of prehistoric diversity in both tools and tasks.

A lack of evidence for strongly gendered task divisions does not, however, mean that the Windover population did not include the concept of gender in their worldview, a notion argued against by the appearance of a number of female-only and male-only artifact types at the site. Rather than being based strictly on tasks, though, gender may well have been expressed through the association of a given gender with certain material or artifact types—males with lithics, females with shell, males with one type of projectile point, females with another. The assemblage at Windover appears to indicate that tasks were not as strongly gender coded as were the tools used to perform the task, a concept that reflects gender ideology rather than gender role (Spector and Whelan 1989).

Only further study at terrestrial sites of similar age, as permitted by the preservation of appropriate cultural and skeletal materials, will determine if task division at Windover was typical of prehistoric North American populations. Rather than the "man the hunter" model so often reflected at sites with poor organic preservation, the materials from Windover suggest that at least some prehistoric populations instead "shared the load" more evenly than is typically thought.

REFERENCES

Andrews, R. L., James M. Adovasio, and D. G. Harding. 1988. An interim report in the conservation and analysis of perishables from the Windover Archaeological Project,

Florida. Paper submitted to the Windover Archaeological Project, Florida State University, Tallahassee.

Beriault, John, Robert Carr, Jerry Stipp, Richard Johnson, and Jack Meeder. 1981. The archaeological salvage of the Bay West site, Collier County, Florida. *Florida Anthropologist* 34 (2):39–58.

Dickel, David N. 1988. Analysis of mortuary patterns at the Windover site. Paper submitted to the Windover Archaeological Research Project, Florida State University, Tallahassee.

Dickel, David, and Glen H. Doran. 1988. Radiometric chronology of the Archaic Windover archaeological site (8BR246). *Florida Anthropologist* 41 (3):365–80.

Dickel, David N., C. Gregory Aker, Billie K. Barton, and Glen H. Doran. 1989. An orbital floor and ulna fracture from the early Archaic of Florida. *Journal of Paleopathology* 2 (3):165–70.

Doran, Glen H. 1986. National register of historic places inventory, nomination form. On file with the Florida Department of State, Tallahassee.

———. 1992. Problems and potential of wet sites in North America: The example of Windover. In *The wetland revolution in prehistory*. Edited by Bryony Coles, pp. 125–34. Exeter, U.K.: University of Exeter.

Doran, Glen H., and David N. Dickel. 1988. Radiometric chronology of the Archaic Windover archaeological site (8BR246). *Florida Anthropologist* 41 (3):365–80.

Doran, Glen H., David N. Dickel, and Lee A. Newsom. 1990. A 7,290-year-old bottle gourd from the Windover site, Florida. *American Antiquity* 55 (2):354–60.

Gordon, Claire C., and Jane E. Buikstra. 1981. Soil pH, bone preservation, and sampling bias at mortuary sites. *American Antiquity* 46 (3):566–71.

Hall, Robert L. 1976. Ghosts, water barriers, corn, and sacred enclosures in the eastern Woodlands. *American Antiquity* 41 (3):60–64.

Hamlin, Christine M. 1998. Labor division in an early Archaic Florida population: The archaeological evidence for gender roles at the Windover site (8BR246). Master's thesis, Department of Anthropology, Florida State University, Tallahassee.

Hauswirth, William W., C. N. Dickel, Glen H. Doran, Philip J. Laipis, and David N. Dickel. 1991. 8000-year-old brain tissue from the Windover Site: Anatomical, cellular, and molecular analysis. In *Human paleopathology: Current syntheses and future options*. Edited by D. J. Ortner and A.C. Aufderheide, pp. 60–72. Washington, D.C.: Smithsonian Institution Press.

Newsom, Lee A. 1998. The paleoethnobotany of Windover (8BR246): An Archaic period mortuary site in central Florida. Paper submitted to the Windover Archaeological Research Project, Florida State University, Tallahassee.

Penders, Thomas E. 1997. A study of the form and function of the bone and antler artifacts from the Windover archaeological site (8BR246), Brevard County, Florida. Master's thesis, Florida State University, Department of Anthropology, Tallahassee.

Rothschild, Nan A. 1990. *Prehistoric dimensions of status: Gender and age in eastern North America*. New York: Garland Publishing.

Spector, Janet D., and Mary K. Whelan. 1989. Incorporating gender into archaeology courses. In *Gender and anthropology: Critical reviews for research and teaching*. Edited by Sandra Morgen, pp. 65–94. Washington, D.C.: American Anthropological Association.

Tuross, Noreen, Marilyn L. Fogel, Lee Newsom, and Glen H. Doran. 1994. Subsistence in the Florida Archaic: The stable-isotope and archaeobotanical evidence from the Windover site. *American Antiquity* 59 (2):288–303.

Ubelaker, Douglas. 1978. *Human skeletal remains: Excavation, analysis, interpretation.* Chicago: Aldine.

8

Grave Goods Do Not a Gender Make: A Case Study from Singen am Hohentwiel, Germany

Emily Weglian

The study of gender in archaeology can have a significant impact on any attempt to analyze mortuary contexts. Traditionally, gender and sex are conflated into a single category in European archaeological interpretations. Archaeologists have often looked at grave good assemblages and assigned the individual in the grave to a male or female category with or without the benefit of biological sexing, and sometimes in the complete absence of skeletal material. In order to consider gender, one need not reject biological sex as a significant and relevant factor, but limiting understanding of gender to our modern sex categories disguises any potential variation in a community. One good way to begin reconstructing gender categories in mortuary analysis is to look at those burials that have been considered anomalous.

Before proceeding to archaeological analyses, I need to define gender and the gender terminology I will use in this chapter. I follow Gilchrist's definition of gender as "the cultural interpretation of sexual difference that results in the categorization of individuals, artefacts, spaces and bodies" (1999, xv). I will use Nanda's (2000, 1) terminology regarding gender diversity or gender variation to discuss varying cultural constructions of sex and gender systems. Gender diversity/variation allows one to discuss gender categories beyond male and female without making presumptions about the form these categories may take. A transgendered individual is one who changes, whether temporarily or permanently, completely or partially, from one gender category to another.

Most of the cemeteries from the end Neolithic and early Bronze Age in Europe have been interpreted assuming the existence of only two genders that correlate exactly with biological sex. One can explain much of the burial data from the end Neolithic and early Bronze Age using an exclusively sex-based gender, but this masks the potential effects of gender variability, and such an approach does not account for all of the burial evidence. In order to view the evidence holistically, especially that which is anomalous and problematic, scholars need to reexamine traditional ideas of sex and gender. In this chapter, I critique traditional classifications and assumptions about sex and gender as well as the gendered assumptions associated with certain categories of grave goods for the end Neolithic and early Bronze Age using statistical analysis and modern anthropological and archaeological gender theory.

In this chapter, I will use an analysis of the cemetery at Singen am Hohentwiel in southwestern Germany that dates from about 2175 to 1950 B.C. (calibrated) to propose gender categories through analysis of biological sex and grave goods (fig. 1). Krause published the initial analysis of this cemetery (1988). He categorizes this component of the cemetery as early Bronze Age, but I have argued elsewhere that it makes more sense to consider this cemetery as belonging to one mortuary archaeological phase that spans the end Neolithic and the earliest portions of the early Bronze Age, a time period that runs from roughly 2300 to 1700 B.C. (Weglian 1999). I will present the evidence, and then evaluate the possibility for a one-gendered, two-gendered, or three- or more-gendered system at the cemetery of Singen. In order to accomplish this, I challenge the stereotypical categories embedded in much European archaeology using examples of anomalous graves within what is traditionally considered a rigid sex/gender scheme. I hope to offer a way to start thinking about different possible gender systems in prehistoric societies from a mortuary perspective.

THE CEMETERY AT SINGEN

The graves that archaeologists most often find from the end Neolithic and early Bronze Age in temperate Europe are inhumation burials. Individuals were usually buried in flexed positions on either their right or left sides, a dichotomous pattern that typifies many of the cemeteries across Europe. A number of scholars have attempted to analyze such cemeteries according to either biological sex, with the assumption that this dichotomy directly reflected male and female sex/gender categories (Randsborg 1973; Shennan 1975), or with an informed gender approach (Rega 1996).

At Singen, the graves are aligned on a north-south axis and are facing east. Biological females are usually buried on their right sides with their heads in the southern portion of the grave. Biological males tend to be buried on their left sides with their heads in the northern portion of the grave. Children's

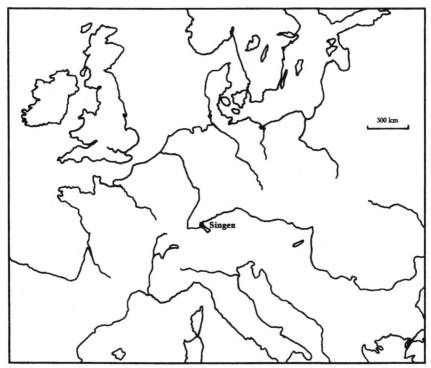

Figure 1.   Map of Europe showing the location of the site of Singen.

graves also follow a bipolar orientation (Krause 1988, 43), and their grave goods seem to adhere to the general distributions of grave goods for left- or right-lying individuals in adult contexts. For instance, where there is skeletal evidence to designate age and burial position, awls in children's graves are found only in those graves with right-lying individuals, a pattern reflecting that found in adult graves. Rega describes the same phenomenon at the early Bronze Age cemetery of Mokrin in the Banat region of former Yugoslavia (1996). Children's graves are more difficult to assess in terms of how biological sex relates to gender because of the difficulties of sexing the skeletons, although there are now some methods for sexing juveniles with permanent teeth (Rega 1999). The skeletal material at Singen was analyzed before any reliable methods for sexing children's skeletons were developed, but a reanalysis of the skeletal collection could reveal new data.

According to Krause, the graves at Singen contain a fairly large number of grave goods, especially goods made of bronze, and he considers Singen to be a rich cemetery for the end Neolithic and early Bronze Age. Archaeologists have assumed for many years that grave goods at Singen and other cemeteries were placed into graves according to the biological sex of the interred individual. As a result, burials from these time periods are still interpreted by many archaeologists in terms of a strict two-gendered system consisting of males and females, which correlates almost exactly with modern Western European notions of the male and female genders. Archaeologists have also assigned certain categories of grave goods to these male or female sex/gender categories, thereby imbuing the artifact categories with "maleness" or "femaleness." For instance, traditionally, scholars considered daggers a male grave good because they are often found in graves associated with males. There is an underlying assumption that the daggers are part of male weaponry, which in turn reinforces the idea that daggers equal maleness and always indicate a male grave. Assumptions such as these cause problems for scholars wanting to study the end Neolithic and early Bronze Age from an engendered perspective.

Archaeologists in the past used their "common sense" to interpret the evidence before them. They did not recognize or admit that their own cultural assumptions and assertions had an impact on their interpretation of prehistoric social organization, including gender. This does not mean that these archaeologists were less than observant, but they were not using rigorous analytical techniques now available. However, not all archaeologists, even today, avail themselves of newer theories and methodologies. In this instance, the result is a confused archaeological interpretation that conflates sex and gender.

An obvious place to start countering rigid archaeological sex/gender interpretations is to examine the burials in cemeteries that contradict or ignore the "norm." In the cemetery at Singen, for instance, there are several examples of exceptions to what Krause (1988, 43) calls "strict rules and rites" of the early Bronze Age burial tradition. Unfortunately, these anomalous graves are glossed over as individuals who were buried "wrong" (i.e., in a nonnormative way: a biological male buried in the female position and a biological female buried in the typical male position), and are interesting only in their strangeness. When members of a community take care in burying an individual, however, the grave is probably "right" and the interpretation wrong. But what is "wrong" in terms of biological sex may be perfectly correct in terms of gender.

ATYPICAL GRAVES

I begin by examining two graves from Singen that are certainly puzzling if biological sex equaled gender in prehistoric European societies. The analysis of the graves begins to make more sense if one uses gender as a primary category that is informed by biological sex.

The individuals from both Grave 71 and Grave 74 appear to be buried contrary to the dichotomous rule if biological sex alone is the regulating factor governing burial position. Some archaeologists argue that it is best to think of gender as a continuum (Arnold n.d.) and complementary (Joyce 1992). However, the strict dichotomous pattern for body position at Singen at first obscures gender as interconnected and continuous. There are no exceptions to this pattern at the cemetery at Singen in the graves where enough skeletal material was preserved to indicate body position. In graves where there is no skeletal evidence, the orientation and size of the graves indicate conformity to the general pattern of individuals buried either on their right or left sides. For the purposes of this analysis, I will assume that, for the most part, left-lying skeletons in graves indicate individuals belonging to a male gender category, and right-lying skeletons indicate a female gender category. These are not exclusive, but I believe that for the majority of individuals in the cemetery at Singen, this generalization holds true. The atypical graves allow me to make a case for alternative gender categories while standardizing the majority of burials that belong to the male or female gender category.

According to Gerhardt, the physical anthropologist who analyzed the skeletons from Singen, the individual buried in Grave 71 was a very old male (Gerhardt 1964 cited in Krause 1988, 327). The skeleton was on its right side with the skull toward the southwest, the typical position for *females*. There were three large rocks and some smaller ones placed over the body, and there were no grave goods preserved with this skeleton. Krause suggests that this male buried as a female provides evidence for *Totenfurcht*, or fear of the dead, at the cemetery at Singen (1988, 45). There are many examples from ethnographic, ethnohistorical, and historical sources where the living's fear of the dead influences burial (Barber 1988). In the case of Grave 71, the idea is that burying the individual in an "incorrect" position would confuse the dead individual, and the stones placed at the top of the grave would ensure that the body could not move. These measures were intended to keep the dead individual safely in his grave where he would cause no harm to the living. Pauli was one of the first scholars to introduce this concept of the "dangerous dead" to archaeological interpretation (Pauli 1984), and other archaeologists have recognized and defined deviance in mortuary ritual in similar terms (Pader 1982). Unfortunately, the concept of *Totenfurcht* often surfaces fortuitously in mortuary scholarship when scholars feel the need to explain away unusual burials.

In the case of Grave 71, a biological male buried in the typical female position is not incomprehensible if analyzed in terms of gender. This individual could very well be a male gender variant, and often such individuals would in some way fill a female role in the community (Nanda 2000). The extent to which this individual filled such a role is a matter of speculation, and the lack of any remaining grave goods precludes further interpretation for this particular study.

Grave 74 belongs to grave group III at Singen (fig. 2). The individual from Grave 74 is biologically a young adult female (Krause 1988, 329). The body had been placed with stone piles at the head and the feet. Originally, the body was placed on its left side, the typical male pattern, but at some point, the upper part of the body tipped onto its stomach, probably indicating that the body decayed faster than its coffin. What remained of a bronze bracelet was on the right wrist, and in the area of the throat, there was a small bronze pin. Krause proposes two possibilities for interpreting this grave. The first is that the physical anthropologist assigned this individual the wrong sex, and it is in fact an extremely gracile male (Krause 1988, 45–46). The cranium from Grave 74 provided the only means for sexing the individual because the distinguishing parts of the pelvis were missing. The second possibility is that this individual is a biological female who is buried strangely considering her biological sex. Krause believes that this individual is in fact a female buried as a male, but not because he recognizes the possibility of a female gender variant belonging to a transgendered category. Instead, he claims that there are several strange burials in grave group III, and within this context another strange burial loses some of its oddity (Krause 1988, 43). Perhaps a disjunction between sex and gender categories rather than just arbitrary oddity is part of what defines this grave group. Regardless, out of thirteen skeletons that are fairly securely sexed, two do not fit the "strict rules and rites" that Krause imagines for this cemetery. These two burials constitute 15 percent of the graves that are sexed with a good degree of certainty.

Graves 71 and 74 provide evidence that there are exceptions to the traditional "rules" governing burial patterns. The burial position seems to be flexible, at least in terms of biological sex, so perhaps grave good categories also have a greater flexibility in terms of sex/gender than previously thought. I now consider several categories of grave goods, their legitimacy as distinct groups, and their traditional gender assignments.

THE GRAVE GOODS

In this section, I will discuss the kinds of artifacts found in the graves at Singen and I will evaluate whether or not they cross the traditional categories of biological sex and/or burial orientation. Simple statistics are applied to a

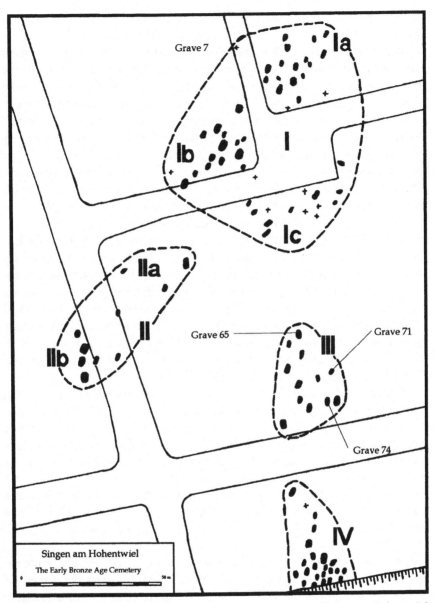

Figure 2. Grave groupings at the early Bronze Age cemetery at Singen am Hohentwiel (adapted from Krause 1988, 28).

sample of twenty-eight graves for which body position could be determined with a good degree of certainty from the skeletal evidence. Only data from such graves is used to analyze the statistical relationship between grave good categories and body position. The chi-square test for goodness-of-fit and the chi-square test for independence of variables are applied. Sample sizes from this cemetery are rather small, so Yate's correction for continuity is applied to all of the chi-square tests to minimize the possibility of rejecting a null hypothesis when a relationship between variables is actually not statistically significant. Despite the fact that the sample sizes are small, it is still a useful exercise to perform some simple statistical tests to verify my conclusions. Otherwise, I run the risk of perpetuating the same kinds of abstracted generalizations that traditional archaeologists used and misused in creating their conclusions about burial position, grave goods, and sex.

Eisner (1991) analyzed the later provincial Roman cemetery from Oudenberg in Belgium, and reports similarities in interpretations in terms of the traditional sex/gender assumptions and biases to the cemetery at Singen. Even without an explicit description of male and female grave goods, Eisner had little difficulty in identifying grave good categories that scholars had "sexed" male or female (Eisner 1991, 354). For instance, in the literature, goods that archaeologists considered nonfunctional (e.g., jewelry, combs, hair pins, gaming pieces) were female, and functional items (e.g., knives, buckles, clasps, metal tools) were male.

In the case of Singen, and the end Neolithic and early Bronze Age in general, some of the same assumptions cloud archaeological interpretation. Scholars generally "sex" many of the categories of goods in end Neolithic and early Bronze Age cemeteries such as awls, daggers, and pins. Krause claims that the dagger is the most important accoutrement in a male grave (Krause 1988, 106), implying its importance as a weapon or a tool. Awls seem to be associated with female graves, presumably an indication of female domestic duties. However, Eisner asserts that, "There may be other criteria for the classification of grave goods which have little or nothing to do with sex" (Eisner 1991, 354).

The first step in analyzing the grave good data is to test whether or not the distribution of certain grave goods is in fact random across the sample of right- and left-lying individuals. I performed a chi-square test for independence of variables in order to analyze the data (table 1). The null hypothesis stated that pins, bracelets, awls, and daggers are distributed randomly across graves of right- and left-lying individuals. The null hypothesis was rejected at a (0.01) level of significance. This outcome indicates that archaeologists have been correct in their observations that there are varying distributions of grave goods in graves containing right-lying and left-lying individuals.

Table 1

left-lying individuals
right-lying individuals
3 degrees of freedom
$\div^2_c = 11.4117$
when $á = 0.01$, $\div^2 = 9.210$

H_o: pins, bracelets, awls, and daggers are distributed randomly across graves of right- and left-lying individuals

pins	bracelets	daggers	awls
2	3	9	0
9	9	2	6

PINS AND BRACELETS

Bronze pins represent the most prevalent grave good category at Singen. There are twenty-nine pins that come from graves in the cemetery, and no grave with a single individual has more than one pin. There are three different types of pins: rudder shaped, disc shaped, and Horkheimer (Krause 1988). Horkheimer pins are rolled slightly at the top of the head, and a metal wire is wound about the neck of the pin. Krause states that rudder-shaped pins are found exclusively in female graves at Singen (1988, 105), but the other types of pins appear in graves of both left- and right-lying skeletons (Krause 1988, 45). There are eleven pins in the sample of twenty-eight graves. Nine of these pins come from graves with right-lying skeletons, and two from graves with left-lying skeletons. I used a chi-square test for goodness-of-fit to determine whether or not, statistically speaking, the small number of pins in the typical male burial context was significant (table 2). My null hypothesis stated that the distribution of pins is random among graves with right- and left-lying skeletons. At a significance level of (0.05), the null hypothesis was not rejected, indicating that pins do not form an exclusive grave good category for graves with either right- or left-lying skeletons. That some "male" graves contained pins is, statistically speaking, expected.

Bronze bracelets are the second most prevalent grave good in the cemetery at Singen. Bracelets are not specific to graves containing either right-lying or left-lying skeletons, but at Singen, more bracelets come from graves with right-lying skeletons. Bracelets are ususaly found on the right wrist in both right- and left-lying graves, and it is unusual for an individual to wear more than one bracelet (Krause 1988, 106). I performed a chi-square test for

Table 2

left-lying individuals
right-lying individuals
1 degree of freedom
$\div \, ^2{}_c = 3.2727$
when á = 0.05, $\div \, ^2 = 3.841$

H_o: the distribution of pins is random among graves with right- and left-lying skeletons

pins	expected number of pins
2	5.5
9	5.5

goodness-of-fit for bracelets from the graves in the sample (table 3). There were three bracelets from the burials of left-lying skeletons and nine from the graves of right-lying skeletons. The null hypothesis stated that bracelets are distributed randomly among all of the graves. The null hypothesis was not rejected at a significance level of (0.05). Bracelets, therefore, are not a significant category of grave goods for distinguishing sex or gender at Singen in relation to body positioning.

AWLS

Awls are the fourth most prevalent grave good from the cemetery at Singen. (I will return to daggers, the third most prevalent grave good, shortly.) Krause

Table 3

left-lying individuals
right-lying individuals
1 degree of freedom
$\div \, ^2{}_c = 2.0833$
when á = 0.05, $\div \, ^2 = 3.841$

H_o: the distribution of bracelets is random among graves with right- and left-lying skeletons

bracelets	expected number of bracelets
3	6
9	6

claims that awls are found exclusively within the female burial pattern (1988, 106). At Singen, awls are found in three graves of biologically female individuals. There are two children's graves with awls, and a third probable child's grave. Of these three graves, two of them probably contained right-lying, flexed individuals with their heads to the south—the typical position for females. There are three other graves that definitely contained awls, and where enough skeletal evidence is preserved, these follow the female burial pattern. I performed a goodness-of-fit chi-square for the null hypothesis that stated: awls are distributed randomly among all graves in the sample. At a significance level of (0.05), the null hypothesis was rejected (table 4). Awls are grave goods that are not distributed randomly among graves with right- and left-lying individuals, and at Singen, of the twenty-eight graves analyzed, awls only come from those with right-lying individuals. There is no evidence from the data from Singen that contradicts the assertion that awls belong to an exclusively female gender category.

DAGGERS

According to Krause, the most important male grave good is the dagger, which is usually found next to the pelvis or the arms (1988, 106). Archaeologists generally consider daggers tools or weapons, and, following modern cultural biases, scholars often attribute a male character to grave goods such as daggers. However, much of the bronze work from the earliest phases of the Bronze Age in temperate Europe is nonfunctional and ornamental. Even items such as daggers were probably limited in value as weapons or tools.

Table 4

left-lying individuals
right-lying individuals
1 degree of freedom
$\div{}^2_c = 4.1667$
when $á = 0.05$, $\div{}^2 = 3.841$

H_o: the distribution of bracelets is random among graves with right- and left-lying skeletons

awls	expected number of awls
0	3
6	3

Therefore, it is most likely best to think of the daggers as ornamental or symbolic in nature.

Five graves with daggers contain biologically male individuals at Singen, and another three adult graves contain daggers where the sex of the individual is unknown. There is a dagger that came from a child's grave, and one from another grave that Krause believes contained a child. There are six daggers from graves with little or no skeletal evidence and therefore no good evidence for sex or body position. Two of the graves with daggers have female individuals lying on their right sides, the typical female position. With the exception of these two graves, all of the graves with preserved skeletal material follow the typical burial pattern for males. There are some differences in the positions of daggers relative to the body for the graves of the biological males versus the biological females. Krause indicates that the daggers are placed near the shoulders of the female, rather than next to the pelvis or the arms, as in the graves with biological males who are buried following the typical male pattern (1988, 106).

Grave 7 contains an individual, most likely a female, who is a young adult (Krause 1988, 298). This individual has her hands in front of her face with a rudder pin and a dagger underneath the right hand. There is a bracelet on the right lower arm, a bone button in front of the face, and an awl south of the skull. In front of the forehead are the remains of a silver ring. The grave has a simple construction: there were four stones that may have acted as wedge stones for a tree-trunk coffin (1988, 298). This female has six grave goods when the norm is one to two preserved grave goods, and she has a dagger in the grave as well as a silver ring, this in a cemetery where silver is rare. She is certainly an exception in several categories of analysis.

The individual from Grave 65 also had a dagger in the grave and is certainly biologically female, but she was substantially older than the female from Grave 7 when she died. This individual was also buried with a large number of grave goods relative to other burials in the cemetery. Excavators found a large rudder pin across the chest, a bracelet on the right elbow, and a small dagger on the chest underneath the chin. Archaeologists also found an awl in this grave, but the records do not indicate where it was placed in relation to the body. The construction of this grave is more complex than that of Grave 7. Both of these females have a rather extraordinary set of burial goods accompanying them. They conform to the typical female gender pattern in terms of orientation of the body and the presence of awls and rudder pins.

I used the chi-square test for goodness-of-fit with the null hypothesis that daggers will be distributed evenly among graves of left-lying and right-lying individuals (table 5). The null hypothesis was not rejected at a significance level of (0.05). The results of this test do not support the idea that daggers form a grave good category restricted to the male pattern at Singen. The two females buried with daggers are not atypical in their body positioning and do not seem to belong to a female gender variant category. They stand out because of the presence of daggers in their graves and because they have a greater number of grave goods than average. These two graves seem to fit solidly into the female burial pattern, based on several criteria—the placement of the body, the presence of awls and rudder pins, and their biological sex. The presence of daggers in the graves does not by itself indicate a probability for transgendered individuals in these two graves.

Eisner tackled a similar problem at the cemetery at Oudenberg where assumptions about grave goods and their gendered nature led archaeologists to misinterpret the meaning of certain grave goods because gender was given preference as their most important characteristic. Eisner used statistical tests to demonstrate that there were certain grave goods that were exclusively male, but not all male graves had these grave goods. "The overwhelming emphasis in the Oudenberg cemetery does not seem to be one of sex differentiation, but of affiliation. If a dichotomy must be set up, I propose that a military:civilian one is more *apropos*" (Eisner 1991, 356). The cemetery at Singen provides another similarity to Oudenberg both in terms of the evidence and in terms of the traditional assumptions that color interpretations. Daggers are not found exclusively in male graves, and statistical tests indicate that archaeologists should reconsider the association of daggers first and foremost with a gender category, in this case, the male gender category. Daggers could instead indicate, for instance, membership in a social group that tends to be mostly male, but not exclusively so. They could indicate some kind of special status, or even have been gifts from male relatives (Shennan 1993;

Table 5

left-lying individuals
right-lying individuals
1 degree of freedom
$\div^2_c = 3.2727$
when $\acute{a} = 0.05$, $\div^2 = 3.841$

H_o: the distribution of daggers is random among graves with right- and left-lying skeletons

daggers	expected number of daggers
9	5.5
2	5.5

Renfrew 1986), a contentious stance that is uncritically accepting of a double standard of interpretation (Ehrenberg 1989; Hodder 1991; Stalsberg 1991). These two females seem wealthy in terms of grave goods when compared to others in the cemetery. Perhaps the presence of daggers in these two graves particularly indicate that these females occupied a social status that most individuals in the female gender category did not share.

I have used some simple statistical methods to interpret the possibility for gendered categories of grave goods. Only awls form an exclusively female-gendered grave good category in terms of body position within a grave. Having analyzed the results of the statistical tests and observations from atypical graves, I now consider the gender system of the community that buried its dead at Singen.

WHAT KIND OF GENDERED SYSTEM?

The data indicate that, at least at Singen, one cannot explain the evidence solely by a rigid set of rules based not too subtly upon an idealized view of the Western European two-gendered system. Scholars need to consider the possibilities for other kinds of gender systems during the end Neolithic and early Bronze Age.

Some scholars have discussed one-gendered (Fisher 1998; Shepherd 1998), as well as three- or more-gendered systems (Joyce 1992; Nanda 2000). Shepherd has argued that the Vikings placed all individuals into either a male gender category or a nonmale category (1998). What is practically speaking a female category is always negatively defined in terms of not being male, so there is only one positive gender. A value, such as courage or a sense of honor was considered male, while activities that led to trouble, for instance gossip, fit into the nonmale category. All individuals had parts of their character that were male and parts that were nonmale, and actions and activities were gendered appropriately. An individual could also change genders in the course of his or her life. For instance, an older male who was no longer self-sufficient and required care would acquire nonmaleness in Viking society.

The Viking gender system highlights another conceptual problem implicit in many archaeological interpretations: is gender central to concepts of personhood? In a case study from Papua New Guinea, Meigs discusses the gender system of the Hua of the eastern highlands (1990). The Hua categorize people according to the gendered substances with which each person has had bodily contact. "The result is that a genitally male person may be classified as female, and a genitally female person as male. In such cases, it seems clear that concepts of personhood, including notions of moral worth, agency and autonomy, are gendered, but that they are not gendered in the sense that they correspond to the discrete binary categories female and male when these are premised on the discrete categorization of biological sex differences evidenced by external genitalia" (Moore 1993, 202). There are many other ethnographic accounts of people who attribute aspects of maleness and femaleness to all individuals in the community (Bloch 1988; Bloch and Parry 1982; Diemberger 1993; Dureau 1991).

Age too can greatly affect mortuary treatment, because age also helps to define and create concepts of personhood. In many prehistoric cemeteries, infants and small children are missing from the burial population. The inclusion of children in Bell Beaker cemeteries represents a significant change in mortuary practices in prehistoric temperate Europe (Harrison 1980). Morris (1987) discusses political implications for the inclusion or exclusion of infants, children, and subadults from Attic cemeteries, and Rega (1996) demonstrates that infants under one year of age are not buried in the cemetery at Mokrin. Pader (1982) demonstrated that all children in Anglo-Saxon cemeteries were basically gendered female until they reached adolescence, and artifact assemblages associated with adolescent males are gendered male. Older individuals of a society can also be accorded special treatment. At Mokrin, graves of older individuals look "poor" in comparison to younger adults (O'Shea 1996).

Eisner's study of the cemetery at Oudenberg could serve as a model for identifying a one-gendered system archaeologically. Her analysis showed that the grave goods only formed an exclusive grave good category in the context of military males (1991, 356), so the individuals buried with weapons would represent the positive category, and civilians a nonmilitary category. In Eisner's study, these artifact categories may inform the archaeologist about gender categories. Females were not associated with military paraphernalia, but then neither were all of the men. Nevertheless, military accoutrements do indicate membership in the male gender category, but archaeologists must recognize that these items are not sole indicators of a male gender category.

In a male-focused, one-gendered system, children would probably fall into the nonmale category, as they do in Anglo-Saxon England (Pader 1982). In the Viking example, because children as well as older people are "weak" and require care, they would be considered nonmale. If this gender status were reflected in the burial practice, then the cemetery at Singen does not seem a likely candidate for such a system because the children are also buried in the typical bipolar pattern (Krause 1988, 43). The evidence offered by pins and bracelets could potentially support the proposition of a one-gendered system at Singen. Perhaps the presence of pins and bracelets in graves with right-lying individuals would support the possibility for some males acquiring this "nonmaleness" at some point in their lives. On the other hand, there is no good evidence that pins are grave goods that should be thought of first and foremost in terms of gender. In a single gender system, one might also assume that there would be categories of grave goods that were exclusively male and did not occur in any female or children's graves. Such a category does not exist at Singen, but awls are an exclusive category of grave goods, and statistical analysis revealed that they are exclusively female. Perhaps Singen represents the first example of a female/nonfemale system of gender attribution, but the lack of ethnographic or ethnohistoric evidence indicating the existence of such a society makes this seem unlikely. Singen looks at first glance like a good candidate for a two-gendered system. The dichotomous burial practice works in many cases as an indication of gender differences. However, the grave good associations do not support a strict two-gendered system. The biological females from Grave 7 and Grave 65 were buried in the typical female position and both have awls in their graves, reinforcing the interpretation that they belonged to a female gender category. However, both females also had daggers buried with them, something that is rarer for individuals buried on their right sides. These two graves indicate that a primary understanding of daggers should not be solely one of gender. A two-gendered system based upon the traditional interpretation of grave goods as gendered items does not hold up very well under careful analysis. The only grave goods that are perhaps good indicators of gender are awls, and not all graves of right-lying individuals contained awls. There is no grave good that provides the same service for male-gendered burials.

The individuals from Grave 71 and Grave 74 were buried contrary to their biological sex and are potential gender variants. This weakens the case for a two-gendered system that equates gender and biological sex. The lack of preserved grave goods in these two burials is unfortunate in one respect, because their presence would increase our understanding of how strongly different categories of grave goods were infused with gender qualities. The fact that both of these graves lack any discernible grave goods could also be meaningful, but it is too difficult to analyze such negative evidence in a responsible way. Regardless, these two individuals indicate that there is a great likelihood for gender categories beyond the traditional male and female categories. If individuals who were of one biological sex and belonged to the opposite gender were never recognized as different at the biological level, then a strict two-gendered system could still be posited. However, ethnographic evidence of transgendered individuals makes this unlikely (Kulick 1998; Manalansan IV 1995; Nanda 2000; Phillimore 1991; Whitehead 1981).

The cemetery at Singen provides some good evidence for greater gender diversity, with three or four recognized genders. These could be one comprehensive or two separate gender categories that include male and female gender variations, or a range of gender varieties that span a spectrum of gender variability. Grave 71 and Grave 74, which contain the individuals buried contrary to their biological sex, are located in the same part of the cemetery with otherwise "different" individuals, according to Krause (1988, 43). This evidence could indicate that transgendered individuals were in fact regarded differently from the majority of the population, but within the context of several other atypical burials, this does not necessarily indicate anything important in terms of gender categories. Further study of end Neolithic and early Bronze Age gender categories at other cemeteries in southwestern Germany would enhance archaeologists' understanding of gender categories, in general, and the status of those individuals who fall outside of the traditional ideal of male and female gender categories.

CONCLUSION

Burials of individuals that contradict the norm for their sex may serve as indicators of a social system with more than two genders. From the burial evidence at Singen, I have argued for the probable existence of gender diversity beyond the categories of male and female. The two individuals buried contrary to the general trend of males and females indicate that gender roles may not always correspond closely with biological sex, at Singen particularly, and during the end Neolithic and early Bronze Age generally. But where do these individuals fit within the larger social framework? Perhaps gender categories were relatively flexible in a community such as the one that buried its dead at Singen. The majority of individuals may have belonged to the male and female categories, but there is good evidence that numerous constructions of gender were common and accepted in the end Neolithic and early Bronze Age communities of southwestern Germany.

REFERENCES

Arnold, Bettina. 2001. "Sein und Werden": Gender as process in mortuary ritual. In *In pursuit of gender*. Edited by Sarah M. Nelson. Walnut Creek, Calif.: AltaMira.

Barber, Paul. 1988. *Vampires, burial, and death: Folklore and reality*. New Haven, Conn.: Yale University Press.

Bloch, Maurice. 1988. Death and the concept of person. In *On the meaning of death: Essays on mortuary rituals and eschatological beliefs*. Edited by Sven Cederroth. Uppsala Studies in Cultural Anthropology No. 8, pp. 11–29. Stockhom: Almqvist & Wiksell.

Bloch, Maurice, and Jonathan Parry. 1982. Introduction: Death and the regeneration of life. In *Death and the regeneration of life*. Pp. 1–44. Cambridge, U.K.: Cambridge University Press.

Diemberger, Hildegard. 1993. Blood, sperm, soul, and the mountain. Gender relations, kinship, and cosmovision among the Khumbo (N.E. Nepal). In *Gendered anthropology*. Edited by Teresa del Valle, pp. 88–127. New York: Routledge.

Dureau, Christine M. 1991. Death, gender and regeneration: A critique of Maurice Bloch. *Canberra Anthropology* 14 (1):24–44.

Ehrenberg, Margaret. 1989. *Women in prehistory*. London: British Museum.

Eisner, Wendy R. 1991. The consequences of gender bias in mortuary analysis: A case study. In *The archaeology of gender: Proceedings of the twenty-second annual Chacmool conference of the Archaeological Association of the University of Calgary*. Edited by Dale Walde and Noreen D. Willows, pp. 252–357. Calgary: University of Calgary.

Fisher, Genevieve. 1998. Battle-stirrers or peace-weavers? Militaristic imagery in the construction of early Anglo-Saxon female identity. Paper presented at the sixty-third annual meeting of the Society for American Archaeology, March 25–29, Seattle.

Gerhardt, Kurt. 1964. *Schädel-und Skelettreste der frühen Bronzezeit von Singen/Hohentwiel*. Freiburg: Badische Fundberichte, Sonderheft 5.

Gilchrist, Roberta. 1999. *Gender and archaeology: Contesting the past*. New York: Routledge.

Harrison, Richard J. 1980. *The Beaker folk: Copper Age archaeology in Western Europe*. London: Thames and Hudson.

Hodder, Ian. 1991. Gender representation and social reality. In *Gender and archaeology: Proceedings of the twenty-second annual Chacmool conference of the Archaeological Association of the University of Calgary*. Edited by Dale Walde and Noreen D. Willows, pp. 11–16. Calgary: University of Calgary.

Joyce, Rosemary. 1992. Images of gender and labor organization in Classic Maya society. In *Exploring gender through archaeology: Selected papers from the 1991 Boone conference*. Edited by Cheryl Claassen, pp. 63–70. Madison, Wis.: Prehistory Press.

Krause, Rüdiger. 1988. *Die Endneolitischen und frühbronzezeitlichen Grabfunde auf der Nordstadtterrasse von Singen am Hohentwiel*. Forschungen und Berichte zur Vor-und Frühgeschichte in Baden-Württemberg Vol. 32. Stuttgart: Konrad Theiss Verlag.

Kulick, Don. 1998. *Travestí: Sex, gender, and culture among Brazilian transgendered prostitutes*. Chicago: University of Chicago Press.

Manalansan, Martin F. IV. 1995. Speaking of AIDS: Language and the Filipino 'gay' experience in America. In *Discrepant histories: Translocal essays on Filipino cultures*. Edited by Vicente L. Rafael. Philadelphia: Temple University Press.

Meigs, Anna S. 1990. Multiple gender ideologies and statuses. In *Beyond the second sex*. Edited by Peggy Reeves Sanday and Ruth G. Goodenough, pp. 101–12. Philadelphia: University of Pennsylvania Press.

Moore, Henrietta L. 1993. The differences within and the differences between. In *Gendered anthropology*. Edited by Teresa del Valle, pp. 193–204. New York: Routledge.

Morris, Ian. 1987. *Burial and ancient society: The rise of the Greek city state*. Cambridge, U.K.: Cambridge University Press.

Nanda, Serena. 2000. *Gender diversity: Cross-cultural variations*. Prospect Heights, Ill.: Waveland Press.

O'Shea, John. 1996. *Villagers of the Maros: A portrait of an early Bronze Age society*. New York: Plenum.

Pader, Ellen-Jane. 1982. *Symbolism, social relations, and the interpretation of mortuary remains*. British Archaeological Reports International Series 130. Oxford, U.K.: Archaeopress.

Pauli, Ludwig. 1984. *The Alps: Archaeology and early history*. Translated by E. Peters. London: Thames and Hudson.

Phillimore, Peter. 1991. Unmarried women of the Dhaula Dhar: Celibacy and social control in northwest India. *Journal of Anthropological Research* 47 (3):331–50.

Randsborg, Klavs. 1973. Wealth and social structure as reflected in Bronze Age burials: A quantitative approach. In *The explanation of culture change: Models in prehistory*. Edited by Colin Renfrew, pp. 565–70. London: Duckworth.

Rega, Elizabeth. 1996. Age, gender, and biological reality in the early Bronze Age cemetery at Mokrin. In *Invisible people and processes: Writing gender and childhood into European archaeology*. Edited by Jenny Moore and Eleanor Scott, pp. 229–47. London: Leicester University Press.

———. 1999. The gendering of children in the early Bronze Age cemetery at Mokrin. In *Gender and material culture in historical perspective: Studies in gender and material culture*. Edited by Moira Donald and Linda Hurcombe. New York: Macmillan.

Renfrew, Colin. 1986. Varna and the emergence of wealth in prehistoric Europe. In *The social life of things*. Edited by Arjun Appadurai, pp. 1–18. Cambridge, U.K.: Cambridge University Press.

Shennan, Stephen J. 1993. Settlement and social change in central Europe 3500–1500 B.C. *Journal of World Prehistory* 7:121–61.

Shennan, Susan E. 1975. The social organisation at Branç. *Antiquity* 49:279–87.

Shepherd, Deborah. 1998. The elusive warrior maiden tradition, archaeology, and the social meaning of bearing weapons in north European society before the Christian conversion. Paper presented at the sixty-third annual meeting of the Society for American Archaeology, March 25–29, Seattle.

Stalsberg, Anne. 1991. Women as actors in north European Viking Age trade. In *Social approaches to Viking studies*. Edited by Ross Samson, pp. 75–83. Glasgow: Cruithne Press.

Weglian, Emily J. 1999. Political uses of bronze: Cultural changes and contacts in the end Neolithic and early Bronze Age in southwestern Germany. Master's thesis, University of Minnesota.

Whitehead, Harriet. 1981. The bow and the burden strap: A new look at institutionalized homosexuality in native North America. In *Sexual meanings: The cultural construction of gender and sexuality*. Edited by Sherry B. Ortner and Harriet Whitehead, pp. 80–115. Cambridge, U.K.: Cambridge University Press.

Weapons, Women, Warriors

9

Decoding the Gender Bias: Inferences of Atlatls in Female Mortuary Contexts

Dianna L. Doucette

The value and significance of grave goods in mortuary contexts has long been debated by archaeologists and social anthropologists alike. One point of view is that grave offerings represent the person in death as that individual was in life. Winters, in his paper "Value Systems and Trade Cycles of the Late Archaic," has defined the value of grave goods as follows: "grave goods represent appropriate equipment for the deceased in terms of the norms of the culture, and thus in general reflect concepts of a society as they pertain to the status and roles of the two sexes and the various age groups, regardless of the idiosyncratic behavior of any individual member of the society" (1968, 208). Likewise, as Rothschild has stated, "it is assumed that distinctions visible in mortuary practices reflect status distinctions visible during life. If patterns exist in mortuary practices, it is assumed that they relate to the structural divisions in society" (1979, 660). It is within this paradigm that the subject of this chapter is based, not because it is the only interpretation behind the meaning of grave goods, but because it is the point of view taken by the original Indian Knoll authors and others (Winters 1968) and those views are to be challenged. However, I would like to stress that although Winters and Rothschild suggest that mortuary practices are idealized reflections of the practical, daily social relations that are components of social organization, behaviors surrounding death do not necessarily represent behaviors in daily life. Some social anthropologists view burial practices more for the living than for the dead, because death is a disruption in the social structure, and it becomes a time for people to review and renew their social connections (Bloch and Parry 1982, 36; Chesson 1999, 140–42).

In order to explore the bias that has surrounded grave goods with regard to gender, I use the example of the atlatl and its interpretation as a grave good in burials at the Indian Knoll site along the Green River in western Kentucky and at the Annasnappet Pond site in Carver, Massachusetts (fig. 1). There is very little evidence for Archaic period burials (circa 9000–4000 B.P.) in the eastern woodlands of the United States, thus it is hard to compare the mortuary practices from either of these sites with a "norm." In this paper, I first present an abbreviated background of archaeological mortuary research, followed by a brief description of the Indian Knoll site in Kentucky, and a review of the literature surrounding the atlatl interpretations from Indian Knoll. From this base I introduce the Annasnappet Pond site as a way to reevaluate some of the older interpretations from Indian Knoll. Finally, I present the problems and implications of gender bias in the mortuary analysis of grave goods.

BACKGROUND

The study of mortuary practices and behavior by archaeologists has played a crucial role in identifying the social (Binford 1971; Brown 1995) and ideological (Hodder 1984) worlds in which people lived during prehistoric times. Several types of attributes are selected in mortuary analysis to obtain information about the status (rank, age, gender) and social complexity of the people in question (Brown 1995), including, (1) biological conditions of the human remains (Gau and Lee 1993; Konigsberg and Buikstra 1995; Milner 1995; Larsen 1997), (2) the spatial configuration of cemeteries (Goldstein 1981, 1995), (3) the presence/absence and configuration of primary and secondary burials (Kuijt 1996; Chesson 1999), (4) energy expenditure on the grave and its components (Tainter 1978), and (5) the value and significance of grave goods (Winters 1968; Rothschild 1979; Carr 1995). Mortuary analysis is one of the few avenues of research on the organization of gender in prehistoric societies. This is because, in many cases, the sex of the individual remains can be absolutely identified in a grave, thus providing an association for the surrounding grave goods within a gendered context. However, it is this association that needs to be approached with caution. Traditionally, comparisons between males and females (as well as young and old) with respect to the types of burial tombs and the types of grave have been made using ethnographic analogy (e.g., the direct-historical approach). Traditional views need to be challenged and great care needs to be taken so as not to project the present onto the past, especially with reconstructions of gender and when "assigning" gender to cultural material. Of course, all archaeological interpretation projects the present onto the past, at least to some degree, but what

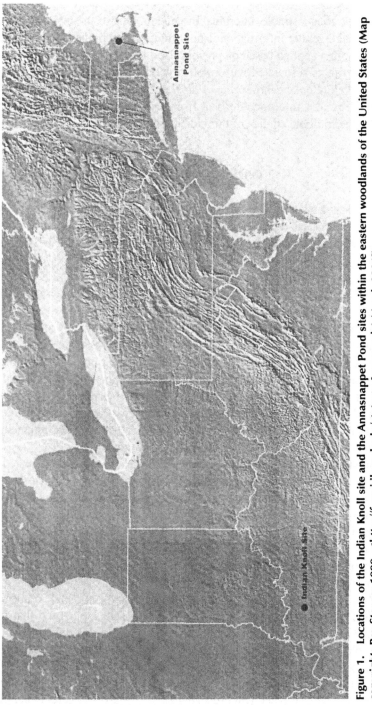

Figure 1. Locations of the Indian Knoll site and the Annasnappet Pond sites within the eastern woodlands of the United States (Map copyright: Ray Sterner 1999. <http://fermi.jhuapl.edu/states> [accessed 1 March 2001]).

we should avoid is a simple, uncritical projection. One of the main problems is that although gender information is not often reliable in the archaeological record, it is often applied based on preconceived notions of what roles should be. Thus, artifacts associated with implied gender activities become gender specific as well (Conkey and Spector 1984). As I demonstrate in this chapter, this type of gender inference derived from grave goods is clearly demonstrated by the multiple studies of the Indian Knoll site.

THE INDIAN KNOLL ATLATLS

Indian Knoll is a shell midden site in Kentucky with radiocarbon dates ranging from 6100 ± 315 years B.P. to 4508 ± 365 B.P. (Winters 1974, xviii). It was first identified by Moore while investigating the Green River territory in his steam-powered yacht *Gopher* in 1916, and again by Webb in the 1930s and 1940s. More than 1,000 burials were excavated at this site (230 by Moore, 880 by Webb), of which 76 included polished drilled stones and antler bone atlatl hook components (fig. 2). Thirteen of the 76 graves containing atlatls were female burials, and, in total, about one-third as many atlatls were found in the graves of females as were found with males. Prior to Webb's investigations, however, the polished stones and bone hooks from Indian Knoll graves were not in fact identified as atlatl components. Throughout the history of investigations at Indian Knoll, various interpretations of these grave goods and how they might have functioned were presented. These interpretations included banner stones, netting needles and sizers, hair ornaments, ceremonial stones, and, finally, atlatl hooks and weights.

When Moore (1916) first realized that the antler hooks were repeatedly found in association with drilled, polished stones, he interpreted them as netting needles and the stones as net spacers or sizers around which the cords of a fishnet were thrown to give them uniformity and size in a net under construction. He also noted that the stones were often broken, and sometimes fragments were scattered in the grave. This led Moore to suggest that the breakage observed had been intentional, perhaps ceremonial at the time of interment.

In 1917, in consultation with Moore, Moorehead and George H. Pepper of the R. S. Peabody Museum in Andover, Massachusetts, suggested that the stones and antler hooks were possibly hair ornaments. Based on the location of the hooks and stones in the graves, they surmised that the stone had been attached to the hook by a wooden plug, and the hook was assumed to have been thrust through a braided scalp lock where, by catching in the hair, the ornament was held in place (Moorehead 1917, 379–80). As ceremonial ob-

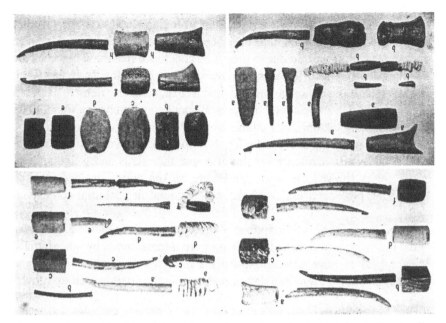

Figure 2.   Representative atlatl weights and antler bone hooks from the Indian Knoll
site (after Webb 1946, fig. 28).

jects, they were called banner stones and were thought to have adorned staffs.
In New England, these stones often took the form of whale tails because
whales were regarded with superstition or reverence, and were thus the greatest prize for coastal hunters (Moorehead 1917; Willoughby 1935).

Moorehead, on the other hand, who called the stones "problematicals" in
his book *Stone Ornaments of the American Indian* (1917), had yet another
theory for the "banner stones" that were found in places far away from
whales, such as Kentucky. He suggested that they represented the great thunderbird and called them "thunderbird ceremonials" (Moorehead 1917, 424).
He thought the head of a bird could have been attached to the top of the stone,
with feathers attached to the bottom of the stone to represent the tail
(Knoblock 1939).

Although these artifacts were found in both male and female graves, none
of these men specifically referred to gender in their interpretations of the objects. Perhaps there was no separation of gender when discussing these different interpretations because the interpretations of atlatls as netting needles and
sizers, as hair ornaments, or ceremonials did not fit any particular age or sex
stereotype. It was not until these artifacts were identified as hunting tools that
they became problematic as grave goods in female burials.

It was Webb who saw, when he returned to Indian Knoll twenty years after Moore, that the antler hook must have been attached to the stone by a wooden shaft that had disappeared due to decay; he concluded that these objects were weighted atlatls. One of Webb's main reasons for excavating the Indian Knoll site was to specifically obtain information as exact and as extensive as possible on the burial associations of the atlatl hooks and weights (Webb 1946, 159). Assigning the objects a utilitarian value might explain their use. Webb also felt the weighted atlatls were highly important practical tools in the social economy. His evidence for this was that the atlatls and weights found in the graves showed use wear, some were broken during use and repaired (suggesting prolonged use), and many were found in nonburial contexts as well.

According to Webb's descriptions of the atlatl burials at Indian Knoll, most of the individuals were flexed and many were intruded upon by other burials. They appear to have only contained the atlatls' components (hooks and weights) and not the attached dart apparatus that the atlatl is used to throw.

> From a careful study of this body of artifacts, their position in the graves, and their association with each other, the conviction that has grown [is] that all of these antler hooks are the distal ends of atlatls . . . and the "banner" stones . . . are all atlatl weights. This belief rests on the assumption that the body of the atlatl was made of wood . . . perhaps 40 cm long. One end of this wooden bar was worked to a cylinder about 13 mm. in diameter. On this end was slipped a "banner stone," having a longitudinal perforation of the proper size, and following it, an antler hook, conically reamed at its base, was attached. . . . Now if atlatls were made in such ways and were placed in burial associations, it would be expected that generally the more indestructible parts of stone and antler would be found together in combination of weight and hook. . . . Obviously, the wooden body of the atlatl, with its lashings would long since have disappeared, but the relatively indestructible portions, hooks, weights and handles would remain in association in the grave together with any asphalt which had been used in their original attachment. This seems to be precisely what has happened. (Webb 1946, 321–22)

Webb never mentions the possibility of the darts being included in the burials, and based on the photographs of the burials in his report (see Webb 1946), it also does not appear that the pits were excavated much beyond the space in which the flexed individual lay. The fact that the hooks and weights were close to the upper body suggests that the dart or spear points (if a complete, attached atlatl/dart/foreshaft assemblage was present) would have extended beyond the feet of the individual.

Like Moore, Webb also felt that the atlatls played a part in the ceremonial preparation of the grave based on the fact that some of the weights (about one-third) were intentionally broken. But he also was more inclined to call them ceremonial because they were found in female burials as well as in male burials. In fact, Webb was astonished to find that approximately 18 percent of the burials with atlatls were female because, in his opinion, the atlatl was clearly a tool primarily intended for male use: "It is hardly to be supposed that . . . women would have any practical use in life for an atlatl. . . . such occurrences represent true burial offerings to the dead of artifacts primarily intended for the use of men" (Webb 1946, 330).

THE ANNASNAPPET POND ATLATLS

Recent excavations at the Annasnappet Pond site have shed new light on the technological composition and use of atlatls and, in turn, have led to a critical reconsideration of their use as grave goods in terms of gender in an Archaic society.

The Annasnappet Pond site, located in southeastern Massachusetts, was excavated as part of a cultural resource management project by Public Archaeology Laboratory, Inc., (PAL) of Rhode Island between 1992 and 1995. The site is multicomponent and yielded evidence of occupation ranging from the late Paleoindian to the Middle Woodland (11,000–1000 B.P.) periods. The largest occupation at the site was during the Middle Archaic period (8000–5500 B.P.). In addition to a large base camp, a human burial was found dating to the early part of the Middle Archaic period. At the top of a sandy knoll, PAL archaeologists identified a deep burial pit feature that contained cremated human bone fragments with two polished stone atlatl weights aligned with two large Middle Archaic projectile points (fig. 3; Doucette and Cross 1998). This type of projectile point is referred to as a Neville point, first named by Dincauze (1976) in her book on the site of the same name, and is the equivalent of Stanley points of the southeast (Cross 1999). The burial yielded an uncalibrated radiocarbon date of 7570 ± 150 B.P. (Doucette and Cross 1998), making it the earliest burial to be found in Massachusetts, one of the earliest in the northeast, and the first Neville-complex burial to be identified.

Although the burial pit (which measured approximately 2 meters north/south by 1.5 meters east/west) was large enough to have contained the remains of an extended adult, the cremated bone fragments were found concentrated in the center of the pit. The bone fragments did not appear to be articulated in any way, and it appears from their clustered position within the burial shaft that they could have been contained within a pouch or otherwise wrapped, and placed in the grave as an offering. There is no evidence to suggest that the bones were burned in situ, and it is almost certain that unburned bone would not have been preserved in the well-drained, acidic soils of the

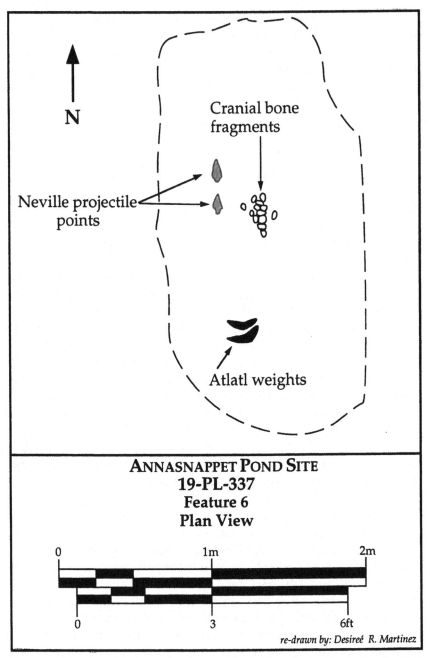

Figure 3. Plan view of the Annasnappet Pond burial feature (feature 6), showing the location of the atlatl weights in relation to the Neville projectile points (after Doucette and Cross 1998).

site, even as an organic stain or shadowy image. The human cranial fragments may have derived from an ancestor, relative, friend, or enemy as a symbol of personal identity. In other words, they do not necessarily represent the cremated skeletal remains of the person for whom the mortuary feature was created (Doucette and Cross 1998). In the absence of any other examples of Neville-complex burials from this time period in the northeast, it is important that archaeologists remain receptive to a wide spectrum of possible interpretations.

Overall, the Annasnappet burial contained the two winged atlatl weights, three Neville projectile points, a Neville drill, and a possible chipped-slate *ulu* preform. The position of the objects suggests that two atlatls and two dart assemblies (consisting of shafts and tips, or shafts, foreshafts, and tips) were included in the burial in an articulated position, just as the antler hooks and atlatl weights probably were at Indian Knoll (fig. 4). The atlatl hooks and handles at Annasnappet were likely made of wood, as were the spear shafts, thus, they would not have been preserved. The importance of the Annasnappet burial lies in the fact that the postition of the projectile points allows us to estimate the length of the dart shafts, which are approximately 125 centimeters long (given the position of points relative to the atlatl weights and to the overall length of the pit). This contrasts strongly with the estimates of 180- to 250-centimeters-long throwing spears that have been presented in the archaeological literature; it is possible that longer spear shafts were the exception rather than the rule. It has long been hypothesized that these longer dimensions would require a lot of upper-body strength, thereby supposedly inhibiting their use by women. However, the dimensions determined from the *in situ* artifacts at Annasnappet Pond suggest otherwise. The shorter estimated length of the Annasnappet atlatls underscores the ease with which these atlatls could have been used by almost anyone.

The other point to consider with the Annasnappet Pond burial is the inclusion of cremated human bone. What kind of social implications surround it? Was it an ancestor, or an enemy, as a Wampanoag Native American visitor to the site suggested? Certainly the "bones of an enemy" would imply that warfare existed in some form during the Middle Archaic period. Were atlatls weapons of warfare, as well as hunting tools? If so, can they still be considered grave goods befitting a female grave?

DISCUSSION

At the time when Webb discovered the utilitarian value of the grave goods at Indian Knoll, archaeology was a male-dominated field. Ethnographic studies

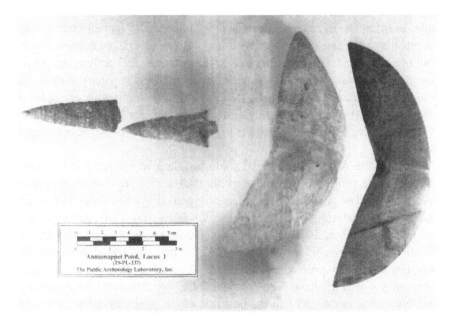

Figure 4. Alignment of the Neville points and atlatl weights in the Annasnappet Pond burial. The two atlatl weights were found eighty centimeters south of the two Neville points (after Doucette and Cross 1998; photo by Kirk VanDyke).

focused on male burial ritual, early ethnohistories of the Native Americans were interpreted and written by men, and ethnographies on living hunter-gatherer groups around the world were primarily being undertaken and written by men. It was an androcentric and biased view of gender roles: men hunted and women gathered. But even in the late 1960s, Winters (1968), who believed that status and role differences in life are reflected in treatment at death, offered several possible explanations for the presence of atlatls in female graves including ceremonial inclusions or special gifts passed down through the family. He also suggested that the Indian Knoll culture may have included a "platoon of Amazons . . . defending the Green River mussel beds against the onslaught of intruders," or finally (last and least on Winters' list) the women may have actually hunted (1968, 206–7).

In fact, because Winters felt that all burial goods should have a practical value, he even wondered if the various components of the atlatl were used differently by the women. One wonders what kind of uses Winters had in mind for the atlatl. Why would a women take a perfectly useful atlatl and use it for something other than hunting? The whole realm of what Winters calls ceremonial objects (as opposed to utilitarian objects) at Indian Knoll— including medicine bags, turtle rattles, and flutes—were more often buried with women than with men (although according to Winters, women would not have been shamans or flute players), leading him to believe that women were not just "chattel" but were "accorded at least as much attention in death as the males, even though an individual male might surpass any female in total quantity of grave goods" (1968, 207). Winters divided the artifacts found in the Indian Knoll burials into those that were solely associated with males, solely associated with females, and those associated with both males and females but primarily with males. Axes, bone awls, fishhooks, groundhog incisors, antler drills, flakers, antler chisels, and animal bones and jaws of several species were solely associated with males. Domestic equipment (pestles and nutting stones), certain ornaments (bone beads), and processing equipment (gravers) were predominantly associated with females. Predominantly in male association, but also found with females, were weapons or weapon components (projectile points, atlatl weights, atlatl hooks and handles), general utility artifacts (knives, scrapers), fabricating and processing tools (drills, various types of bone awls), and items of uncertain function such as bone pins. Winters also notes that men were associated with a greater variety of artifacts, especially concentrations of processing tools. Consistent with his utilitarian interpretation of grave goods, he indicates that a pestle could be found in a male grave without indicating the grinding of seeds or other foods on his part. If the tool was "new," the association could be based upon his role in the manufacture of these items, or, in the instance of a heavily battered specimen, he could have used it as a hammer stone (1968, 206). Winters gives a much more detailed description and interpretation of male grave goods than he does of female grave goods. It should be noted, however, that the number of burials with atlatls where the sex of the individual could not be determined is still relatively high for the Indian Knoll site (fourteen out of seventy-six), and it is possible that some of these were women.

Conkey and Spector (1984, 11) point out that a problem with androcentric interpretations is that they have preconceived or a priori expectations about what males and females did, what materials they manufactured, used, or exchanged, and what the archaeological association of materials with either sex might mean. These androcentric views assume that the objects associated with women were organic and therefore did not preserve in the archaeological record. When stone tools are found in a burial (including spear points and atlatl weights), they are typically interpreted as associated with a male burial, and the osteological examination of that individual, often on poorly preserved bone, could also be biased. As with everything else, osteological knowledge was not as precise when the Indian Knoll site was excavated as it is today (Rothschild 1979, 660). Because of the antiquity of the bone and the limited knowledge of sexual dimorphism at the time, misidentification of the sex of

Archaic human skeletal remains ultimately could have significantly affected the gender roles associated with certain objects found in the burials at Indian Knoll.

Of course, we also have to consider whether grave offerings are really representations linked to the deceased person, or special items for the living and given to the deceased as a gesture. Rothschild, who looked at mortuary behavior and social organization at Indian Knoll, notes that Mauss's book *The Gift* (1967) best explains why the dead receive grave goods and the variety of customs encountered in relation to their distribution. Mauss believes that importance lies not necessarily in what grave goods are offered, but that what individuals were buried with may be less important than that they are buried with anything at all (Mauss quoted in Rothschild 1979, 661). However, this study suggests that if we assume grave goods are representative of the deceased person in life, we should not jump to conclusions based on modern gender roles or gender stereotypes.

FEMALE HUNTERS AND THE MECHANICS OF THE ATLATL

The pervasive myth that women cannot be hunters stems from uncritically viewing the past through the lens of the present. Burial interpretations tend to be based on twentieth-century behavioral ideals and may have little to do with the Archaic cultures (Eisner 1991, 352). It is not feasible to assume that women waited for men to bring home the meat, or that they waited for men to make them a stone tool. It is not even realistic at any time during history or prehistory. Women have always been able to survive by themselves. It is true that men may have assumed certain roles such as hunting during childbearing times, but women were not always pregnant. Hunter-gatherer societies generally are made up of small families and have low population densities. Issues of mobility, caloric intake, and the possible strenuous activities of women (such as hunting), often resulted in long birth spacing.

One of the most studied contemporary hunter-gatherer groups is the !Kung of the Kalahari Desert in Africa. Although women of the !Kung tribe do not practice large-mammal hunting, they do hunt smaller animals and collect hunting information (Lee 1968). There are also many other hunter-gatherer groups in which women hunt, including the Chipewayan of northwestern Saskatchewan (Brumbach and Jarvenpa 1997) and the Mbuti pygmy tribe of the Democratic Republic of Congo rain forest (Lee and DeVore 1968). Size does not seem to be an important component of hunting, considering the short stature of the Mbuti pygmy women, which is most likely smaller than that of most Archaic Native American women. I have a female friend in Washington state who, for three years in a row, has won the one-shot antelope hunt with a bow and arrow. She not only kills the animal herself, but cleans it and uses it to feed her family of four through the winter.

There are no reasons why a woman could not have used an atlatl for hunting, and women could have engaged in hunting with atlatls routinely. Let us consider the tools in question here and their applicability to hunting. In a series of experiments with atlatls, Hill concluded that the "records indicate that anyone whose muscular coordination is good can within a short time become an efficient user of the throwing stick" (Hill 1948, 42). The morphology of a weighted atlatl serves as a balancing technique, which would lessen the need for great strength and could have been easily used by women and children (John Cross, personal communication; Cross 1999).

The mechanics of the atlatl are such that throwing a spear with more power and accuracy is made easier. Webb describes the physical principles involved in using an atlatl as being similar to those of using a baseball bat. In both cases, the force acting through the hand or hands on the instrument causes it to produce a change of the momentum in the projectile (Webb 1950, 392). Webb adds that although the added atlatl weights may have been decorative or ceremonial (totemic), their most important function was to give a sense of balance to the spear thrower by moving the center of percussion nearer to the spur on the atlatl shaft (Webb 1950, 353). Cross (1999) has argued that in the forested setting of the eastern woodlands, atlatl technology was developed to hunting deer at short range (i.e., ambush conditions from a blind or tree stand [see Churchill 1993]). Few of the experimental measures that have been used to assess atlatl performance and the feasibility of weighted adjuncts (e.g., distance, force of impact) are sensitive to the "real world" conditions of hunting deer in wooded environments. What is needed, Cross believes, is a system that delivers a projectile accurately over short-to-moderate distances with a minimum of body motion. The weighted atlatl and the shorter dart/foreshaft/ shaft assembly are well matched to this requirement. In fact, it is likely that some spear shafts were shorter than others, based on environmental conditions or even gender in order to make the handling processes easier.

Amazons or not, hunting or warring, there is no compelling reason why women could not have participated in such activities, as seen in the examples above. Far too much emphasis is placed on the slight physical advantage that men possess, based on nineteenth- and twentieth-century gender stereotypes. Conkey and Spector state that because many archaeologists follow a systemic approach, they rarely consider the sources of change in society, the roles played by individuals, small groups, or even the role of personal choice, focusing instead on broad processes and on functionalist explanations (Conkey and Spector 1984, 23). The notion of "Man the Hunter" comes from ethnographic analogies, and we should not discount the fact that social environmental conditions during the Middle and late Archaic periods may have been very different than any analogous situation today (Chilton 1994).

VALUE JUDGMENT

Any discussion involving a gender issue cannot avoid discussion of the value judgments placed on male and female tasks in general. Twentieth-century models of Archaic period life are filled with the biases and struggles of their creators, which are projected on past peoples. Somewhere along the way, scientists decided that men hunted, which was valuable, and women took care of children and gathered plants, which wasn't as valuable or important. Rosaldo (1974), among others (Dahlberg 1981; Conkey and Spector 1984; Gero 1991; Chilton 1994), wrote about placing more value on women's roles in gathering, toolmaking, and child care as opposed to giving men all the power as hunters. This was an important distinction based on the "Man the Hunter" and "Woman the Gatherer" concept, and her basic point was that gatherers play an equally if not more important role in foraging societies. The concepts of "Man the Hunter" and "Man the Hunting Toolmaker" (i.e., projectile points and atlatl weights) were combined with the fact that stone tools are the artifacts that survive longest in the archaeological record. This has resulted in extreme emphasis being placed on hunting as the major subsistence activitiy. Preconceived notions of gender roles divert attention from consideration of the broader aspects of subsistence.

It is true even among modern hunter-gatherer groups (e.g., the !Kung), as it most likely was during the Archaic period also, that the gathering of fruits, vegetables, and cereals (plant products), was the major subsistence source, whereas meat was a supplement (Lee and Devore 1968; Chilton 1994). Also, if men were the primary hunters and went off on prolonged hunting trips leaving the women and children behind, it seems unlikely that the women sat idly by during more than a million years of male hunting activities (Lee and DeVore 1968). The value placed on men and men's work has masked not only the value of what women did (and do), but, also, it has tended to rule out the possibility that women could have performed the same basic tasks as men. The question to be asked is: Could men have performed some of the same tasks as women? We know for a fact of two important tasks that were impossible for men—childbirth and breast-feeding—but it wasn't these things that would have kept women from small-game hunting or extensive foraging.

Hrdy points out in her book *Mother Nature* that !Kung women in the last months of pregnancy could carry at least sixty pounds of provisions using a kaross, or a leather sling, which would also serve for towing other small children (Hrdy 1999, 198). Thus, pregnancy does not become an inherently limiting factor in terms of women contributing to the division of labor. The other facts to consider, with no less weight, revolve around feedback loops that resulted in birth spacing and in women who were child-free. The ideal birth spacing of three to five years among hunter-gatherers is contingent upon the mother's breast-feeding habits, as well as her workload, overall health, and environmental conditions (Hrdy 1999, 194). However, a woman may choose not to have children, or she could opt to have just one, based on the quality of life she could offer the child. Lastly, and likely not uncommon, conception is not always possible due to the factors listed above, especially in regard to workloads and the overall health of the woman. In cases of infertility or childlessness by choice, a woman could have certainly retained the same level of activity throughout her adult life, giving her time to master certain tasks as well as any other child-free member of her extended family.

SUMMARY

In this chapter, I have attempted to highlight two issues: the various interpretations of the atlatl over the past 100 years, and the problems with the direct-historical and systemic approaches when applied to aspects of gender during the Archaic period. Moore, Moorehead, and Willoughby all suggested gender-neutral functions for the objects. Webb's interpretation of the drilled stones and antler hooks in the Indian Knoll burials as atlatl weights and atlatl hooks was important. However, it was not until this functional interpretation came to light that the perplexing gender questions began, as well as questions as to how to interpret grave goods. The second issue is the ideology governing the inclusion of weighted atlatls (and grave goods in general) in female and male burials. Winters believed that they were a direct reflection of the person in life—an atlatl in a male grave meant that he was a hunter, and an atlatl in a female grave meant that she was in some way associated with a hunter. It was not until the 1980s that this image of "female-not-the-hunter" was questioned by Conkey and Spector (1984). Besides pointing out that women could have been hunters, they also addressed concerns regarding the value judgment placed on hunters as compared to gatherers.

Excavations at the Annasnappet Pond site confronted many of the same questions that Moore and Webb faced at Indian Knoll during the first half of the century. A grave was found with atlatls, projectile points, and an *ulu* preform but without human remains to determine the sex of the buried individual. However, the position of the atlatl weights in relation to the projectile points suggests that the spear shaft was not as long as those typically portrayed in the literature, and experiments performed with atlatls also suggest that they can easily be used by anyone who possesses a certain amount of coordination. It was, then, concluded, that the gender of the individual was inconclusive based on the presence of hunting tools in the burial.

Several possible interpretations were considered by Moore, Moorehead, Willoughby, and Webb when interpreting the function of the atlatl weights—from net hooks and sizers, to ceremonial objects, to hair ornaments, to atlatls with weights. However, this determination did not extend quite so far when considering why these objects were part of a female burial. We know today from seeing trends change even within our lifetimes that the past was often very unlike the present. It is important for us to be critical when projecting the present onto the past, although this appears to some extent to be unavoidable in archaeological interpretation. As it turns out, the "Man the Hunter" scheme doesn't work in the present, either—women still hunt today! There is no reason why the women at Indian Knoll, Annasnappet Pond, or anywhere else could not have made and even used the tools so often associated with men in the literature. There has been a certain amount of closed-mindedness in the past that is finally being modified by more thoughtful considerations of gender, burial traditions, and the possibilities of scientific evidence. Particularly, if adequate evidence is lacking, all options must be considered, even the one that suggests females hunted using atlatls.

ACKNOWLEDGMENTS

I would like to thank the editors, Bettina Arnold and Nancy Wicker, for all of their hard work in pulling this together—from the conference to the book. The Annasnappet Pond excavation was conducted through PAL as part of a cultural resource management project supported by the Massachusetts Highway Department. I would like to extend special thanks to John Cross, the principal investigator, for his continued support and brilliant ideas throughout the project and beyond. Thanks also go to Deborah Cox and John Rempelakis for the opportunity to work on Annasnappet Pond, and for their constructive comments on the final technical report. The project could not have existed without the dedicated and excellent crew at PAL, to whom I am grateful. The ideas expressed in this chapter grew out of numerous discussions with John Cross, Elizabeth Chilton, and Holly Herbster. Valuable editing advice and useful comments on an earlier draft were provided by Elizabeth Chilton and Yun Kuen Lee.

REFERENCES

Binford, Lewis R. 1971. Mortuary practices: Their study and their potential. In *Approaches to the social dimensions of mortuary practices*. Edited by James A. Brown, pp. 6–29. Society for American Archaeology, Memoir 25. Washington, D.C.: Society for American Archaeology.

Bloch, Maurice, and James Parry. 1982. Introduction: Death and the regeneration of life. In *Death and the regeneration of life*. Edited by Maurice Bloch and James Parry, pp. 1–44. Cambridge, U.K.: Cambridge University Press.

Brown, James A. 1995. On mortuary analysis—with special reference to the Saxe-Binford Research Program. In *Regional approaches to mortuary analysis*. Edited by Lane Anderson Beck, pp. 3–26. New York: Plenum.

Brumbach, Hetty Jo, and Robert Jarvenpa. 1997. Woman the hunter: Ethnoarchaeological lessons from Chipewyan life-cycle dynamics. In *Women in prehistory*. Edited by Cheryl Claassen and Rosemary A. Joyce, pp. 17–32. Philadelphia: University of Pennsylvania Press.

Carr, Christopher. 1995. Mortuary practices: Their social, philosophical-religious, circumstantial, and physical determinants. *Journal of Archaeological Method and Theory* 2 (2):105–200.

Chesson, Meredith S. 1999. Libraries of the dead: Early Bronze Age charnel houses and social identity at Urban Bab edh-Dhra', Jordan. *Journal of Anthropological Archaeology* 18 (2):137–64.

Chilton, Elizabeth. 1994. In search of Paleo-women: Gender implications of remains from Paleo-Indian sites in the northeast. *Bulletin of Massachusetts Archaeological Society* 55:8–15.

Churchill, Steven E. 1993. Weapon technology, prey size selection, and hunting methods in modern hunter-gatherers: Implications for hunting in the Paleolithic and Mesolithic. In *Hunting and animal exploitation in the later Paleolithic and Mesolithic of Eurasia*. Edited by Gail Larsen Peterkin, Harvey M. Bricker, and Paul Mellars, pp. 11–24. AP3A Vol. 4. Washington, D.C.: American Anthropological Association.

Conkey, Margaret, and Janet Spector. 1984. Archaeology and the study of gender. *Advances in archaeological method and theory*. Vol. 7. Edited by Michael B. Schiffer, pp. 1–38. New York: Academic Press.

Cross, John. 1999. By any other name . . . : A reconsideration of Middle Archaic lithic technology and typology in the northeast. In *The archaeological northeast*. Edited by Mary Ann Levine, Kenneth Sassaman, and Michael S. Nassany, pp. 57–74. Westport, Conn.: Bergin and Garvey.

Dahlberg, Frances, ed. 1981. *Woman the gatherer*. New Haven, Conn.: Yale University Press.

Dincauze, Dena F. 1976. *The Neville site: 8,000 years at Amoskeag, Manchester, New Hampshire*. Peabody Museum Monographs 4. Cambridge, Mass.: Peabody Museum Press.

Doucette, Dianna, and John R. Cross. 1998. Archaeological investigations at the Annasnappet Pond site, Carver, Massachusetts. PAL Report 580. Pawtucket, R.I.: Public Archaeology Laboratory, Inc.

Eisner, Wendy R. 1991. The consequences of gender bias in mortuary analysis: A case study. In *The archaeology of gender: Proceedings of the twenty-second annual Chacmool conference*. Edited by Dale Walde and Noreen D. Willows, pp. 352–57. Calgary: University of Calgary.

Gau, Qiang, and Yun Kuen Lee. 1993. A biological perspective on Yangshao kinship. *Journal of Anthropological Archaeology* 12 (3):266–98.

Gero, Joan. 1991. Genderlithics. In *Engendering archaeology: Women in prehistory*. Edited by Joan M. Gero and Margaret W. Conkey, eds., pp. 163–93. Oxford, U.K.: Basil Blackwell.

Goldstein, Lynne. 1981. One-dimensional archaeology and multi-dimensional people: Spatial organization and mortuary analysis. In *The archaeology of death*. Edited by Robert Chapman, Ian Kinnes, and Klavs Randsborg, pp. 53–69. Cambridge, U.K.: Cambridge University Press.

———. 1995. Landscapes and mortuary practices: A case for regional perspectives. In *Regional approaches to mortuary analysis*. Edited by Lane Anderson Beck, pp. 101–21. New York: Plenum.

Hill, Malcolm W. 1948. The atlatl or throwing stick: A recent study of atlatls in use with darts of various sizes. *Tennessee Archaeologist* 4 (4):73–44.

Hodder, Ian. 1984. Burials, houses, women and men in the European Neolithic. In *Ideology, power and prehistory*. Edited by Daniel Miller and Christopher Tilley, pp. 51–68. Cambridge, U.K.: Cambridge University Press.

Hrdy, Sarah Blaffer. 1999. *Mother nature*. New York: Pantheon.

Knoblock, Byron W. 1939. *Bannerstones of the North American Indian*. LaGrane, Ill.: The author.

Konigsberg, Lyle W., and Jane E. Buikstra. 1995. Regional approaches to the investigation of past human biocultural structure. In *Regional approaches to mortuary analysis*. Edited by Lane Anderson Beck, pp. 191–219. New York: Plenum.

Kuijt, Ian. 1996. Negotiating equality through ritual, A consideration of late Natufian and prepottery Neolithic A period mortuary contexts. *Journal of Anthropological Archaeology* 15:313–36.

Larsen, Clark Spencer. 1997. *Bioarchaeology: Interpreting behavior from the human skeleton*. Cambridge, U.K.: Cambridge University Press.

Lee, Richard. 1968. What hunters do for a living, or, how to make out on scarce resources. In *Man the hunter*. Edited by Richard B. Lee and Irven DeVore, pp. 30–48. Chicago: Aldine.

Lee, Richard B., and Irven DeVore. 1968. Problems in the study of hunters and gatherers. In *Man the hunter*. Edited by Richard B. Lee and Irven DeVore, pp. 3–13. Chicago: Aldine.

Mauss, Michel. [1925] 1967. *The gift*. Translated by I. Cunnison. Reprint, New York: W. W. Norton.

Milner, George R. 1995. An osteological perspective on prehistoric warfare. In *Regional approaches to mortuary analysis*. Edited by Lane Anderson Beck, pp. 221–24. New York: Plenum.

Moore, Clarence B. 1916. Some aboriginal sites on the Green River, Kentucky. *Journal of the Academy of Natural Sciences of Philidelphia* Vol. 16 (3).

Moorehead, Warren K. 1917. *Stone ornaments of the American Indian*. Andover, Mass: Andover Press.

Rosaldo, Michelle. 1974. Woman, culture, and society: A theoretical overview. In *Women, culture, and society*. Edited by Michelle Rosaldo and Louise Lamphere, pp. 17–42. Stanford, Conn.: Stanford University Press.

Rothschild, Nan. 1979. Mortuary behavior and social organization at Indian Knoll and Dickson Mounds. *American Antiquity* 44 (4):658–70.

Tainter, Joseph A. 1978. Mortuary practices and the study of prehistoric social systems. In *Advances in archaeological method and theory*. Vol. 1. Edited by Michael B. Schiffer, pp. 105–41. New York: Academic Press.

Webb, William. 1946. Indian Knoll, Site Oh2, Ohio County, Kentucky. Pt. 1. *Reports in Anthropology* Pt. 1, 4 (3). Lexington: University of Kentucky Press.

———. 1950. The Read shell midden. *Reports in Anthropology* 7 (5). Lexington: University of Kentucky Press.

Willoughby, Charles. 1935. *Antiquities of the New England Indians*. Cambridge, Mass.: Peabody Museum.

Winters, Howard. 1968. Value systems and trade cycles of the late Archaic in the Midwest. In *New perspectives in archeology*. Edited by Sally Binford and Lewis Binford, pp. 175–222. Chicago: Aldine.

———. 1974. Introduction. *Indian Knoll*. Rev. ed. Knoxville: University of Tennessee Press.

10

Warfare and Gender in the Northern Plains: Osteological Evidence of Trauma Reconsidered

Sandra E. Hollimon

This chapter is a reconsideration of osteological evidence of violent conflict among Arikara-affiliated groups of the upper Missouri River. In a previous work, I interpreted osteological indicators of violence from a relatively androcentric viewpoint (Hollimon 1999, 35–36). At that time, I may have appeared to subscribe to the notion that Arikara women cowered in their doorways or cornfields during raids upon their villages and gardens. I have since reevaluated that position and have endeavored in this chapter to consider other interpretations of these data. I employ information about alternative gender roles among northern Plains women that may have included warrior statuses and use this ethnographic and ethnohistoric information to examine patterns of combat-related trauma and their demographic distribution.

It is also my intention to expand the examination of gender in the archaeological record of the northern Plains. While there have been several recent analyses that consider the genders of "woman" and "man," there have been relatively few studies that also consider genders other than these two (see Duke 1991; Whelan 1991).

PREHISTORIC VIOLENCE IN THEORETICAL PERSPECTIVE

Recent anthropological research concerning violent conflict has examined archaeological examples in several prehistoric and ethnographically documented cultures (Martin and Frayer 1997; Owsley and Jantz 1994). Among these studies are those that explicitly employ sex and/or gender as analytical categories (e.g., Bovee and Owsley 1994; Ewers 1994; Lambert 1997; Martin 1997; Owsley 1994; Robb 1997; Walker 1997; Wilkinson 1997). Such analyses provide comparative data and interpretive frameworks for the examination of both gender and violence in prehistoric societies.

THE ARIKARA AND THEIR NEIGHBORS

This chapter examines osteological evidence from archaeological sites, the majority of which has been attributed as Arikara-affiliated (see Blakeslee 1994). The level of cultural and economic exchange among groups in the upper Missouri interaction sphere warrants the inclusion of ethnographic and ethnohistoric information about other northern Plains groups in this analysis; these groups include speakers of Caddoan languages (e.g., the Pawnee), as well as those who spoke Siouan languages. These groups varied in subsistence and settlement patterns, but display many cultural similarities, such as an emphasis on warfare (Robarchek 1994).

Given that linguistic analysis estimates the separation of the Arikara from the Skiri Pawnee around A.D. 1400, it is not surprising that many aspects of these cultures are quite similar (Rogers 1990, 24; see also Murie 1981, 29–30). The convergence of the Arikara with the Mandan and Hidatsa at Like-A-Fishhook Village resulted in many cultural similarities as well (Parks 1996, 11, 14; Rogers 1990, 24). Therefore, ethnographic and ethnohistoric information concerning these cultures are particularly useful as interpretive sources for this analysis.

GENDER DIVERSITY IN NORTHERN PLAINS SOCIETIES

The presence of "multiple" genders (more than two) in native North American societies has been extensively documented among Plains groups (see Callender and Kochems 1983; Roscoe 1987, 1998). Most of the historic and anthropological literature in this area has focused on the gender colloquially referred to as *berdache*, a category of gender occupied by individuals exhibiting male genitalia who adopt certain aspects of occupation and dress that are associated with women, or a distinct third gender in those cultures. Indeed, the term was initially applied to third-gender males in Plains societies by French-speaking traders and explorers (see Roscoe 1998, 7–8, 173–78).

The focus on alternative genders occupied by morphological males has "crowded out" much discussion of female role variation (Jacobs 1968; Medicine 1983). Perhaps this is due in part to the relative inability to detect cross-dressed females who occupy a masculine (or nonfeminine) role.

> Male observers seemed to be acutely aware of the male in woman's dress, but it is very likely that they would not have noticed the female who appeared as a small boy or as a young man participating with the other boys or men in tribal societies. (Cromwell 1997, 128)

However, alternative genders held by persons with female bodies have been documented among Plains groups. Among the Cheyenne, some females who participated in warfare were identified as members of a gender other than "woman" (Roscoe 1998, 75). It appears that for some North American groups, a combination of characteristics qualified a female person as belonging to a named "fourth gender"; these include participation in male-dominated subsistence activities such as hunting, inclusion in war parties as armed combatants, occasional and/or partial cross-dressing, sexual activity with women, and refusal to marry men (see table 1; Roscoe 1998, 73–75). Other Plains societies with such female roles include the Pend d'Oreille (Kalispel) (De Smet 1905), the Crow (Denig 1930), and the Blackfoot (Schultz 1916, 1919). Alternative male genders have been documented among the Arikara, Mandan, Hidatsa, Pawnee, and most divisions of the Sioux, but apparently these groups lacked a linguistically marked analogous female category (see Roscoe 1998, Tribal Index; Douglas Parks, personal communication 1999).

WARRIOR WOMEN AND "MANLY HEARTS"

As Medicine (1983, 267) notes, the phenomenon of warrior women challenges assumptions about the male-dominated social and political organization of Plains groups. This female role alternative, while exhibiting parallels with the *berdache* gender, was not its mirror image (Medicine 1983, 268–69; see also Roscoe 1998). In some societies, females who were considered "manly-hearted" or who participated in traditionally male activities were not considered members of a gender category different from "woman"; their gender was not reclassified when they adopted the status (Roscoe 1998, 85). For example, among the Blackfoot, ethnographic research during the 1930s documented manly-hearted women; all were married to men, all were wealthy, and the majority were over the age of fifty (Lewis 1941, 176–80, 185), suggesting that age and socioeconomic standing were at least as impor-

Table 1. Selected Alternative Female Roles in Northern Plains Groups

Role	Gloss	Group	Reference
sakwo'mapi akikwan	boy-girl	Blackfoot	Schultz 1919, 38
ninauposkitzipxpe	manly-hearted woman	Piegan	Lewis 1941, 143
ninawaki	manly-hearted woman	Piegan	Seward 1946, 120
female "berdache"		Piegan	Schaeffer 1965, 228ff
hetaneman		Cheyenne	Petter 1915, 1116; Grinnell 1923 (2):39
Woman Chief (personal name)		Crow	Denig 1961, 196ff., Kurz 1937, 213f.
winox:tca' akitcita	women police	Dakota/Santee	Landes 1968, 57, 69
bloka egla wa ke	thinks she can act like a man	Lakota	Medicine 1997, 142
okitcitakwe	warrior woman	Ojibwa	Skinner 1914, 486
Cta-wi-rakuh-wari' (personal name)	Woman Who Goes As A Warrior	Pawnee	Murie 1981, 156
Cakaruhku (personal name)	Women Count Coup On Enemy With Goods	Pawnee	Murie 1981, 199

tant in identifying a manly-heart as her "masculine" behavior (Roscoe 1998, 85–86; see also Kehoe 1995, 115–16).

A role similar to the "manly-hearted" woman was described among the Pawnee. A Skiri bundle tradition describes a poor young woman who was the first female to set out with a war party (Murie 1981, 156). She counted coup, stole a hide, and upon return to her village, her name was changed from White Woman to Woman Who Goes As A Warrior. She was welcomed by the men in the war party, because she brought them luck and was skillful at capturing ponies by leading the mare from the enemy village, with the ponies following behind. Her desire to go to war came from a dream, in which her brother gave her instructions regarding a bundle and the use of its contents. She refused many suitors, but finally married and had a son, who became a successful warrior himself (Murie 1981, 156–58). In fact, one of Murie's consultants was named Woman Count Coup On Enemy With Goods (1981, 199). This association of supernatural power and success at warfare is also found in the example of the Pawnee named War Leader Woman who was considered to be particularly powerful (Weltfish 1965, 336).

Another Skiri tradition describes a war celebration among an enemy group, in which women dressed as men danced around a captive, mocking him (Dorsey 1904, 317). This tradition echoes the activity of a Pawnee woman's society that comprised "single women, old maids, and widows," whose regalia mimicked that of men. These women taunted and tortured war captives (Murie 1914, 598–99).

A Hidatsa narrative details the exploits of Wolf Woman, who was born human, but became a wolf. She would join war parties of her choice, and was well respected by the community. She never made love to a man, and lived as a virgin, passing on the wolf ceremony rite to her niece (Beckwith 1932, 242). In some respects, her behavior fits the description of a female whose gender was something other than "woman" (see above).

Some northern Plains traditions describe instances where women came to the aid of their male loved ones. A Lakota narrative describes a woman who rescued her husband held captive by the Crow. She scalped the enemy, and for her deed, "which was the kind that only men are able to do," was elevated to the status of beloved (first) wife (Rice 1994, 33). A Crow oral history depicts a situation where a mother dispatched her son's enemy by smashing the assailant's head with her hatchet; subsequently, her son's name became He-kills-with-his-mother (Lowie 1918, 253).

GENDER AND WARFARE

The stereotypical image of a Plains Indian is that of a man, clad in a feathered war bonnet, seated on a pinto, and wielding a spear or bow and arrow. This image reinforces the idea that warfare was a male pursuit among Plains people. However, the presence of "nonmen" in Plains war parties is an underrepresented aspect of these practices. Indeed, the presence of women, *berdaches*, and alternative-gender females in warfare belies the notion that only "real men" participated in organized conflict on the Plains. An example can be found in the career of Osch-Tisch, a Crow who earned the name Finds Them and Kills Them in 1876, when fighting in the Battle of the Rosebud (Roscoe 1998, 30). The description of this battle by a woman named Pretty Shield included not only the *bote* (alternative gender) Osch-Tisch, but a woman as well, named The Other Magpie, who was a "wild one . . . both bad and brave" (Linderman 1932, 227–31). The prestige and wealth that Osch-Tisch had already accumulated during two years of the battle are reflected in the dress and ornaments shown in a photograph of the *bote* and a companion, who may have been The Other Magpie (see Roscoe 1998, 33–34).

Berdaches joined war parties either as combatants or performing other functions among the Lakota, Crow, and Cheyenne (see Callender and Ko-chems 1983, 448–49; Roscoe 1998, 14, table 1.1). Indeed, among the Chey-enne, these people were considered to bring good luck and were desired members of war parties (Hoebel 1978, 83). Lowie (1935, 48) describes a Crow bate (his spelling) who "had once fought valiantly in an encounter with the Dakota." An additional example can be found among the Osage. In 1840, Tixier noted an Osage warrior named *la Bredache* (Tixier's spelling), who was one of the most distinguished braves (McDermott 1940, 234).

A Pawnee tradition, called "The Moon Medicine," describes a boy, Taihip-irus, who is influenced by the moon, and grows up with womanish ways. De-spite his womanly demeanor, Taihipirus became a successful warrior, aiding his war parties with help from Mother Moon (Dorsey 1904, 199–203). (For a description of moon influence on a Pawnee "Half-Man-and-Half-Woman" see Dorsey 1904, 237–38).

An association between nonnormative women and warfare is displayed in the symbolism of Double Woman dreamers in northern Plains societies. Women who dreamed of this figure were given sexual license that was un-available to normative women, and they could publicly enact the dream; dur-ing a trance induced by the enactment, these women might obtain power to make medicines or war shields, among other skills (Wissler 1912, 94; see also DeMallie 1983, 241; Hassrick 1964, 230–31).

The gender role designated "warrior woman" can be distinguished from the occasional participation of women in war parties. The woman warrior fre-quently engaged in battle, was successful at it, and the warrior status was a clear part of the woman's identity (Roscoe 1998, 76). This suite of character-istics can be contrasted with the occasional participation of Plains women in warfare, such as accompanying a husband, or a widow taking part in a re-venge raid (see Ewers 1994, 328–31). While there is a lack of published eth-nographic or ethnohistorical documentation on alternative female gender roles in Arikara society, these phenomena are widespread throughout the Plains area (for examples see Denig 1961, 200; Lowie 1922, 341, 363–64; McAllester 1941, 597; Medicine 1983, 273–74; Roscoe 1998, 75–76; Schaef-fer 1965, 224–35; Seward 1946, 112–24; Weist 1983, 263).

Medicine (1983, 268) suggests that the warrior woman role was a culturally accepted position that accorded women power and prestige in a realm that is usually defined as masculine. It is also possible that this prestige system was attractive to Plains people of any gender (woman, man, *berdache*, and so on). While warfare may have been dominated by men, it was not the exclusive domain of men.

Ethnographic and ethnohistoric information concerning gender roles, ac-tivities, and the ideology of warfare, can be used to interpret the archaeological record of the northern Plains. These sources provide data that shed light on the circumstances of prehistoric and historic conflicts among northern Plains groups.

WARFARE ON THE NORTHERN PLAINS

Documented warfare in the northern Plains has a considerable time depth, ranging from circa A.D. 900 to the historic period (Blakeslee 1994, 24–25; Owsley 1994). Archaeological evidence, such as village fortification, and osteological evidence, such as indications of scalping and other trauma, provide this record of warfare in the prehistory and history of the Missouri Trench (Owsley 1994, 334–35). According to these data, the first dramatic rise in conflict occurred during the Initial Coalescent variant of the Plains Village pattern, circa A.D. 1300 to 1550; these battles presumably took place between ancestral Mandan and Arikara populations who were vying for resources (Olsen and Shipman 1994, 384). Examples of large-scale warfare, including massacres, can be seen in the osteological series from the Fay Tolton site (Hollimon and Owsley 1994), and the later Arikara-affiliated Crow Creek (Willey 1990) and Larson sites (Owsley, Berryman, and Bass 1977). These data clearly indicate that all degrees of warfare (raids, skirmishes, battles, and massacres) were employed during the precontact period.

As middlemen in trade on the upper Missouri River, the more sedentary Arikara came into contact with equestrian groups of the northern Plains during the protohistoric period. While the Cheyenne, Assiniboine, and Sioux were attracted to Arikara villages by exchange opportunities, the agricultural surpluses, horses, and other goods made these sites inviting targets for raids (Owsley 1994, 333–34). At one time or another, the Arikara counted among their enemies the Assiniboine, Crow, Mandan, Hidatsa, and especially the Sioux (Abel 1939; Brackenridge 1904; Larpenteur 1962; Nasatir 1952; Thwaites 1904).

IDEOLOGY: THE SCALPED MAN

The mythologized historical character of the Scalped Man provides insight into the ideology of warfare among Caddoan groups. In Arikara, Pawnee, and Wichita folklore, the figure of the Scalped Man has been elaborated to include roles such as benefactor or bestower of supernatural power, comic, and bogeyman (Parks 1982, 47; see also Dorsey 1995, 274–75). The Arikara verb "to scalp" literally means to ruin, and according to historic sources, a scalping victim who survived was considered no longer human. He was forced to live outside the pale of human society, as a solitary, frightening figure who might steal food, and who maintained essentially a nocturnal existence (Parks 1982, 49; see also Gilmore 1933).

A Pawnee story describes the interaction between Coyote and Scalped Woman (Dorsey 1906, 428–29; Parks 1982, 56). As expected, Coyote wishes to have sexual relations with her, and ultimately succeeds, living with Scalped Woman as his wife for several years thereafter (Dorsey 1906, 428–29). This suggests a possible gender difference in the way that scalping survivors were regarded. Perhaps scalped women were not banished from society; it is also possible that this practice changed during the early historic period, when the oral histories were collected by ethnographers. Archaeological evidence suggests that females, males, and children who survived scalping were allowed to remain in their villages, because their remains have been found in village and cemetery contexts (Hollimon and Owsley 1994, 352).

OSTEOLOGICAL EVIDENCE OF WARFARE

Several skeletal markers can be used as indirect indicators of violent interaction, ranging from interpersonal fights to full-scale massacres involving hundreds of victims. Embedded projectile points, cranial cuts and lesions indicative of scalping, and traumatic injuries suggesting perimortem mutilation have been found among skeletal series from the northern Plains. Perimortem mutilation includes the disarticulation of the limbs, hands and feet, decapitation, depressed cranial fractures, traumatic dental avulsions, and scalping (Owsley 1994, 335).

Osteological evidence of warfare, including scalping and perimortem mutilation, has been documented among several Arikara skeletal series (Olsen and Shipman 1994; Owsley 1994, 335). These include Crow Creek (39BF11), the site of a massacre (Willey 1982, 1990), Larson (Olsen and Shipman 1994, 385; Owsley, Berryman, and Bass 1977), Leavenworth (Olsen and Shipman 1994, 384), Mobridge (Owsley 1994), and Sully (Hollimon and Owsley 1994).

DEMOGRAPHIC PATTERNS OF NORTHERN PLAINS WARFARE THROUGH TIME

Crow Creek (Initial Coalescent)

The fortified village of Crow Creek was the site of a massacre at roughly A.D. 1325 (Willey 1990, 3). Extensive perimortem mutilation was present on the majority of the 486 individuals represented by the skeletal remains, which probably constituted about 60 percent of the village population (Willey 1990, xv). These mutilations include those described above, as well as snapping and splintering of limb bones suggesting dismemberment, and possible tongue and nose removal (Willey 1990). Adults, adolescents, and children were scalped; nearly 90 percent of all crania show evidence of scalping (Willey 1990, 113).

As inferred from archaeological skeletal remains, patterns of age and sex are exhibited in northern Plains warfare during the Coalescent Tradition, circa A.D. 1600 to 1832 (Owsley 1994, 339–42). In a sample of 751 adult and sub-adult crania from archaeological sites along the Missouri Trench, a total of 41 displayed cuts indicative of scalping. The risk of scalping for females and males was roughly equal (5.3 percent and 6.7 percent, respectively). Through time, however, the risk of being scalped apparently increased dramatically for males, while there was a smaller decrease for females during the early historic period (Owsley 1994, 341; this may be an artifact of sampling variation).

The majority of these scalped males were aged between twenty and thirty-four years, suggesting that they were young warriors killed during raids or in defense of the village, while the scalped females were more evenly distributed across age categories (Owsley 1994, 341–42). However, if the patterns of female and male victims are drawn only from the scalped sample, we see that 77 percent of scalped females were thirty-four years or younger, while 82 percent of scalped males were of these ages.

Owsley (1994, 341) interprets the high proportion of young males with scalping wounds as a reflection of the differences between women's and men's activity patterns, with females of all ages participating in the gathering of firewood and agricultural labor, leaving them susceptible to attack while away from the village. I would suggest that the basic premise of his argument is correct, but that some of the female scalpings may have been a result of active participation in raids or village defense. Given that equal numbers of scalped females and males were found in cemetery contexts, it would appear that their injuries and deaths occurred near the village. Had significant numbers of males died away from the village, a disproportionate sex ratio would have been observed in the cemetery assemblage; such a sex ratio was not observed, suggesting that young females and males were both at risk for violent death (see Owsley 1994, 341).

An ethnographic example can be found among the Osage. Sources describe cases where the village was defended by women alone, who would inflict severe casualties on the enemy. Women would also scalp their victims as a method of revenge (McDermott 1940, 219).

The Over Collection

Olsen and Shipman (1994) examined thirty-eight individuals from the Over Collection (Owsley and Jantz 1994, ix) displaying evidence of cuts and/or other forms of perimortem treatment. These skeletons come from archaeological sites that span the period between A.D. 400 and 1832, and likely represent ancestral Mandan and Arikara populations in South Dakota (Olsen and Shipman 1994, 377–78). While this sample contained more males than females (a ratio of 2:1), skeletons of both sexes exhibited cuts and traumatic injuries that are likely indicators of violent conflict (Olsen and Shipman 1994, 386).

It has been suggested that the intrusion of Arikara groups in the Mandan area during the Coalescent period was characterized by violent interaction. Osteological evidence indicates that this hypothesis is correct, in that battle-related trauma and perimortem mutilation dramatically increased after the arrival of the Arikara (Olsen and Shipman 1994, 377).

DISCUSSION

The demographic patterns of osteological indicators of violence can be viewed in several ways. It is not my intention to suggest that all female skeletons displaying traumatic injuries represent "women warriors" or other alternative female roles. However, I do suggest that at least some of these injuries may have been incurred during conflicts where the women were not passive victims, but may have been active combatants. If we automatically assume that young male skeletons showing these injuries are the remains of warriors, and that analogous female skeletons are not, should we not examine this assumption? The conventional wisdom that Plains warfare was the pursuit of young men might be more accurately viewed as the pursuit of young persons, be they women, men, or individuals of other genders.

It is possible that the frequency of Arikara female participation in warfare rose throughout the Coalescent period. Perhaps the decline in population, and the attendant reduction of the male fighting force, resulted in a greater number of women taking up arms (Owsley and Bass 1979, 151). Historical sources indicate a steady depopulation among the Arikara, and a decline in the number of warriors.

> This nation formerly so numerous, and which according to their reports, could turn out four thousand warriors is now reduced to about five hundred fighting men. (Nasatir 1952, 299)

The need for warriors, of any gender, may have provided opportunities that previously went unfilled by women.

Alternatively, the activities of Arikara warriors may not have differed tremendously from those performed by other villagers. Krause (1972, 109) points out that village defense is more important among horticulturalists such as the Arikara, who did not have large masses of warrior troops to sustain extended campaigns away from the village. Under such circumstances, a male Arikara warrior, defending his village, may not have engaged in activities that differed significantly from an Arikara woman who was in the same position (see the Osage example above). The massacre sites of Crow Creek and Larson display archaeological and osteological evidence suggesting that women, men, and children were at equal risk for violent death during village raids. Old, young, warriors, gardeners, doctors, dreamers, women, and men: all of these roles and statuses were indiscriminately killed.

CONCLUSION

Evidence of violent conflict from the northern Plains can be interpreted in light of alternative genders and roles in these societies. The anthropological analysis of warfare benefits from a consideration of the roles played by women, men, and members of other genders. Increasing attention to the phenomenon of women who wage war demands a reconsideration of archaeological evidence from the northern Plains. Future research should focus on aspects of organized conflict in which the participants are not exclusively men.

ACKNOWLEDGMENTS

This work was supported in part by a postdoctoral fellowship at the Smithsonian Institution, National Museum of Natural History.

REFERENCES

Abel, Annie H., ed. 1939. *Tabeau's narrative of the upper Missouri.* Norman: University of Oklahoma Press.

Beckwith, Martha Warren. 1932. *Myths and hunting stories of the Mandan and Hidatsa Sioux.* Publications of Folk-Lore Foundations 12. Poughkeepsie, N.Y.: Vassar College.

Blakeslee, Donald J. 1994. The archaeological context of human skeletons in the northern and central Plains. In *Skeletal biology in the Great Plains: Migration, warfare, health, and subsistence.* Edited by Douglas W. Owsley and Richard L. Jantz, pp. 9–32. Washington, D.C.: Smithsonian Institution Press.

Bovee, Dana L., and Douglas W. Owsley. 1994. Evidence of warfare at the Heerwald site. In *Skeletal biology in the Great Plains: Migration, warfare, health, and subsistence.* Edited by Douglas W. Owsley and Richard L. Jantz, pp. 355–62. Washington, D.C.: Smithsonian Institution Press.

Brackenridge, Henry M. 1904. Journal of a voyage up the Missouri performed in eighteen hundred and eleven. In *Early western travels, 1748–1848.* Edited by Reuben G. Thwaites. Cleveland: Arthur H. Clark.

Callender, Charles, and Lee M. Kochems. 1983. The North American berdache. *Current Anthropology* 24:433–56.

Cromwell, Jason. 1997. Traditions of gender diversity and sexualities: A female-to-male transgendered perspective. In *Two-spirit people: Native American gender identity, sexuality, and spirituality.* Edited by Sue-Ellen Jacobs, Wesley Thomas, and Sabine Lang, pp. 11–142. Champagne: University of Illinois Press.

DeMallie, Raymond. 1983. Male and female in traditional Lakota culture. In *The hidden half: Studies of Plains Indian women.* Edited by Patricia Albers and Beatrice Medicine, pp. 237–65. Washington, D.C.: University Press of America.

De Smet, Pierre-Jean. 1905. *Life, letters, and travels of Father Pierre-Jean De Smet, S.J., 1801–1873.* Vols. 2 and 3. Edited by Hiram M. Chittenden and Alfred T. Richardson. New York: Francis P. Harper.

Denig, Edwin T. 1930. Indian tribes of the upper Missouri. Edited by J. N. B. Hewitt. *Bureau of American Ethnology Annual Report* 46. Washington, D.C.: Bureau of American Ethnology.

———. 1961. *Five Indian tribes of the upper Missouri.* Edited by John C. Ewers. Norman: University of Oklahoma Press.

Dorsey, George A. 1904. *Traditions of the Arikara.* Washington, D.C.: Carnegie Institution of Washington.

———. 1906. *The Pawnee: Mythology (Part I).* Washington, D.C.: Carnegie Institution of Washington.

———. 1995. *The Mythology of the Wichita.* Edited by Elizabeth A. H. John. 1904. Reprint, Norman: University of Oklahoma Press.

Duke, Philip. 1991. Recognizing gender in Plains hunting groups: Is it possible or even necessary? In *The archaeology of gender: Proceedings of the twenty-second annual Chacmool conference of the Archaeological Association of the University of Calgary.* Edited by Dale Walde and Noreen Willows, pp. 280–83. Calgary: University of Calgary.

Ewers, John C. 1994. Women's roles in Plains Indian warfare. In *Skeletal biology in the Great Plains: Migration, warfare, health, and subsistence.* Edited by Douglas W. Owsley and Richard L. Jantz, pp. 325–32. Washington, D.C.: Smithsonian Institution Press.

Gilmore, Melvin R. 1933. The plight of living scalped Indians. *Papers of the Michigan Academy of Science, Arts, and Letters* 19:39–45.

Grinnell, George B. 1923. *The Cheyenne Indians: Their history and ways of life.* 2 vols. New Haven, Conn.: Yale University Press.

Hassrick, Royal B. 1964. *The Sioux.* Norman: University of Oklahoma Press.

Hoebel, E. Adamson. 1978. *The Cheyenne: Indians of the Great Plains.* New York: Holt, Rinehart and Winston.

Hollimon, Sandra E. 1999. Sex, health, and gender roles among the Arikara of the Northern Plains. In *Reading the body: Representations and remains in the archaeological record*. Edited by Alison Rautman, pp. 25–37. Philadelphia: University of Pennsylvania Press.

Hollimon, Sandra E., and Douglas W. Owsley. 1994. Osteology of the Fay Tolton site: Implications for warfare during the initial middle Missouri variant. In *Skeletal biology in the Great Plains: Migration, warfare, health, and subsistence*. Edited by Douglas W. Owsley and Richard L. Jantz, pp. 345–53. Washington, D.C.: Smithsonian Institution Press.

Jacobs, Sue-Ellen. 1968. Berdache: A brief review of the literature. *Colorado Anthropologist* 1:25–40.

Kehoe, Alice B. 1995. Blackfoot persons. In *Women and power in native North America*. Edited by Laura F. Klein and Lillian A. Ackerman, pp. 113–25. Norman: University of Oklahoma Press.

Krause, Richard A. 1972. *The Leavenworth site: Archaeology of an historic Arikara community*. University of Kansas Publications in Anthropology 3. Lawrence, Kans.

Kurz, Rudolph Friedrich. 1937. *Journal of Rudolph Friedrich Kurz 1846–1852*. Translated by Myrtis Jarrell. Edited by J.N.B. Hewitt. In Bureau of American Ethnology Bulletin 15. Washington, D.C.: Bureau of American Ethnology.

Lambert, Patricia M. 1997. Patterns of violence in prehistoric hunter-gatherer societies of coastal southern California. In *Troubled times: Violence and warfare in the past*. Vol. 3 of *War and society*. Edited by Debra L. Martin and David W. Frayer, pp. 77–109. Amsterdam: Gordon and Breach.

Landes, Ruth. 1968. *The Mystic Lake Sioux*. Madison: University of Wisconsin Press.

Larpenteur, Charles. 1962. *Forty years a fur trader on the upper Missouri: The personal narrative of Charles Larpenteur*. Minneapolis: Ross and Haines.

Lewis, Oscar. 1941. Manly-hearted women among the north Piegan. *American Anthropologist* 43:173–87.

Linderman, Frank B. 1932. *Red mother*. New York: John Day Company.

Lowie, Robert H. 1918. Myths and traditions of the Crow Indians. *Anthropological Papers of the American Museum of Natural History* 25 (1).

———. 1922. The religion of the Crow Indians. *Anthropological Papers of the American Museum of Natural History* 25 (2).

———. 1935. *The Crow Indians*. New York: Farrar and Rinehart.

Martin, Debra L. 1997. Violence against women in the La Plata River Valley (A.D. 1000–1300). In *Troubled times: Violence and warfare in the past*. Vol. 3 of *War and society*. Edited by Debra L. Martin and David W. Frayer, pp. 45–75. Amsterdam: Gordon and Breach.

Martin, Debra L., and David W. Frayer, eds. 1997. *Troubled times: Violence and warfare in the past*. Vol. 3 of *War and society*. Amsterdam: Gordon and Breach.

McAllester, H. 1941. Water as a disciplinary agent among the Crow and Blackfoot. *American Anthropologist* 43:593–604.

McDermott, John F., ed. 1940. *Tixier's travels on the Osage prairies*. Norman: University of Oklahoma Press.

Medicine, Beatrice. 1983. "Warrior women"—sex role alternatives for Plains Indian women. In *The hidden half: Studies of Plains Indian women*. Edited by Patricia Albers and Beatrice Medicine, pp. 267–77. Washington, D.C.: University Press of America.

————. 1997. Changing Native American roles in an urban context. In *Two-spirit people: Native American gender identity, sexuality, and spirituality*. Edited by Sue-Ellen Jacobs, Wesley Thomas, and Sabine Lang, pp. 119–42. Urbana and Chicago: University of Illinois Press.

Murie, James R. 1914. Pawnee Indian societies. *Anthropological Papers of the American Museum of Natural History* 11 (7).

————. 1981. *Ceremonies of the Pawnee*. Edited by Douglas R. Parks. Washington, D.C.: Smithsonian Institution Press.

Nasatir, Abraham P., ed. 1952. *Before Lewis and Clark*. St. Louis: St. Louis Historical Documents Foundation.

Olsen, Sandra L., and Pat Shipman. 1994. Cutmarks and perimortem treatment of skeletal remains on the northern Plains. In *Skeletal biology in the Great Plains: Migration, warfare, health, and subsistence*. Edited by Douglas W. Owsley and Richard L. Jantz, pp. 377–87. Washington, D.C.: Smithsonian Institution Press.

Owsley, Douglas W. 1994. Warfare in coalescent tradition populations of the northern Plains. In *Skeletal biology in the Great Plains: Migration, warfare, health, and subsistence*. Edited by Douglas W. Owsley and Richard L. Jantz, pp. 333–43. Washington, D.C.: Smithsonian Institution Press.

Owsley, Douglas W., and William M. Bass. 1979. A demographic analysis of skeletons from the Larson site (39WW2), Walworth County, South Dakota: Vital Statistics. *American Journal of Physical Anthropology* 51:145–54.

Owsley, Douglas W., and Richard L. Jantz, eds. 1994. *Skeletal biology in the Great Plains: Migration, warfare, health, and subsistence*. Washington, D.C.: Smithsonian Institution Press.

Owsley, Douglas W., Hugh E. Berryman, and William M. Bass. 1977. Demographic and osteological evidence for warfare at the Larson site, South Dakota. *Plains Anthropologist* 22 (78):119–31.

Parks, Douglas R. 1982. An historical character mythologized: The Scalped Man in Arikara and Pawnee folklore. In *Plains Indian studies: A collection of essays in honor of John C. Ewers and Waldo R. Wedel*. Edited by Douglas H. Ubelaker and Herman J. Viola, pp. 47–58. Washington, D.C.: Smithsonian Institution Press.

————. 1996. *Myths and traditions of the Arikara Indians*. Lincoln: University of Nebraska Press.

Petter, Rodolphe. 1915. *English-Cheyenne dictionary*. Kettle Falls, Wash.: The author.

Rice, Julian. 1994. *Ella Deloria's "The Buffalo People."* Albuquerque: University of New Mexico Press.

Robarchek, Clayton A. 1994. Plains warfare and the anthropology of war. In *Skeletal biology in the Great Plains: Migration, warfare, health, and subsistence*. Edited by Douglas W. Owsley and Richard L. Jantz, pp. 307–16. Washington, D.C.: Smithsonian Institution Press.

Robb, John. 1997. Violence and gender in early Italy. In *Troubled times: Violence and warfare in the past*. Vol. 3 of *War and society*. Edited by Debra L. Martin and David W. Frayer, pp. 111–43. Amsterdam: Gordon and Breach.

Rogers, J. Daniel. 1990. *Objects of change: The archaeology and history of Arikara contact with Europeans*. Washington, D.C.: Smithsonian Institution Press.

Roscoe, Will. 1987. Bibliography of berdache and alternative gender roles among North American Indians. *Journal of Homosexuality* 14 (3–4):81–171.

———. 1998. *Changing ones: Third and fourth genders in native North America.* New York: St. Martin's.

Schaeffer, Claude E. 1965. The Kutenai female berdache: Courier, guide, prophetess, and warrior. *Ethnohistory* 12 (3):193–236.

Schultz, James W. 1916. *Blackfeet tales of Glacier National Park.* Boston: Houghton Mifflin.

———. 1919. *Running Eagle: The warrior girl.* Boston: Houghton Mifflin.

Seward, Georgene H. 1946. *Sex and the social order.* New York: McGraw-Hill.

Skinner, Alanson. 1914. Political organization, cults, and ceremonies of the Plains-Ojibway and Plains-Cree Indians. *Anthropological Papers of the American Museum of Natural History* 11 (6).

Thwaites, Reuben G., ed. 1904. *Original journals of the Lewis and Clark expedition 1804–1806.* New York: Dodd, Mead and Co.

Walker, Phillip L. 1997. Wife beating, boxing, and broken noses: Skeletal evidence for the cultural patterning of violence. In *Troubled times: Violence and warfare in the past.* Vol. 3 of *War and society.* Edited by Debra L. Martin and David W. Frayer, pp. 145–179. Amsterdam: Gordon and Breach.

Weist, Katherine. 1983. Beasts of burden and menial slaves: Nineteenth-century observations of northern Plains Indian women. In *The hidden half: Studies of Plains Indian women.* Edited by Patricia Albers and Beatrice Medicine, pp. 29–52. Washington, D.C.: University Press of America.

Weltfish, Gene. 1965. *The lost universe.* New York: Basic.

Whelan, Mary K. 1991. Gender and historical archaeology: Eastern Dakota patterns in the nineteenth century. *Historical Archaeology* 25 (4):17–32.

Wilkinson, Richard G. 1997. Violence against women: Raiding and abduction in prehistoric Michigan. In *Troubled times: Violence and warfare in the past.* Vol. 3 of *War and society.* Edited by Debra L. Martin and David W. Frayer, pp. 21–43. Amsterdam: Gordon and Breach.

Willey, Patrick S. 1982. Osteology of the Crow Creek massacre. Ph.D. diss., University of Tennessee, Knoxville.

———. 1990. *Prehistoric warfare on the Great Plains: Skeletal analysis of the Crow Creek massacre victims.* New York: Garland.

Wissler, Clark. 1912. Societies and ceremonial associations in the Oglala Division of the Teton-Dakota. *Anthropological Papers of the American Museum of Natural History* 11 (6).

Index

About the Contributors

BETTINA ARNOLD is associate professor in the Department of Anthropology at the University of Wisconsin–Milwaukee. Her area of expertise is early Iron Age Europe, but she has participated in archaeological projects ranging from the middle Bronze Age through the Roman period. She is the director of a long-term, collaborative research project in southwest Germany that combines conventional analysis of burials dating to the late Hallstatt period with the analysis of ancient DNA in order to reconstruct aspects of social organization. Her research interests include European prehistory, Celtic Europe, the archaeology of gender, mortuary analysis, material culture as a system of communication, and ethical issues in archaeology, including the use and abuse of the past for political purposes.

BARBARA A. CRASS completed her Ph.D. in anthropology at the University of Wisconsin–Milwaukee, specializing in mortuary analysis, archaeology of the arctic regions, and circumpolar folklore. She is currently an adjunct professor in anthropology at the University of Wisconsin–Oshkosh. Her research is concerned with an integrative approach to archaeology, folklore, and gender in the Arctic.

DIANNA L. DOUCETTE is a Ph.D. candidate in the Department of Anthropology at Harvard University. Her research in New England archaeology focuses on identifying early and middle Archaic Native American cultural histories (ca. 9000–6000 B.P.) by looking at spatial complexity through feature analysis. This work includes an examination of site formation processes using micromorphology and chemical analysis of soils. Her other research specialties include lithic and mortuary analysis. She has been involved in cultural resources management for the past eighteen years. From 1995 to 1997 she served as the Native American Graves Protection and Repatriation Act (NAG-

PRA) coordinator of New England at Harvard's Peabody Museum of Archaeology and Ethnology.

ANNE-SOFIE GRÄSLUND is associate professor of archaeology at the University of Uppsala, Sweden. Her research concentrates on religion of the second half of the first millennium A.D., especially the Viking Age. Topics of interest to her include conversion and art, rune stones, burial customs, and gender. She is the author of *Birka I: The Burial Customs—A Study of the Graves on Björkö* (Stockholm 1980) and numerous articles in journals and conference proceedings.

CHRISTINE HAMLIN is a Ph.D. candidate at the University of Wisconsin–Milwaukee. Her research interests include British prehistory (with an emphasis on the Late Iron Age and the Roman period), mortuary archaeology, gender studies, religious syncretism in colonial contexts, and human osteology.

SANDRA E. HOLLIMON teaches anthropology at Sonoma State University and Santa Rosa Junior College. She is senior prehistoric archaeologist with the Anthropological Studies Center, Sonoma State University. Her research interests include gender systems, sexuality, and the prehistory of California and the Northern Plains. Some of her recent articles have appeared in *Archaeologies of Sexuality* (Routledge) and *Reading the Body* (University of Pennsylvania Press).

TIANLONG JIAO is a doctoral student in anthropology at Harvard University, specializing in Chinese Neolithic and Bronze Age archaeology. He has been involved in excavations in Shandong, Ningxia, and Hubei Provinces and in Hong Kong. His M.A. thesis explored the prehistoric cultures of the Lingnan area of Southern China from the late Pleistocene to early Holocene. His current research investigates the earliest dispersal of Austronesians, working at Neolithic sites in Fujian and Guangdong areas of Southeast China. He is co-author of five books published in China.

JODIE A. O'GORMAN is assistant professor of anthropology and assistant curator in the Museum at Michigan State University. She received her doctorate in 1996 from the University of Wisconsin–Milwaukee and, prior to moving to the Great Lakes State, served as director of research at the Center for American Archeology in Kampsville, Illinois. Her research interests include the interplay of gender, death, household dynamics, and social organization within the late prehistoric and early historic societies of the North American midcontinent.

ELEANOR SCOTT obtained a B.A. and a Ph.D. in archaeology at the University of Newcastle upon Tyne and is now a senior lecturer in archaeology at King Alfred's University College, Winchester, UK. Her research centers on the archaeology of the Roman world, focusing in particular on gender, children, and the life cycle. Her published works include *The Archaeology of Infancy and Infant Death* (1999) and *Invisible People and Processes: Writing Gender and Childhood into European Archaeology* (1997), coedited with Jenny Moore. She is currently writing books about Roman villas and children in antiquity and is researching infancy and disability.

ANNE STALSBERG is associate professor and chief curator of archaeology at the Museum of Natural History and Archaeology at the Norwegian University of Science and Technology in Trondheim, Middle Norway. Born in 1943 in Norway, she was educated at the University of Oslo and the Lomonosov University of Moscow, and was awarded an M.A. from the University of Oslo in 1974. Her research has included several visits to the Soviet Union/Russia and the Ukraine and has earned her a Fulbright fellowship at the University of Minnesota. Her specialties include Russian-Scandinavian Viking Age relations, female roles in the Viking Age, Viking Age swords, and the archaeology of settlement.

EMILY J. WEGLIAN is an advanced graduate student in the Department of Anthropology at the University of Minnesota–Minneapolis, specializing in European prehistory. She earned her B.A. at Miami University in Ohio and her M.A. at the University of Minnesota. She has participated in several excavations in Germany and Denmark. Her interests include social stratification, chronology construction, and gender in temperate Europe, especially of the end Neolithic period and early Bronze Age. She is a frequent contributor to organized sessions at professional conferences.

NANCY L. WICKER is professor of art history and director of Scandinavian studies at Minnesota State University–Mankato. She specializes in Scandinavian Iron Age archaeology and early medieval art history. Dr. Wicker has published on Scandinavian Migration period bracteates, Scandinavian animal-style art, female infanticide during the Viking Age, and relationships between archaeology and art history. Her research has been funded by the National Endowment for the Humanities, the American Philosophical Society, the American-Scandinavian Foundation, the American Council of Learned Societies, and the International Research and Exchanges Board. She has also edited *From the Ground Up: Beyond Gender Theory in Archaeology* (1999) with Bettina Arnold.